CW00794235

Professional Police Practi

Scenarios and Dilemmas

Professional Police Practice

Scenarios and Dilemmas

Edited by

PAJ Waddington, University of Wolverhampton, UK

John Kleinig, John Jay College of Criminal Justice, CUNY, New York and CSU, Canberra, Australia

Martin Wright, University of Wolverhampton, UK

OXFORD
UNIVERSITY PRESS

Great Clarendon Street, Oxford, OX2 6DP,
United Kingdom

Oxford University Press is a department of the University of Oxford.
It furthers the University's objective of excellence in research, scholarship,
and education by publishing worldwide. Oxford is a registered trade mark of
Oxford University Press in the UK and in certain other countries

First Edition published in 2013

Impression: 1

British Library Cataloguing in Publication Data
Data available

ISBN 978–0–19–963918–2

Printed and bound in Great Britain by
CPI Group (UK) Ltd, Croydon, CR0 4YY

Acknowledgements

Like any volume of this kind, a great many people have contributed to its successful publication. Foremost amongst those are the contributors who were prepared, as many others were not, to confront police practice dilemmas of wickedly contrived difficulty. To each of them, the editors are enormously grateful.

We are also grateful to Oxford University Press for whom this collection is just one aspect of its growing involvement in and commitment to the development of professional police practice. Two of the editors (Waddington and Wright) are also editors of *Policing: A Journal of Policy and Practice*, also published by OUP. Without the support and sometimes the cajoling of Peter Daniell and Lucy Alexander, we doubt if this volume would ever have come to fruition.

The editors hope that this is merely the initiation of a series of publications in which you, the readership, participate fully in developing scenarios and venturing to say how they should be resolved. We believe that this is an effective medium through which to develop a growing professional consciousness amongst police officers throughout the world.

Contents

List of Contributors

Steve Darroch Inspector Steve Darroch joined the New Zealand Police as a Cadet in 1981. He has worked as a Detective, Community Policing Centre Manager, and Area Commander. He is currently the Policing Development Manager in Eastern District based in Napier. Steve has professional and academic interests in Crime Sciences, Police Innovation, and the prevention of major social problems through the application of science to problem analysis. Steve is particularly interested in effective policing and the role of policing in addressing crime and related problems in neighbourhoods and communities. Steve completed his PhD, evaluating the development of Intelligence-led Policing in New Zealand, at Griffith University Queensland Australia in 2009.

Jenny Fleming Professor Jenny Fleming is Chair of Criminology and co-Director of the Institute of Criminal Justice Research at the University of Southampton, Hampshire, UK. Professor Fleming was previously the Director of the Tasmanian Institute of Law Enforcement Studies at the University of Tasmania, Australia. For over twenty years Professor Fleming has worked on a formal and informal basis with police agencies and police associations in Australia, the United Kingdom, Scotland, Canada, the Netherlands, the United States, and New Zealand. Professor Fleming has worked on a range of projects including: the implementation of community policing strategies; building capacity and engagement for police leadership; the provision of criminal justice services to the mentally ill; the policing of anti-social behaviour and alcohol-related violence, police management of adult sexual assault, creating local partnerships, and the politics of law and order. She has published widely in these areas. She is the Editor of *Australasian Policing: a Journal of Professional Practice, Policy and Research* and is on the editorial board of *Policing: A Journal of Policy and Practice* (UK).

John Kleinig John Kleinig is Professor of Philosophy in the Department of Criminal Justice, John Jay College of Criminal Justice and in the PhD Program in Philosophy, Graduate School and University Center, City University of New York. He is also Strategic Research Professor at Charles Sturt University and Professorial Fellow in Criminal Justice Ethics at the Centre for Applied Philosophy and Public Ethics (Canberra, Australia). He is the author/editor of 18 books, and is currently completing four more: *Patriotism* (with Igor Primoratz and Simon Keller), *The Problematic Virtue of Loyalty, Prisoners' Rights* (ed), and *Ends and Means in Policing*.

Monique Marks Professor Monique Marks is based in the Community Development Programme at the University of KwaZulu-Natal in South Africa. She is also a Research Associate of the Centre of Criminology at the University of Cape Town.

She has published widely in the areas of youth social movements, ethnographic research methods, police labour relations, police organisational change, and security governance. She has published four books: *Young Warriors: Youth Identity, Politics and Violence in South Africa*; *Transforming the Robocops: Changing Police in South Africa*; *Police Occupational Culture: New Debates and Directions* (edited with Anne-Marie Singh and Megan O'Neill); and *Police Reform from the Bottom Up: Officers and their Unions as Agents of Change* (edited with David Sklansky).

Michael Messinger Michael Messinger joined the Metropolitan Police Service in 1966 and retired in 2006. As a Chief Superintendent he commanded the MPS Discipline Office; was responsible for policing in the West End; and delivered public order policing in Central London for three years. On promotion to Commander he undertook the role of overseeing the implementation of operational technology throughout the MPS. For the last ten years of his service he was responsible for public order policing, emergency planning, business continuity within the MPS, uniform counter-terrorism policing, consequence management coordination, and CBRN issues. He commanded the policing of six Notting Hill Carnivals and the funerals of Princess Diana and the Queen Mother, and the Golden Jubilee celebration of Her Majesty the Queen. He also oversaw all the 'Stop the War' demonstrations in central London as well as the State visit of the President of the United States of America (George W Bush). He was a member of the several ACPO committees that related to his role. In particular he was a member of the Public Order Committee and was Secretary of the Emergency Procedures Committee, dealing with emergency and contingency planning, consequence management, and business continuity. He was a member of the London Emergency Service Liaison Panel (LESLP) and oversaw the delivery of the evacuation plan for London.

Peter Neyroud Peter Neyroud is a practitioner and academic. A police officer for 30 years, from Constable to Chief in Thames Valley, he set up and led the National Policing Improvement Agency. He carried out a fundamental Review of Police Training and Leadership which has led to the creation of the National College of Policing. Since 2010, he has been a Resident Scholar at the Jerry Lee Centre for Experimental Criminology at the Institute of Criminology at Cambridge. His research includes a major randomised controlled trial of offender desistance policing. He is a Visiting Professor at Chester University, a Visiting Fellow at Teeside University, and the Editor of *Policing: a Journal of Policy and Practice*. His published works cover police ethics, leadership, the history of the police, and crime harm. He has been awarded a QPM (2004) and a CBE (2011).

Juani O'Reilly Juani O'Reilly is a Federal Agent with the Australian Federal Police (AFP). She joined the AFP in 1981 and has performed duties in a range of positions, investigating and managing serious and organised criminal activity within ACT Policing and national operational areas. She has broad experience in managing major investigations. Juani has been involved in joint operations at both the international and state level. Juani was the inaugural Federal Agent in Residence at the Australian National University's Research School of Social Science and bore primary responsibility for managing the 'Governance of Illicit Synthetic Drugs' research project. Juani served with the International Deployment Group for two years where she was a key contributor to the research project 'Policing the Neighbourhood: Australian Police Involvement in Peace Keeping, Capacity Building and Development'. Juani was awarded an AFP National Manager's Certificate in appreciation of her professionalism and dedication in the area of research and strategic relationships with tertiary institutions. Juani has authored or co-authored book chapters and journal articles relating to a broad range of strategic policing issues.

Colin Paine Colin Paine is a local police area commander in Thames Valley Police and was recently promoted to the rank of Superintendent after the astonishingly short period of ten years in the police. He studied Philosophy and Theology at Oxford University from 1996 to 1999 and recently completed the police executive programme, acquiring a Masters in Applied Criminology and Police Management at the University of Cambridge.

Vern Neufeld Redekop Over the last two decades, Vern Neufeld Redekop has been preoccupied with the questions of 'How and why do individuals and groups commit atrocities?' and 'How can parties be reconciled in wake of grievous harm?' He has pursued these questions theoretically and practically. The practical side of his experience was developed when he was President of the Canadian Institute for Conflict Resolution. There he guided the development of Third Party Neutral training and gave oversight to its application in Rwanda and Bosnia Herzegovina (among other contexts). He also used two-day open-ended seminars on deep-rooted conflict and reconciliation, with people from around the world, as contexts for participatory action research that would hone the ideas and processes he was working on. In this context he was invited to address issues of 'crowd control'. He used the principles of Community-Based Conflict Resolution to hold three-day seminars with protester and police. At one point he facilitated a group of 85 angry protesters and fourteen police following a G20 protest that had gone off the rails, from a policing perspective. The ideas and processes had an impact on public order policing practice and police, particularly with the Ottawa Police and the Royal Canadian Mounted Police. They also provided a basis for a book he wrote with his former student, the late Shirley Paré, *Beyond Control: A Mutual Respect Approach to Protest Crowd—Police Relations*.

Sarah Stewart Sarah Stewart is a police officer of fifteen years' experience, after a short career as a teacher. After working as a frontline officer for five years she moved to Wellington where she became a Detective investigating numerous serious crime and homicide operations. In 2007 she was deployed to the Solomon Islands where her role was to investigate the homicides and serious crimes that were carried out by one of the militant groups during the civil war. After a year she returned to New Zealand, periodically visiting the Solomon Islands for homicide trials. She was promoted to Sergeant in charge of all response staff in the Art Deco city of Napier. Now she holds the rank of Senior Sergeant and tactical coordinator where her role is to coordinate workgroups and tactics to reduce and prevent crime in the area. She has completed a Masters degree in Strategic Studies and a Post Graduate Certificate in Applied Leadership.

Sean Tait Sean Tait is coordinator of the African Policing Civilian Oversight Forum in his native South Africa. He is a graduate in criminology from the University of Cape Town's Centre of Criminology. He has worked as Director of the Open Society Foundation for South Africa's Criminal Justice Initiative, and as director of a South African NGO, UMAC, working inter alia on issues of policing, crime prevention, conflict management, and human security

PAJ Waddington PAJ Waddington, BSc, MA, PhD, is Professor of Social Policy and Honorary Director of the Central Institute for the Study of Public Protection at the University of Wolverhampton. He has published eight books and numerous scholarly articles in the field of criminal justice and criminology. He is (with Martin Wright) series editor of *Policing Matters*, which publishes textbooks for vocational policing-related courses. He is also General Editor (with Peter Neyroud) of *Policing: A Journal of Policy and Practice*. He has written three book-length reports, including the official report on the policing of the Boipatong massacre in South Africa in 1992. He has given evidence to numerous inquiries related to policing and served on the Independent Advisory Group to the inquiry into the policing of the G20 protests in 2009 held by Her Majesty's Chief Inspector of Constabulary and on the ACPO working party implementing the recommendations of HMCIC.

He has lectured to academic and criminal justice practitioners throughout Europe, North and South America, South Africa, Australia, New Zealand, and the Middle East. He has been an external examiner at many universities in the UK and elsewhere.

Martin Wright Martin Wright retired from the West Midlands Police after thirty years' service in 2009. In his own time, Martin completed an undergraduate degree in Law and a Masters degree in security management. In 1999, he was the only police officer ever to be granted a Doctoral Scholarship by the Association of British Insurers to undertake research into radio links and public reassurance, at the University of Leicester. He is currently the Director of the Central Institute for the Study of Public Protection and Head of Department of Uniformed Services at the University of Wolverhampton, with responsibility for pioneering BSc (Hons) degrees in Policing, Fire & Rescue, and Armed Forces. Students on all three degrees are selected entirely on intellectual merit, but are required to join auxiliary volunteer branches of each of these uniformed services during their studies. He has co-authored and co-edited several books and articles, and is also Managing Editor of *Policing: a Journal of Policy and Practice*.

List of Abbreviations

ACC	Assistant Chief Constable
ACT	Australian Capital Territory
AFP	Australian Federal Police
Ch Insp	Chief Inspector
Ch Supt	Chief Superintendent
CHIS	covert human intelligence source
CNC	Civil Nuclear Constabulary
D Comm	Deputy Commissioner
Det Ch Insp	Detective Chief Inspector
Det Insp	Detective Inspector
HMCIC	Her Majesty's Chief Inspector of Constabulary
HMRC	Her Majesty's Revenue and Customs
IAG	Independent Advisory Group
IFC	Inter-Faith Council
Insp	Inspector
IPCC	Independent Police Complaints Commission
LGBT	lesbian, gay, bisexual and transgender
NSW	New South Wales
PCC	Police and Crime Commissioners
Sgt	Sergeant
SOCO	Scenes of Crime Officer
Supt	Superintendent

PART ONE

Police Practice and Ethics

1

Introduction

PAJ Waddington

This volume was intended to break new ground in several directions not all of which have been realised. In this introduction, I want to describe what the volume was intended to achieve and the changes that it has undergone in the process of its production.

Police Culture

I have long been a vocal critic of how 'police culture' is conceptualised by academic criminology (Waddington, 1999a, 1999b, 2008, 2012), not because I find the chatter of the police canteen or personnel carrier edifying, but because this concept has been used as a lazy way of explaining police (mis)behaviour. If officers act improperly it is tempting to attribute it to the malign influence of their culture and demand that it should change. It is another incarnation of what Wilson once described as the 'good man' theory of policing—this notion insisted that in order for policing to change 'good people' should be recruited and trained, and their virtue should be defended by strict rules backed by threats of draconian punishment (Wilson, 1968). One need not even apologise for the sexism of the phrase, since it is still male police officers who are seen as perpetuating a masculine ethos that often serves to exclude and marginalise their female peers. I have never been persuaded that this was an accurate portrayal of policing. Some might say that I am betraying the fact that I began my working life as a police officer, but others who did the same and followed the same course into academic life were not so afflicted. Ad hominem criticism is the academic equivalent of 'playing the man, not the ball' in soccer. My background may have disposed me to look kindly on my former colleagues, but what really impressed me was the dedication and quality of the young people whom I accompanied on routine patrol as part of my research fieldwork. They loved policing and wanted to do a good job.

Denunciation is easy, but police culture is not easily changed, indeed it persists quite tenaciously. One of the few research projects that did not succumb to lazy theorising about police culture suggests why police culture is so immutable. Janet Chan studied closely the New South Wales police during a period of radical reforms following a scandal that claimed the careers of many of its most senior officers (Chan, 1996, 1999, 2003, 2009). A new Commissioner was appointed with a wholly new mandate for the organisation. Commissioner Avery was a prominent advocate of community policing and his goal was to instil in the NSW police this ethos. One obvious means of doing so was to recruit and train the right people to do the right thing. The training regime was thoroughly overhauled and infused with the values of community policing. The trainers were carefully selected from those committed to the Commissioner's vision. The first cohorts of recruits were selected from the 'brightest and best' of their generation: liberally minded young people from diverse ethnic backgrounds and gender balanced—a reformer could not wish for more! During the first month at the police academy the liberal values and commitment of these recruits to the community policing ethos not only remained undimmed, but was enhanced. After completing a month's initial training, the recruits were entrusted to field training officers who had been equally carefully selected to introduce the recruits to the realities of police work. At the conclusion of that first period of police work, those young people returned to the academy with attitudes and inclinations indistinguishable from generations of hard-bitten veteran cops.

What had gone wrong? How did Chan explain it? Using the conceptual framework of Pierre Bourdieu she distinguishes between the 'field' and 'habitus' within which Australian police officers work. She concluded that the origins of the culture lay less inside the police station, canteen, or personnel carrier than it did in Australian society into which its colonial heritage was deeply etched, not least in the treatment afforded to the Aboriginal population (Chan, 1997). This created a 'field' in which conflicts were played out and dilemmas created to which the 'habitus' of assumptions, beliefs, stereotypes, and much else were an adaptation. I don't find the 'field'–'habitus' conceptualisation particularly helpful, however I do agree entirely with the underlying proposition that police culture, like other cultures, represents collective attempts to resolve recurring problems, issues, dilemmas, and conflicts. The implication is that Commissioner Avery tried to wish away the culture he had inherited, without being able to change the underlying conditions that gave rise to it.

When it was first coined by academic researchers, 'police culture' *was* seen as an adaptation to the realities of police work, and there was also tacit acknowledgement that those realities of police work are not capable of being wished away at all. Classical research (Skolnick, 1966; Manning, 1997; van Maanen, 1978; Bittner, 1970, 1985, 1990; Punch, 1979; Rubenstein, 1973) emphasised how the culture emerged out of the fundamentals of police work: the need to be suspicious and peer beyond surface appearances; to dissemble and lie so as to manipulate the behaviour of others; and perhaps most fundamental of all, to use force as an instrument of one's work. Yet, in some respects there were, even in this early work, striking disconnections between the realities of policing and the rhetoric of police officers. Punch and Naylor (1973) drew attention to the indefinitely wide role of the police, which effectively meant that they were a 24/7 multi-functional social service, but few police officers were prepared to embrace such a conception of themselves. Indeed, they saw 'do-gooders' such as social workers to be interfering and naïve 'challengers' who thought they knew better how to deal with criminals and ne'er-do-wells than did the police (Holdaway, 1983). An even more striking disconnection is the contradiction between most police officers' commitment to 'crime-fighting' and the reality of policing in which only a minority of tasks conform to this image and those that do are often lengthy, tedious, and unrewarding, such as processing a juvenile shoplifter through the system that concludes with a formal warning (Waddington, 1993). Such realities are often dismissed by officers as mere distractions from the 'real job' of catching criminals. However, denial is as much a cultural coping strategy as many others. John Brewer described how officers of the Royal Ulster Constabulary culturally inoculated themselves against the threat that they would be killed or mutilated by terrorists (Brewer, 1990) and Malcolm Young showed how officers ward off the psychological implications of close encounters with death, especially gruesome deaths, by the adoption of 'black humour' (Young, 1995; Henry, 2004).

Denial comes at a price, however, for it impedes the development of more effective ways of coping with the awkward realities of police work. It allows fictions to be maintained despite daily experience to the contrary. It can even foster mental ill-health, as when the 'John Wayne syndrome' prevents officers admitting that they have been disturbed by their experience and do not seek counselling. Most of all, it discourages officers from confronting the dilemmas and difficulties that their work imposes. Policing is erected on a lie and buttressed by elaborate rhetorical support. The 'lie' is that policing is fundamentally about law enforcement, which protects the wholly innocent from the depredations of depraved criminals who are clearly and unambiguously guilty of the crimes of which they are accused, even if the perversity of the criminal justice system obstructs their conviction. Such a view denies the realities that police do many more tasks than enforce the law; that victims of crime are often also offenders and, if not, are legally, morally, and socially tainted; that the obligation to act on the basis of suspicion entails 'reading between the lines', 'joining the dots', and 'putting two and two together' and all of it in a hurry—a recipe for error; and that the criminal justice process demands that all doubt must be extinguished before conviction can be secured. Taken together policing is institutionally conducive to what the 19th century pioneering sociologist, Emile Durkheim, described as 'anomie': an aversive condition associated with social dysfunction and personal distress. The culture that officers create is institutionalised denial of the anomic nature of their calling.

Those who have written about police culture or simply employed it as a ready explanation for their critical observations often do so from an explicitly normative stance: police culture is to be deplored and changes demanded. I share many of their aspirations. Having spent a career studying police officers from the relative comfort of the 'groves of academe', I have now committed the autumn of my career to making a small contribution to the professionalisation of policing through establishing a three-year undergraduate university degree in policing. However, change cannot be achieved simply as an act of will. If police culture is to change then the circumstances that encourage it must change. Yet, the fundamentals of policing cannot easily be changed, if at all. What point is there in a police officer who does not 'read between the lines' and act on suspicion? The task then is to help the police to confront the realities of their work and construct a professional culture that enables them to cope with those realities. This means identifying the cultural challenges found, not in the canteen or the personnel carrier, but on the streets and in dealing with sometimes difficult people in ambiguous and threatening conditions.

Ethics and Values

Rules

When reformers prescribe changes to the culture of policing, they often do so in terms of infusing officers with higher ethical awareness as an inoculation against wrongdoing. There is nothing at all wrong with ethical awareness: exemplary standards of conduct are the hallmark of professionalism. Police officers are often ready to point to the stringent disciplines under which they work: in England and Wales[1] the Police and Criminal Evidence Act and associated codes of practice prescribe in exquisite detail how officers must treat those they stop and search, arrest, charge, detain, interrogate, and much else. Internal disciplinary regulations stipulate the minutiae of how they conduct themselves. Also, it is often overlooked that whilst police officers have been described as merely 'citizens in uniform', they are required by law to conduct themselves in accordance with standards that do not apply to fellow citizens. As occupants of 'public office' they may commit offences of 'mis-' and 'malfeasance' and they are liable to the specific offence of 'neglect of duty'.[2] Also, in the performance of their duties they are given exemption from some of the legal standards that would otherwise apply, for example, they are allowed to exceed the speed limit in the performance of their duties, but this is normally hedged around with legal interpretations of

---

[1] Whilst this collection of essays is written by and intended for a readership drawn from across the world, each of the contributors (including the editors) will, of necessity, be writing from a perspective coloured by the particular jurisdiction in which they work. The United Kingdom is an assemblage of jurisdictions, with some marked differences amongst them. In this chapter and other contributions throughout the text, I will be writing from the perspective of the jurisdiction of England and Wales.

[2] I am indebted to Martin Wright for this information.

what exactly is in the 'performance of their duties'. More commonly officers must rely on having 'lawful authority or excuse' for performing acts that would otherwise violate the law. Officers can also expect not only to have their evidence tested in the witness box, but also to have their personal competence and integrity questioned. Whilst officers might rely on powers that are available to anyone, they can expect to be held to a higher standard of propriety and competence. For example, s 3 of the Criminal Law Act 1967 grants to 'any citizen' the power to use 'such force as is reasonable' to prevent crime and apprehend offenders. Police officers are afforded no special status in this legislation, but what does 'reasonableness' amount to? A frightened elderly person alone in their home at night and confronting a burglar will be regarded by the courts quite differently from officers who find themselves in an equivalent position. Ordinary people can be expected to panic in the face of such an unaccustomed threat, but a police officer is equipped with weaponry and trained in its use, and should be familiar with handling volatile people who might put others in fear of harm. Hence, officers can be expected and are required to act with more skill—'who is the professional around here?' Also, in their private lives, police officers find themselves being confined by expectations that do not apply to others. For instance, they must avoid excessive debt, lest they put themselves in a position where third parties (creditors) could exert undue influence over them—an obligation that extends to other members of their family. It is also the case that disreputable conduct that would otherwise not attract a criminal sanction, is more likely to be criminalised if committed by an officer. Plagiarism is a sin that offends academics, but few others. Students on vocational university courses designed to lead to policing careers may find that what the university regards as a 'slap on the wrist' internal matter, will be treated as 'fraud' by their current or prospective employer and that will result in their dismissal or obstruct their recruitment as a police officer.

Rule breaking and 'bending'

One might imagine that given this dense web of restrictions and constraints there is no need to add yet another in the form of standards of professional ethics, but that would be wrong. First, despite such a plethora of rules and procedures, it does not prevent police officers 'bending' and 'breaking' them, indeed to some extent it encourages them to do so. Policing necessarily and unavoidably is an activity that is conducted in conditions of 'low visibility' (Goldstein, 1960). It is relatively invisible in several senses: police actions taken late at night in deserted locations are likely to be witnessed by no one other than those immediately involved. If an officer is alleged to have behaved badly, then it is usually the word of one person against another—a 'swearing contest' (Skolnick and Fyfe, 1993). Moreover, this 'contest' is an uneven one, because the officer is likely to be performing his or her duty, whereas those they are most likely to encounter in such circumstances are young men, intoxicated by alcohol or drugs, whose character is tainted by criminal convictions or some other discreditable features, such as homelessness, a history of mental illness, and so forth. As a result, officers find it easy to repel accusations of wrongdoing (Russell, 1976). Some locations that give rise to complaints may even be more shielded from view, for instance inside a patrol vehicle, or in the cells. Regulatory agencies have, over the years, tried to cast light into these dark corners, but the environment within which the police operate is replete with 'dark corners' that cannot so easily be illuminated. Also, whilst the *behaviour* of officers might be quite open to scrutiny, their motives for acting in a particular way will always be a matter for conjecture. A police officer was caught on video hitting a young woman on the leg with his baton and with his hand across the face during a protest that accompanied the G20 in London in 2009. The officer was prosecuted for assaulting the woman, but the judge dismissed the case on the grounds that the prosecution had not established that his undoubted use of force was *excessive* given the equally undoubted volatility and aggression being shown towards this officer and others by the crowd surrounding them, and the woman's own provocative behaviour (Casciani, 2010). Police officers legitimately perform, as a matter of duty, actions that would in other circumstances be considered exceptional, exceptionable, or illegal (Waddington, 1999b). Arresting and handcuffing someone would be assault in most circumstances, *unless it was a police officer who was making the arrest and applying the handcuffs.*

Secondly, the dense web of rules and procedures tends to be overwhelmingly punitive—a 'punishment-centred' bureaucracy (Kelling and Kliesmet, 1996). Writing about the Metropolitan Police in the 1980s—an organisation that hardly enjoyed (at that the time) public acclaim for the standards of propriety exhibited by its officers, Smith and Gray observe:

> It is important to recognise that these [internal disciplinary] rules are almost purely negative in their effect: that is, police officers may be disciplined, prosecuted or otherwise get into difficulties if they are seen to break the rules, but they will not necessarily be praised, enjoy their work or achieve their career objectives if they keep to them. (1983: 169)

It is also a hypocritical bureaucracy (Ericson, 1982), because officers are tacitly encouraged to 'sail close to the wind' in dealing with crime and disorder until 'they overstep the mark' and wrongdoing is exposed, whereupon the organisation rejects them. This is what Punch observed during his fieldwork in Amsterdam, when a specialist drug squad that had been valorised for its successes, was revealed as having corrupt relationships with criminals (Punch, 1985). Punch takes the view that corruption in the police is not so much a problem of 'rotten apples', but is instead a symptom of a 'rotten orchard' (Punch, 2009). Just how expansive that 'orchard' can be has been highlighted by Jyoti Belur's research on lethal 'encounters' between police and suspected criminals in Mumbai. She describes how many of those amongst senior officers, the judiciary, politicians, and even human rights campaigners subscribe to a culture in which the summary execution of suspects accused of serious criminality is tolerated (Belur,

2010). From the comfort of the developed world, one might imagine that such an affliction is not something that the police of England and Wales share. However, the tragic killing by armed police of Jean Charles de Menezes suggests otherwise. He was mistaken for a wanted terrorist in the immediate aftermath of the failed bombing of London underground trains and a bus on 21 July 2005. Without warning, he was shot repeatedly in the head at close range—a tactic then known by the codename 'Kratos'. The Independent Police Complaints Commission conducted an inquiry, which whilst it was critical of the police operation, did not recommend any action against the officers who fired the fatal shots. The IPCC relied upon the advice of HM Government's 'Treasury Counsel' who concluded that such a tactic was, within strict limits, 'lawful' (IPCC, 2007: section 9, especially paragraph 9.2). In other words, and to put it bluntly: if the police form the suspicion, on incredibly slender evidence, that someone is about to commit a 'suicide bombing', it is perfectly permissible in law to sneak up behind them and, as Americans so indelicately put it, 'fill their head with lead'. This seems to be tantamount to saying that when protection of human rights becomes seriously inconvenient, they are not worth the paper they are written on. This isn't only true for the extreme circumstances of suicide terrorism, as Article 15 of the European Convention on Human Rights makes clear:

> In time of war or *other public emergency* threatening the life of the nation any High Contracting Party may take measures derogating from its obligations under this Convention to the extent strictly required by the exigencies of the situation, provided that such measures are not inconsistent with its other obligations under international law. (Italics added)

Of course, the Convention is no more than an international treaty from which any state can derogate at will. Hypocrisy reigns!

It is not only a matter of hypocrisy, which after all oils the machinery of government. The dense web of rules and procedures that surround policing make wrongdoing more, rather than less, likely. How can that be? Because it is so difficult for officers to comply strictly with all the rules that supposedly govern them, this encourages the use of expedients that subvert those rules. Such expedients are actually directly encouraged by the operation of the criminal justice process. When officers present evidence, either in court or statements of arrest and similar documents, they swear that they are not only truthful, but also exhaustive; otherwise, a suitably edited version of events could easily give the appearance of criminality. Hence, officers are bound (as are all witnesses) to tell the '*whole* truth'. However, if they do so, then every prosecution of every minor offender would demand huge investigative effort and soak up resources (for an example, see Waddington, 1999b: 133–4). Moreover, the legal process also entices officers to tell untruths. Research on police use of force, especially lethal force (Manolias and Hyatt-Williams, 1988; Burrows, 1992; Klinger, 2004; Lewinski and Grossi, 1999; Lewinski and Hudson, 2003a; Lewinski, 2008) emphasises how perception is distorted by the stress that officers experience in such life-or-death struggles. Yet, officers are required, when giving evidence, to recount in detail and accurately what exactly happened and in what order. To be exposed as less than entirely certain, would be to jeopardise a prosecution, or indeed in some circumstances an officer's own defence. This problem is simply the most acute end of a much broader spectrum. As Dixon (1997) points out, the criminal justice process involves creating a 'paper reality' and this is conducive to cynicism and tolerance of wrongdoing, such as enhancing evidence to secure a conviction— 'gilding the lily'. Since cynicism and low-level manipulation of evidence is ubiquitous, there is no 'moral high ground' for officers to occupy when deploring the excesses of others, because everyone is tainted, delinquency is a matter of degree. Everyone is also at risk of exposure and so this breeds a culture of solidarity in which it is in each person's self-interest not only to passively tolerate wrongdoing by others, but actively to connive in covering it up.

This may appear an excessively bleak picture, but it is precisely what has come to light in the aftermath of causes célèbres in which wrongdoing has become endemic (Punch, 2009). However, there is a *much bleaker* picture. The pioneering sociologist, Robert Merton (Merton, 1957) developed Durkheim's earlier conception of 'anomie', which he re-defined as a conflict between institutionally approved ends and institutionally approved means. This applies perfectly to police officers who are enjoined to prosecute criminal wrongdoers through a criminal justice process that by design makes conviction difficult to achieve. Merton went on to examine different ways in which people strive to overcome this conflict, one of which he called 'ritualism'—substituting means for ends. This is the disease that infects bureaucracies: it does not matter what is achieved, only that the rules are correctly applied. Such 'ritualism' is actually what the rules and procedures approach mandates. It reached its full malign absurdity during the years of performance management, when officers were instructed to maximise the number of 'sanctioned detections' for specified offences, which encouraged them to make needless arrests for trivial infractions.

Professional standards

Despite the plethora of rules and procedures that govern policing, this still does not impose on police officers standards of conduct that are high enough. The reason is that such rules can only stipulate minimum standards, which if an officer falls below will merit his or her punishment. They are also externally imposed standards, which police officers do not *own* either psychologically or culturally. Such impositions are notoriously ineffectual: people 'jump through hoops' with reluctance, often for the very good reason that the 'hoops' are at best purposeless and may even be counter-productive. Even scrupulous adherence to rules and procedures cannot guarantee a satisfactory level of performance. A pioneer of police research, Egon Bittner, observed:

> The prevalence of regulatory supervision, that is, control that merely measures performance against formulated norms of conduct, can only produce judgement

that the assessed person did nothing wrong. Insofar as this is the case, an incompetent, ineffective, and injudicious officer could remain in good standing in his department provided it cannot be shown by any accepted method of proof that he has violated some expressly formulated norm of conduct. This comes very close to saying that an officer who shows up for work, does what he is told to do and no more, and stays out of trouble meets the criterion of adequacy demanded of him. (Bittner, 1983: 5)

In a revealing piece of research, Bullock and Johnson (2012) examine police compliance with the Human Rights Act (1998), which incorporates into English law the European Convention on Human Rights. What they discovered was that compliance was what might be called 'procedural-ised'; that is, when planning an operation, senior officers would explicitly check off that they had fulfilled their obligations under the Act and often used stock phraseology with which to do so. This was not the internalisation of a human rights consciousness, but an exercise in 'covering one's back' in case of allegations of wrongdoing.

No one can credibly object to organisations explicitly avowing virtue, but equally it is naïve to imagine that the profession of virtue is an effective shield against temptation. Organisations whose primary, in some cases, sole function is the profession of virtue, can and have nonetheless been riven with corruption. The scandals that have rocked the Roman Catholic Church worldwide pay handsome testimony to the frailties of all people no matter what their calling. Successive generations of members of the 'mother of parliaments' were implicated in systematic inflation of their supposed 'expenses', which in some cases represented a clear breach of the criminal law, for which a few were prosecuted and found guilty. Even medicine has played host to some of the vilest criminals on the planet. Harold Shipman has the distinction of being amongst the most prolific and sustained serial killers the world has seen. Suspicions about the deaths amongst his elderly patients were voiced and disregarded, until the accusations became irrefutable (Smith, 2005). The retention of human organs of children who died in the Royal Liverpool and other hospitals, without the consent of the next of kin, was a systematic abuse that continued over a protracted period of time and involved the participation of numerous individual medical practitioners and support staff (Redfern et al, 2001).

What is the alternative? Tom Tyler has recently argued (Tyler, 2011) that in all manner of organisations, people cooperate and strive to fulfil their tasks, not in anticipation of rewards and penalties, but because they are 'self-motivated' by the belief that what they are doing is 'the right thing', which in turn, Tyler argues, is fostered by personnel being treated fairly and with respect. He cites evidence that in commercial organisations, when people are treated fairly and with respect, productivity increases and cooperation with even unpopular decisions of management is secured. The imposition of a plethora of rules and procedures is the opposite of Tyler's prescription. It is the adoption of what he refers to as an 'instrumental' regime in which attempts are made to influence behaviour by the threats of punishment and promises of reward. Instead of being trusted, mistrust is elevated to an organising principle (see O'Neill, 2002 for an excoriating critique of this approach to ethical behaviour). Social psychologists have long been aware that in laboratory experiments subjects can be induced to behave badly—cheat in games or inflict gratuitous pain via electric shocks—by suffering even mild reductions in self-esteem, but are more resilient to such inducements when they are encouraged to feel good about themselves. Police organisations are an egregiously perverse version of this model, since even as 'instrumental' regimes, they are unbalanced—'*punishment*-centred bureaucracies' (Kelling and Kliesmet, 1996). Still more perverse is the chorus of civil libertarian critics who demand ever greater stringency in the investigation of police wrongdoing and severity of punishment! All this succeeds in achieving is reinforcing solidarity coupled with defensiveness, which serves to tolerate poor practice and shield delinquent and incompetent officers. We need to reverse this emphasis and encourage officers to recognise the nobility of their calling; the opportunity they are offered to influence lives for the better; and the extent to which they can be relied upon when 'the going gets tough'; so that they aspire to live up to the values they espouse.

Trust cannot just be demanded; trustworthiness must be earned and the route to that taken by other occupational groups is to become recognised as truly professional. Professionals are trusted because they *hold themselves and their colleagues to a higher ethical standard* than those that are externally imposed. Medical doctors are bound by the civil and criminal law not to be negligent in their treatment of patients, neither to kill nor injure them needlessly. However, they impose upon themselves a much higher duty to 'do *no* harm'. There are surprising similarities between the practice of medicine and the duties of police officers. Both entail inflicting harm in order to do good. The drugs that physicians prescribe are invariably toxic, hence the care that is taken to avoid overdosing, and surgery is inevitably injurious. Doctors must live with the prospect that the treatment they prescribe might do serious harm to some—possibly causing death—albeit to a small minority of their patients. We trust them to do this because we believe that they will be genuinely devoted to maximising the patients' best welfare and not simply trying to avoid penalties for poor practice. Medical ethics committees and practitioners generally agonise about the dilemmas that advances in medicine seem to bring in their wake.

Police officers do harm to some—those they suspect of wrongdoing—in order to safeguard the welfare of others, and their practice too involves ethical dilemmas aplenty. However, there is a significant discontinuity between medicine and policing, which is that whereas medical practitioners overwhelmingly inflict the harm of medication or surgery only with the express consent of the patient (or their guardian) who will suffer it, police officers often act *without the consent* of those who are the most immediate recipients of their actions. It seems to me that this places an additional ethical burden on the police. They must ensure that in exercising *all* their constabulary duties, they do so in accordance with the highest ethical standards. Foremost amongst those must be to avoid any needless trampling on the rights of others. However, this must come from and be owned by the police themselves, for only then will officers aspire to achieve the highest standards when dealing with people whose behaviour can be extraordinarily challenging, even frightening; in circumstances that might be complex and uncertain; and in a context that is morally depraved. This is no small demand, but it is one that I believe police officers would embrace. The point of this collection of essays is not to prescribe what officers must do in any given situation, but to stimulate debates about appropriate courses of action, to encourage greater reflection upon what are all too frequently dismissed as mere routine, and to value the contribution that police officers can make to the well-being of others.

Practice

Competence

Are ethics enough? Policing, like any other profession, must be *practised* in a particular context. An equally important hallmark of professionalism is competence in the purely instrumental requirements of fulfilling one's duties. A surgeon who has imbibed medical ethics would still be less than professional if he or she was unable to use surgical instruments effectively! Policing too involves many practical skills and knowledge. Officers need to be well versed in the law, for whilst policing cannot be defined purely in terms of law enforcement, the law remains a vital component of the 'toolkit' available to officers in dealing with the multifarious problems that they are asked to deal with. When crimes are committed officers need to understand how their duties interrelate with other agencies in the criminal justice system. Statements may need to be taken from witnesses and victims that are literate and fit for the legal purposes for which they will be used. Crime scenes need to be recognised as such and preserved for forensic examination. Physical evidence needs to be recovered and treated appropriately. The police serve not only the criminal justice process, but also a host of other legal institutions to which they might find themselves accountable. Coroners' courts have quite different functions and procedures from those of criminal courts, so do the civil courts, and administrative tribunals of bewildering variety. Neither is the police the only organisation with responsibility for maintaining order and security. The size of the private security industry eclipses that of the police and its operatives have overlapping, yet different, responsibilities, functions, and legal powers.

Officers need also to be aware of the cultural backgrounds of those whom they encounter. A firm hearty handshake may be acceptable to men from a western cultural background, but not necessarily to people from other cultures or indeed to women from any culture. Cultural understanding is just one aspect of wider police intelligence, so that officers can accurately 'read between the lines' to ascertain what is happening, but there should be much more to 'police intelligence' than that. It should include an understanding of the causes and consequences of behaviour, some of which may be aberrant. For instance, police frequently encounter people suffering mental ill-health and should be aware of how various conditions present themselves. Officers should not confuse medical conditions, such as insulin overdose, with offending behaviour, such as drunken disorderliness, even though the presenting symptoms are very similar. Policing is often team-work and it is important that officers understand how their organisa-tion functions so that they can best enlist various specialist services as and when necessary.

Most of all, officers need to use force and weapons effectively, proportionately, and with *controlled* aggression. This is a visceral activity, but it too should rely on a clear understanding of the physical, psychological, and socio-political implica-tions of its use. Officers who have been involved in life and death conflicts, such as lethal encounters, express surprise at the sensory and perceptual distortions they experience—time appearing to slow down, hearing impairments, colour draining from their sight, and tunnel vision (Manolias and Hyatt-Williams, 1988; Klinger, 2004). They should not be surprised: officers should be educated about such matters and be familiar with the implications of combat (Lewinski, 2002a, 2002b; Lewinski and Grossi, 1999; Lewinski and Hudson, 2003a, 2003b; Lewinski, 2008). Because modern western societies tend to abhor violence (Pinker, 2012), police organisations tend to de-emphasise its centrality to the police function, preferring instead to redirect attention to more 'cosy' aspects of policing, such as 'community policing'. However, the use of force is prominent amongst the most controversial and damaging behaviour that has attracted public criticism of the police in all western jurisdictions. Attitudes of some officers towards the use of force tend to bring discredit to the police when they leak into the public domain.

Discretion

In the face of such complexity the exercise of discretion becomes central to the police role. Officers exercise both *de facto* and *de jure* discretion. The common law of England and Wales imposes a duty on officers to exercise their constabulary powers with discretion. Legislation is normally couched in terms of 'a constable *may*' rather than a 'constable *must*'. The constabulary powers exercised by an officer are 'original', which in this context means that they origin*ate* from within the officer: his or her judgement. Again, this is something that the police have institutionally ignored: focusing instead upon officers' grasp of the legal require-ments once those powers are invoked. For example, police in England and Wales are granted powers to stop and search fellow citizens subject to various provisos and procedures. However, Code A of the Police and Criminal Evidence Act makes it plain that people are free to consent to be stopped and searched, provided that the legal provisos exist for a formal legal stop and search should it be necessary—consensual stop and search cannot be used as a means to subvert the restrictions on its use. Automatic recourse by officers conducting stops and searches to a formal script might unnecessarily transform what is bound to be a sensitive encounter into an adversarial confrontation. Yet, it has become a common modus operandi amongst inexperienced officers who are encouraged to stop and search people so as to gain experience in using their powers. Certainly, the research evidence suggests strongly that whereas even amongst those who have been stopped and searched there are few who dispute that the police should possess and exercise this power. What they object to (and do so with disturbing frequency) is the *manner* in which it is done (Miller et al, 2000a; Quinton et al, 2000; Miller et al, 2000b). I suspect that this is because many officers seek to hide behind the formal strictures to protect themselves from complaint. However, 'going through the motions' is hardly a recipe for effective policing. It would surely always be preferable to assess the situation and act accordingly. This, of course, is what acting with discretion entails. Discretion is sensitive to the circumstances, weighing up the merits of the case and dealing with it appropriately. Discretion also means responding to the sensitivities of others. Officers tacitly recognise this: a joke (in very poor taste) that circulated in police circles long ago depicted an officer delivering a 'death message' by asking the woman who answers their knock at the door with the question, 'Are you the widow Jones?' This is the humour that makes one squirm with embarrassment, so egregious is the inappropriateness of the behaviour—it is catastrophically *indiscreet*.

Discretion poses a problem for the police educator: it excludes prescribing *any* course of action in advance, because what is appropriate in one instance may not be appropriate in another. How, then, can the skilled use of discretion be developed? The answer, I think, lies in the notion that every situation needs to be assessed on its merits. An experienced officer, skilled in the use of discretion, does not know what the next situation into which he or she is about to intrude will hold for them. What experience has given them is exposure to many such encounters each of which has been unique. Hence, they expect the unexpected, are alive to the subtleties that indicate the particularities of the circumstances, and are knowledgeable about a variety of strategies and the consequences they have produced in the past. They are equipped to deal with uniqueness and they can enjoy it as one of the challenges and delights of police work—never a dull moment!

However, all of this is predicated not only on exposure, but also upon reflection. The professional officer does not discard experiences as being irrelevant to future events because they are each unique. The professional officer savours those experiences to consider the 'what ifs…?' 'I did X, but what if I had done Y?' This is learning and acquiring skills that can be employed in the next encounter and others beyond.

One learns most from those situations that are most challenging: so far beyond anything else one has encountered that they test one's responses to the full. What challenges police officers repeatedly are dilemmas: how to act appropriately when any course of action conflicts with other desirable goals? This involves the careful weighing of various elements and the more acute the dilemma the

15

more weighing has to be done. It is also an intrinsically intellectual process—not something normally associated with police work, which tends all too readily to be dismissed as requiring no more than the application of 'common sense'. However, adjudicating between mutually exclusive options requires analysis and is admirably well suited to deliberative reflection. Hence, this book was envisaged as a series of challenges, by presenting each contributor with a dilemma that was as irresolvable as I could make it, and inviting them to negotiate a path through the maze.

Only a few accepted the challenge. Thankfully, those most willing to do so were serving or retired police officers. From the academics that were approached only very few were prepared to pick up the gauntlet and Jenny Fleming, Monique Marks, and Vern Redekop are to be congratulated for their intellectual courage. Campaigners and activists—individuals and organisations—were also invited to participate in the hope of stimulating discussion and debate, but none were willing to do so—most of them did not acknowledge receipt of the invitation. I leave readers to draw their own conclusions.

Scenarios

What were the dilemmas with which our contributors were faced and why were they selected? Dealing with the 'why?' first: the decision to formulate fictionalised dilemmas was guided by a series of academic considerations. The conventional method of eliciting views and attitudes is one that provides as little information as possible. For example, an interviewer's questionnaire will ask something like the following:

> Overall, were you satisfied or dissatisfied with the way the police handled this
> matter?
> IF SATISFIED ASK:
> Very satisfied or just fairly satisfied?
> IF DISSATISFIED ASK:
> A bit dissatisfied or very dissatisfied?
> (Home Office, 1992: V. 104)

In other words, the aim is for the interviewer to say as little as possible and leave it to the person to autonomously convert what might have been a complex interaction that included aspects with which they were satisfied and dissatisfied into a composite response. This is not necessarily invalid; after all if we are asked our opinion about a movie, concert, restaurant, or holiday destination, we often compress lengthy and complex experiences into a summary. Voting for a political party at an election comes down to a single choice.

The problem with this methodology is that whilst it might reflect the general mood of how people feel about something—the police—it does little to guide how one might effect change. How should an officer behave in any set of circumstances so as to leave those with whom he or she has had contact with a generally satisfied feeling? The 1992 British Crime Survey, from which the question is taken, goes on to ask questions about the amount and quality of information provided by the police about progress of any investigation and/or prosecution. This may be informative: it reveals that people often feel that they are left in the dark about such matters and they find that dissatisfying. But is that all? If the police and other agencies in the criminal justice system were to keep victims better informed about how their case is progressing, would this transform dissatisfaction into a satisfied response? We do not know.

Over the past half a century an alternative methodology has developed virtually unnoticed and certainly without the obsessive attention that has been given to questionnaire design. It approaches the problem from the opposite direction, providing the interviewee with as much information as possible. Although, he may not have been the first to do so, it was the pioneering child psychologist, Jean Piaget, who popularised the technique with his book *The Moral Judgement of the Child* (1932, see also Kohlberg, 1968). He told children of different ages stories that incorporated a moral dilemma and examined the type of reasoning they employed in coming to their conclusions. He found that as children grew older they tended to use more sophisticated reasoning. In the 1960s Stanton Wheeler (1961) did much the same, but this time with prisoners serving sentences for serious crimes. For example he asked interviewees to imagine that they were passengers in a friend's car, which whilst exceeding the speed limit is involved in a serious accident. Should the interviewee tell the police that their friend was driving in excess of the speed limit? To do so would be a clear violation of the 'no rat' rule amongst prisoners, but Wheeler found that as prisoners approached the end of their sentence, so they began to adjust their normative standards and revise (however rhetorically) their allegiance to the 'no rat' rule. More recently, Vanessa Munro and her colleagues (Finch and Munro, 2005, 2006, 2007; Ellison and Munro, 2009a, 2009b, 2009c) have shown 'mock juries' details of rape cases and asked them to adjudicate on the guilt of the accused. This has produced disturbing evidence that ordinary people apply stereotypical criteria of what constitutes 'normal sex' to the advantage of the accused and disadvantage of the alleged victim.

The advantage of vignettes or scenarios is that they approximate more closely the circumstances in which moral or legal rules are necessarily applied. Frequently, a set of moral or legal principles will prove in practice to be internally contradictory: the rights of one individual or group might, and often do, come into conflict with the rights of others. Inevitably, those who sit in judgement about such rules—such as the law courts—must *balance* one set of precepts against another. How do they do so? How should they? It is difficult to answer these questions save in the context of a particular set of circumstances. The scenario methodology provides those particular circumstances.

There is a related, but distinct, strand of academic thinking that is relevant here and that is that people's decisions generally appear not to be guided by sets of rules. Clifford Shearing and Richard Ericson (1991) argue—using police officers as an example—that cultures contain more 'figurative' than categorical impera-tives and the authors emphasise how stories are important in capturing those elusive notions of what is acceptable or not. Rom Harré and Paul Secord (1972) describe human beings as 'rhetoricians', because we habitually offer narratives of our actions: 'Had a nice day at the office, dear?', 'Yes! You'll never guess who walked in today...'. Richard Ericson (2007) argues that there is an inevitable gulf between the rules that dominate an occupation such as policing and the realities of how people—police officers—actually think and act. The result is that officers are condemned to struggle to fit the facts into a rule-based schema—a process which looks awfully like 'anomie'.

Police officers, it is often observed by researchers, just love telling stories—'war stories'. These are the backbone of the police culture, depicting venality on the part of criminals, gullibility on the part of the public, and heroism by police offic-ers. The approach taken here is to 'go with the flow' of policing. To tell stories and then to examine those stories very closely and ask, what should be done?

The advantage of fictionalising the dilemmas of policing is that it makes them 'safe'. Contributors can free themselves from the shackles of compliance with rules and procedures, and discuss how situations must be negotiated and princi-ples balanced. I believe that it is the beginning of the development of a genuine body of practice knowledge. It is designed to be of assistance to police educators, who we hope will pose these scenarios to their students and then compare stu-dent responses with the responses of contributors. However, it is imperative that no one assumes that these contributors are offering a definitive solution to these imagined dilemmas. The notion that there are, or could be, such definitive solu-tions is utterly alien to the approach that this book is taking.

Structure of the Book

The contributions are organised around a set of five scenarios, each of which poses distinctive dilemmas, not just ethical but also legal and political. To the best of my ability, the dilemmas are as irresolvable as they could be made. As explained earlier, whilst police officers were eager to participate in this venture, academics and especially campaigners and activists were less so. The original aim was to have a police officer's, an academic's, and a campaigner's view of each scenario, so as to engender discussion and debate. Sadly, that was frustrated: only two scenarios have more than a single contribution. Hence, responsibility for stimulating discussion and debate falls to the editors to provide and so following the reflections of our contributors to each scenario there is a commentary that is designed to engender discussion. We wish to make it clear that in doing so, we are not criticising our contributors—that would be impolite! What we are doing is to highlight issues.

In devising the scenarios it was our intention to go well beyond the normally quite cryptic accounts that are used to elicit attitudes and opinions from samples of the population. So, each scenario paints a relatively detailed picture. It also paints a picture that deliberately avoids casting any of the participants in the guise of 'evil', 'venal', or 'deranged' individuals. It is too easy to say, as police officers are often prone to do, that a problem has arisen because of the incompetence or corruption of a particular individual. I was one of that legion of damned, compelled to stay awake late into the night watching successive series of the hugely successful American television programme, *The Shield*. This depicted a squad of LAPD cops who policed the gangs dealing in drugs and vice in a dilapidated, ethnically mixed area of Los Angeles. These cops were also corrupt, indeed their depravity was such that the lead character, 'Vic Mackey', wilfully shot and killed another cop who was trying to infiltrate the squad with a view to exposing them and having them prosecuted. Yet, like millions of other faithful viewers, I sat on the edge of my seat as the noose seemed to tighten progressively around Vic's neck, willing him to find a way of escaping justice. Why? Because, Vic was not wholly bad, nor were those pursuing him beyond blemish. They were all flawed human beings, as we all are. So, in these scenarios pains have been taken to populate each of them with characters who are dedicated cops trying to do the right thing in circumstances that pose irreconcilable dilemmas.

The chapter that follows this introduction considers the utility of scenarios as a means of posing and discussing professional ethics, written by one of the foremost police ethicists, John Kleinig. He reviews the various scenarios and considers the ethical issues that they raise.

Thereafter, the book is organised into five sections, each of which contains the scenario, the contribution(s), and an editorial commentary. Since contributors are drawn deliberately from different jurisdictions, there will inevitably be differences of law and practice amongst them, and some contributors have found it necessary to vary the scenario so that it fits more neatly with the circumstances with which they are most familiar. We welcome this. Policing, because it is so jurisdictionally based, can all too easily become parochial. When the cultural defensiveness of police officers is added to the mix, then there is the danger that any discussion of practice simply re-affirms whatever current practice may happen to be. Hence, we look at some scenarios through the lens of jurisdictions other than those with which we are familiar and that gives greater perspective.

The body of the collection begins with a scenario, at the heart of which are issues of loyalty and suspicion amongst colleagues, as well as issues of rank. Very usefully, we have two quite different perspectives from contributors: one from the perspective of a former English chief officer (Peter Neyroud, assisted by Chief Inspector Colin Paine) and the other from a serving officer in the Australian Federal Police (Juani O'Reilly) aided by one of the few academics willing to grasp an intellectual nettle (Jenny Fleming). The contrast between the top down and bottom up views will, we hope, illustrate nicely the extent to which these issues do not appear the same from different positions within the hierarchical structure of police organisations.

This is followed by a perennial dilemma: managing relations with key figures in communities. For much of its history, the British police generally tried to keep officers apart from the public. The notion that 'community policing' is a return to a style of policing hallowed by tradition could not be further from the truth. Most police forces possessed disciplinary codes that forbade officers from 'idling and gossiping' with the public and 'fraternisation' was frowned upon, for fear that officers would become ensnared in relationships that could prove corrupting. 'Idling and gossiping' is now valorised as 'community policing' and 'gathering intelligence', but it continues to pose the danger that officers might stray into a corrupting relationship. Feldberg coined the phrase the 'free cup of coffee' problem (1985, see also MacIntyre and Prenzler, 1999), but in this scenario it turns out to have been a free cup of very sweet tea! An officer in the New Zealand Police, Sarah Stewart, agreed to take on this challenge at very short notice after another contributor withdrew. Fortune smiled on us, because Sarah has direct experience of participating in an overseas policing mission in which she encountered cultural conflicts of the kind envisaged in the scenario.[3]

Community relations issues are also explored in the next section, where the scenario envisages a conflict amongst different sections of the community that appears to be irreconcilable. Vern Redekop is an advisor to the police in Ottawa and has advised other police forces in various Canadian provinces. He is the author of several books aimed at promoting amongst practitioners a method of negotiating conflicts arising from public protest and similar events. We thought it helpful to pose an acute example to test how this approach would be applied in such challenging circumstances!

The next section addresses one of the most iconic issues of contemporary policing—terrorism. It also explores the difficulties that accompany one of the most favoured police responses to terrorism, the collection of intelligence. It envisages a situation in which the police have secured a covert human intelligence source (a CHIS or informant) within a terrorist network, but one whose 'price' for continued participation as an informant entails that a line of enquiry in a murder investigation should not be pursued. What should the police do when faced with the prospect that investigating properly a high-profile murder threatens to turn off the tap of useful intelligence about the intentions and actions of dangerous terrorists? This challenge was accepted by Steve Darroch, again from the New Zealand Police, who should be congratulated for pointing out that the scenario as originally formulated was *not challenging enough* and who encouraged the editors to revise it in order to make the dilemma more acute!

Terrorism is more than a threat to individuals who might be killed or injured in terrorist attacks, it is a direct threat to the state itself, but it is not the only threat to state interests. Privately owned and run power stations are essential parts of

---

[3] The editors are also grateful to Steve Darroch who recommended Sarah and persuaded her to contribute.

the 'critical national infrastructure'. If the power stops flowing, the pumps cease to work and pretty soon there will be sewage in the streets. So, what should the police do when people wish to protest about plans to build a private power station using technologies of which those protesters disapprove?[4] Protest is more than a right in a democracy, it is positively virtuous, since citizens are actively participating in the process of government. However, suppose that the power company makes it clear that if the protest is allowed to interfere with the operation of the controversial site, then they will withdraw plans for other sorely needed power stations? This is a dilemma that creates a toxic mix of ethics, rights, and politics. To ponder it we have two contributions: first from Monique Marks from the University of Zwazulu Natal and Sean Tait, from the African Policing Civilian Oversight Forum. South Africa is, of course, a country with a very troubled history of policing under the apartheid regime, especially public order policing, so it is particularly welcome to have a contribution from that country. The second contribution is from a former senior officer with long experience of policing all forms of protest in central London (some which were highly controversial and sensitive)—Mick Messinger. What may surprise and delight readers is that contributions from two countries with such different histories of public order policing essentially concur on the main issue.

Conclusion

The editors hope and expect that readers will find this volume interesting, but most of all we hope that you will be stimulated to discuss and debate the issues we raise. We hope that in training and during professional development exercises officers will devise their own irresolvable dilemmas in order to challenge themselves as much as they might challenge colleagues. We also hope that by drawing our contributors from different jurisdictions, this volume might make a small contribution to building an international professional policing consciousness.

References

Belur, J, 'Police "encounters" in Mumbai, India', in JB Kuhns and J Knutsson (eds), *Police Use of Force* (Santa Barbara, CA: Praeger, 2010), pp 52–62.

Bittner, E, *The Functions of the Police in a Modern Society* (Washington, DC: US Government Printing Office, 1970).

Bittner, E, 'Legality and workmanship: introduction to control in the police organization', in M Punch (ed), *Control in the Police Organization* (Cambridge, MA: MIT, 1983), pp 1–12.

---

[4] In this case the technology is nuclear power, but it could be fossil fuel or wind or tidal power—all have their opponents.

Bittner, E, 'The capacity of use force as the core of the police role', in F Elliston and M Feldberg (eds), *Moral Issues in Police Work* (Totowa, NJ: Rowman and Allanheld, 1985), pp 15–26.

Bittner, E, *Aspects of Police Work* (Boston: Northeastern University Press, 1990).

Brewer, JD, 'Talking about danger: the RUC and the paramilitary threat' (1990) 24(4) *Sociology* 657–74.

Bullock, K and Johnson, P, 'The Impact of the Human Rights Act 1998 on Policing in England and Wales' (2012) 52(3) *British Journal of Criminology* 630–50.

Burrows, CS, 'The Use of Lethal Force by Police', *Faculty of Business Studies and Management* (Jordanstown: University of Ulster, 1992).

Casciani, D, 'G20 police officer Delroy Smellie cleared of assault' (*BBC News*, London, 2010).

Chan, J, 'Changing police culture' (1996) 36(1) *British Journal of Criminology* 109–34.

Chan, J, 'Police culture', in D Dixon (ed), *A Culture of Corruption* (Annadale, NSW: Hawkins Press, 1999), pp 98–137.

Chan, J, 'Culture', in A Wakefield and J Fleming (eds), *The Sage Dictionary of Policing* (London: Sage, 2009), pp 72–4.

Chan, JBL, *Changing Police Culture: Policing in a Multicultural Society* (Cambridge: Cambridge University Press, 1997).

Chan, JBL, *Fair Cop: Learning the Art of Policing* (Toronto: University of Toronto Press, 2003).

Dixon, D, *Law in Policing: Legal Regulation and Police Practices* (Oxford: Clarendon, 1997).

Ellison, L and Munro, VE, 'Of "normal sex" and "real rape": exploring the use of socio-sexual scripts in (mock) jury deliberation' (2009a) 18(3) *Social and Legal Studies* 291–312.

Ellison, L and Munro, VE, 'Reacting to rape: exploring mock jurors' assessments of complainant credibility' (2009b) 49(2) *British Journal of Criminology* 202–19.

Ellison, L and Munro, VE, 'Turning mirrors into windows? Assessing the impact of (mock) juror education in rape trials'. *British Journal of Criminology* (2009c) 49(3) 363–83.

Ericson, RV, *Reproducing Order* (Toronto: University of Toronto Press, 1982).

Ericson, RV, 'Rules in policing: five perspectives' (2007) 11(3) *Theoretical Criminology* 367–402.

Feldberg, M, 'Gratuities, corruption, and the democratic ethos of policing: the case of the free cup of coffee', in F Elliston and M Feldberg (eds), *Moral Issues in Police Work* (Totowa, NJ: Rowman and Allanheld, 1985), pp 267–76.

Finch, E and Munro, VE, 'Juror Stereotypes and Blame Attribution in Rape Cases Involving Intoxicants' (2005) 45(1) *British Journal of Criminology* 25–38.

Finch, E and Munro, VE, 'Breaking boundaries? Sexual consent in the jury room' (2006) 26(3) *Legal Studies* 303–20.

Finch, E and Munro, VE, 'The demon drink and the demonized woman: Socio-sexual stereotypes and responsibility attribution in rape trials involving intoxicants' (2007) 16(4) *Social and Legal Studies* 591–614.

Goldstein, J, 'Police discretion not to invoke the criminal process. Low visibility decisions in the administration of justice' (1960) 69(4) *Yale Law Journal* 543–94.

Harré, R and Secord, P, *The Explanation of Social Behaviour* (Oxford: Blackwell, 1972).

Henry, VE, *Death work: Police, trauma, and the psychology of survival* (Oxford: Oxford University Press, 2004).

Holdaway, S, *Inside the British Police* (Oxford: Blackwell, 1983).

Home Office, R a PUS a CPRBMRBL, 'British Crime Survey: Questionnaire', in RAPU Home Office (ed) (London: Home Office, 1992).

IPCC, 'Stockwell One: Investigation Into the Shooting of Jean Charles de Menezes at Stockwell Underground Station on 22 July 2005' (London: Independent Police Complains Commission, 2007).

Kelling, GL and Kliesmet, RB, 'Police unions, police culture, and police use of force', in WA Geller and H Toch (eds), *Police Violence: Understanding and Controlling Police Abuse of Force* (New Haven, CN: Yale University Press, 1996), pp 191–213.

Klinger, D, *Into the Kill Zone: A Cop's Eye View of Deadly Force* (San Francisco, CA: Jossey-Bass, 2004).

Kohlberg, L, 'The child as a moral philosopher' (1968) 2 *Psychology Today* 25–30.

Lewinski, B, 'Biomechanics of lethal force encounters—officer movements' (2002a) 27(6) *The Police Marksman* 19–23.

Lewinski, B, 'Stress reactions related to lethal force encounters' (2002b) 27(3) *The Police Marksman* 23–8.

Lewinski, B and Grossi, D, 'The suspect shot in the back—Is your shooting clean? Understanding the limits of survival psychology' (1999) 24(5) *The Police Marksman* 23–5.

Lewinski, B and Hudson, B, 'The impact of visual complexity, decision making and anticipation. The Tempe Study, experiments 3 & 5' (2003a) 28(6) *The Police Marksman* 24–7.

Lewinski, B and Hudson, B, 'Time to START shooting? Time to STOP shooting? The Tempe Study' (2003b) 28(5) *The Police Marksman* 26–9.

Lewinski, W, 'The attention study: A study on the presence of selective attention in Firearms Officers' (2008) 8(6) *Law Enforcement Executive Forum* 107–39.

MacIntyre, S and Prenzler, T, 'The influence of gratuities and personal relationships on police use of discretion' (1999) 9(2) *Policing and Society* 181–201.

Manning, P, *Police Work: The Social Organization of Policing* (Prospect Heights, IL: Waveland, 1997).

Manolias, M and Hyatt-Williams, A, 'Post-shooting Experiences in Firearms Officers' (London: Joint Working Party on Organisational Health and Welfare, 1988).

Merton, RK, *Social Theory and Social Structure* (New York: Free Press, 1957).

Miller, J, Bland, N, and Quinton, P, *The Impact of Stops and Searches on Crime and the Community* (London: Home Office, Policing and Reducing Crime Unit, 2000a).

Miller, J, Quinton, P, and Bland, N, 'Police stops and searches: Lessons from a programme of research', *Home Office, Briefing Note* (London: Home Office, 2000b), pp 1–6.

O'Neill, O, *A Question of Trust* (Cambridge: Cambridge University Press, 2002).

Piaget, J, *The Moral Judgement of the Child* (London: Kegan Paul, 1932).

Pinker, S, *The Better Angels of Our Nature: A History of Violence and Humanity* (London: Penguin, 2012).

Punch, M, *Policing the Inner City* (London: Macmillan, 1979).

Punch, M, *Conduct Unbecoming: The Social Construction of Police Deviance and Control* (London: Tavistock, 1985).

Punch, M, *Police Corruption: Deviance, Accountability and Reform in Policing* (Collumpton: Willan, 2009).

Punch, M and Naylor, T, 'The police: a social service' (1973) 24(554) *New Society* 358–61.

Quinton, P, Bland, N, and Miller, J, 'Police Stops, Decision-making and Practice', *Police Research Series* (London: Home Office, Policing and Reducing Crime Unit, 2000).

Redfern, SM, Keeling, Dr JW, and Powell, E, *The Royal Liverpool Children's Inquiry Report* (London: House of Commons, 2001).

Rubenstein, J, *City Police* (New York: Farrar, Strauss and Giroux, 1973).

Russell, K, *Complaints Against the Police: A Sociological View* (Leicester: Milltak, 1976).

Shearing, CD and Ericson, RV, 'Culture as figurative action' (1991) 42(4) *British Journal of Sociology* 481–506.

Skolnick, JH, *Justice Without Trial* (New York: Wiley, 1966).

Skolnick, JH and Fyfe, JJ, *Above the Law: Police and the Excessive Use of Force* (New York: Free Press, 1993).

Smith, DJ, 'Shipman: the Final Report', *The Shipman Inquiry* (Crown Copyright, 2005).

Smith, DJ and Gray, J, *The Police in Action* (London: Policy Studies Institute, 1983).

Tyler, TR, *Why People Cooperate: The role of social motivations* (Princeton: Princeton University Press, 2011).

van Maanen, J, *Policing: A View From the Street* (New York: Random House, 1978).

Waddington, PAJ, *Calling the Police* (Aldershot, Hants: Avebury, 1993).

Waddington, PAJ, 'Police (canteen) sub-culture: an appreciation' (1999a) 39(2) *British Journal of Criminology* 286–308.

Waddington, PAJ, *Policing Citizens* (London: UCL, 1999b).

Waddington, PAJ, 'Police culture', in T Newburn and P Neyroud (eds), *Dictionary of Policing* (Cullompton: Willan, 2008), pp 203–5.

Waddington, PAJ, 'Cop culture', in T Newburn and J Peay (eds), *Policing: Politics, Culture and Control* (Oxford: Hart, 2012), pp 89–110.

Wheeler, S, 'Socialization in correctional communities' (1961) 26 *American Sociological Review* 697–712.

Wilson, JQ, 'Dilemmas in police administration' (1968) 28 *Public Administration Review* 407–17.

Young, M, 'Black humour—making light of death' (1995) 5(2) *Policing and Society* 151–68.

Reflections on Teaching Police Ethics with Scenarios

John Kleinig

Introduction

Police training, it has been observed, is not only about 'doing it right' but also about 'doing right'. Its concerns go beyond the development of practical and managerial skills to the exercise of wise ethical judgement. How to accomplish the latter constitutes a perennial challenge. It begins with the ancient question about whether virtue can be taught[1] and narrows to debates about the relative merits of open and closed cases.[2]

In an intensely pragmatic occupation such as policing, one fraught with surprise as well as conflict, it is critical that intending and practising officers are appropriately prepared for the situations that will confront them. Certain time-honoured approaches to teaching ethics—often reflected in the early literature on police ethics—seem particularly unsuited to that task. I have in mind, for example, introductions to moral theory—consequentialism, deontology, natural law theory, contractarianism, and so on—imparted in the hope that an engagement with these highly controversial and rarefied theories and the debates that surround them will have an impact on ground level thinking. Although—in my experience—an approach of this kind may sometimes have connected with the Catholic schooling received by many police officers of Irish and Italian descent, even then it did little more than provide a theoretical scaffolding for familiar moral generalities about honesty or respect for persons or

---

[1] Meno's question to Socrates in Plato, *Meno*. See also Ryle (1972: 434–47).

[2] That is, cases allowing for competing ethical responses and those for which only one ethical response will do. See Cliff and Nesbitt Curtin (2005: 14–17).

justice. Hardly better was the effort of early texts in professional ethics that sought to articulate these moral theories and then ask: what would a consequentialist say about...? Or, how would a Kantian deal with a situation in which...? Not only were seven-league boots required to bridge the gap between such high-level moral theory and the particular practical scenarios that were presented, but the approach's non-prescriptive 'political correctness' did little to encourage students to enhance their own moral judgement. They were simply tasked with determining what a utilitarian or Kantian or...would do—a kind of moral anthropology. Or, not too much better, they were asked to opt for one of these theories and then to work from there, as though 'opting' and applying was what moral deliberation was ultimately about. We have come a fair way since then.

Nevertheless, there is still considerable controversy about what police ethics teaching or training should be doing and how it can best be achieved.

Purpose

In a debate between William Heffernan and myself fifteen years ago, Heffernan drew a distinction between guidance and contested-issues models for teaching police (or any other kind of professional) ethics.[3] The guidance model offers advice on particular ethical issues—say, the acceptance of gratuities, the use of force, or the limits of deception—whereas the contested-issues model seeks to acquaint students with the current state of debate on such matters, without indicating how that debate should play out. Both may offer extended rationales for the views that they consider. However, it is Heffernan's contention that 'grading' in the former case should take into account the conformity of students' views with those of the teacher ('right reason'), whereas a grader in the contested-issues approach would grade simply on the basis of the students' grasp of the contours of the debate. Heffernan argues for the special appropriateness of the contested-issues approach to university-based criminal justice ethics courses, though he allows that police academies might well choose to adopt the guidance model. My own contention in the debate with Heffernan was that the contrast between the two models was too sharply drawn, that teacher neutrality was not only impossible but undesirable, and that students should be graded on the quality of their argumentation, not the congeniality of their views. Insofar as reasonable people could disagree on many of these issues, good reasoning need not imply conformity with a teacher's views. Inter alia, I saw the purpose of a criminal justice ethics course (whether in a university or a police academy) not simply as one that acquainted students with the state of the debate but also as involving what Paolo Freire called conscientisation (*conscientização*), in which

---

[3] Heffernan (1997: 3–20) and Kleinig (1997: 21–31). Each paper includes an Addendum.

an effort is made to heighten students' sensitivity to the moral dimensions of situations, the moral status and relevance of particular practical reasons, and strategies for moral judgement.

Teaching Strategies

As for ways of teaching police ethics and criminal justice ethics more generally, there is a great diversity of options, each of which has its pros and cons.[4] The traditional lecture series, which attempts to cover an area (such as police ethics) by providing a richly textured overview of general and particular issues—say, the role of police, exercising discretion, and using force—has a place, albeit a limited one. Although this format can sometimes be replaced by prescribing a textbook or distributing materials that cover the area, it is probably better suited to those whose interest is in academic research of some kind. For people whose ambitions are essentially practical—those who are or wish to become criminal justice professionals of some kind—approaches that are more closely focused on practical decision making should be closer to centre stage. Not that we are confronted by a simple either/or: for the teacher of police ethics, a critical question will probably be that of determining how much of each of the various approaches is employed and how each is to be integrated into a course.

With respect to courses that focus on critical thinking and decision-making skills, there are many options, from fieldwork and debriefing, the use of film, role playing, debates, expositions and explorations of formal codes of ethics, and of course encounters with and discussions of case studies or scenarios (sometimes characterised as problem-based learning). This is not the place to discuss their comparative merits. Nor is this the place to discuss the relative merits of pervasive and stand-alone ethics teaching.[5] My purpose here is the more limited one of considering the strengths and challenges of using scenarios as a teaching device.

What Are Scenarios?

Briefly, scenarios offer opportunities for practical moral reflection based on situations or sets of circumstances that might be encountered in the *real world*. I say 'might' because some scenarios, such as the well-known 'ticking-bomb argument', seek deliberative responses to situations that are not likely to be encountered, given our world or the limitations of our knowledge.[6] Such *artificial thought*

---

[4] I have discussed some of these in Kleinig (1990: 1–18).

[5] For some of that debate, see, eg, Callahan (1997: 87–102).

[6] For an extended discussion, see Brecher (2007).

experiments are usually designed to stretch our ethical imagination in new directions. There is considerable debate about their usefulness.[7]

Here I focus on realistic scenarios, that is, on decision-making situations that might be encountered in the ordinary course of events. Such scenarios may be *skeletal* or *extended*—the distinction between the two being a matter of degree rather than one of kind. Generally, though, skeletal scenarios—often only a paragraph—seek to get our moral responses (and our reasons for them) to some particular decision (or decision-making option) based on a restricted conjunction of factors. So, for example, a scenario is outlined in which a police officer pulls over a speeding car and discovers that it is being driven by an off-duty police officer. The students are then asked what the officer should do (and why). In some cases, such skeletal scenarios may generate an extensive discussion; in other cases, a more limited response and range of reasons is intended.

Extended scenarios involve greater complexity, by providing background material and often a series of decisional opportunities or points. Setting them up may occupy two or three pages, as in this volume, or, as is the case with the highly professional Harvard Case Program, some ten to twenty pages.[8] Extended scenarios may be contrived or based on actual situations, or (for teaching purposes) comprise some combination of the two.

Both skeletal and extended scenarios may be *open* or *closed*; that is, such scenarios may be designed to allow for 'reasonable disagreement among morally reflective persons' or be intended to evoke a single 'ethical' response. And, a bit confusingly, they may be *open-ended* or *complete*; that is, they may develop a problem situation that then leaves it to students to reflect on how it ought to be resolved, or they may tell a complete story, in which decisions have been made and which then function either to stimulate review or as cautionary tales.[9] (Of course, they may also include elements of both.) Although legal cases may sometimes provide frameworks for complete scenarios, they can also encourage an unfortunate reduction of ethical reflection to legally relevant considerations.[10] Nevertheless, they may also have the salutary value of helping students to distinguish what is morally up for consideration from what is of only legal relevance. The same reductionism may also be found—though perhaps less often—in case decisions (or 'advisories') made by professional bodies.[11]

---

[7] For a variety of positions, see Gendler (2000), Dancy (1985), Kamm (1988), and Walsh (2011).

[8] The Harvard Case Program can be accessed at: <http://www.ksgcase.harvard.edu/>.

[9] A further distinction might be made between extended cases that are *live or ongoing* and those in which the dust has *settled*. See McWilliams and Nahavandi (2006: 421–33).

[10] In part this may arise because students are tempted to hew to the reasoning adopted in legal opinions, but it is also encouraged by the fact that the fact patterns of legal cases have been contracted to those matters that are deemed legally relevant. Added to that is the fact that legal opinions are opinionated—that is, fact patterns are likely to be skewed to the outcome desired by 'the court' or a particular judge. For an entrée to some of the literature, see Menkel-Meadow (2000: 787–816).

[11] One commonly finds 'ethical advisories' issued by the professions (law, medicine, engineering, etc) and only rarely in policing contexts.

Literary cases and films may also constitute fruitful sources of scenarios, though here too students may be limited by what an author or film maker chooses to include/exclude for literary or cinematic rather than straightforwardly ethical purposes.

These various options (artificial/realistic; limited/extended; closed/open; open-ended/complete) do not of course represent exclusive alternatives but are better thought of as poles on multi-dimensional continuums, and it is difficult to say which or what combination is to be preferred. Or at least it is difficult to make that judgement independently of contextual factors. Each might have a place, depending on its pedagogical location. Insofar as a training programme seeks to prepare people for making practical decisions in real-life circumstances, scenarios will usually need to have sufficient complexity and be realistic enough to generate the kind of nuanced deliberation that occupational circumstances require. Although simplified cases are valuable in drawing attention to the relevance of particular considerations, and may even help students to see how tradeoffs are often required, most real-life situations involve a range of factors that give complexity to moral decision making and require a series of judgements to be made. Police officers and those they encounter have histories, families, health issues, and formed expectations, and whether and how these need to be factored in must be considered.

Extended cases can be presented in a variety of ways. They may be presented as hard copy narratives (as in this volume), digital texts with options, film clips, 'clicker' cases,[12] or role plays. Each may have its place.

The Case for Teaching with Extended Scenarios

Although there is an argument (introduced later) for using a variety of teaching strategies when dealing with issues of police ethics, there are several reasons for including extended scenarios.

(1) Extended scenarios can be geared to the complexities of human life and decision making. Although a decision may be called for at point t_0, it is very likely that the decision that must be made at that point will reflect decisions made at t_{-3}, t_{-2}, and t_{-1}. It is important that police officers realise that the decision to be made at t_0 cannot be divorced from other decisions already made, whether or not those earlier decisions should be determinative. This is brought out quite well in 'Community Negotiation', in which Superintendent Wiltshire's decision with respect to the LGBT community does not and cannot take place in a vacuum, but needs to take account of a previous decision she has made with respect to a march by far-right activists. That previous decision may now threaten to limit her

---

[12] See, eg, Herreid (2006: 43–7).

options or she may need to distinguish it in relevant ways so that it does not do so. The point is, how she responds to the proposed opening of 'Queers' must take account of the previous decision she made with respect to the far-right activists. Similar considerations apply in other cases as well. In 'The Free Cup of Coffee Problem', by the time that Chief Inspector Roberts realises that Mr Py Ken is likely to be in violation of an international convention, he has already formed a trusted relationship with Mr Py Ken and has chosen to avert his eyes from lesser legal violations. The point is not that he should not have formed a familiar relationship with Mr Py Ken—there were, after all valuable informational tradeoffs to be gained—but that these past decisions serve to blur bright lines and make his current decision more difficult to make, morally as well as psychologically. To take just one more case, in 'Intelligence', Detective Chief Inspector Bhat's previous decisions concerning informant Clive Brown cannot but colour her dealings with Chief Superintendant Dalrymple over the next strategies to be taken in the murder case. Even though she might point out the weakness of the evidence, she knows that she has good reason to think that if the raid takes place she risks losing the cooperation of her prize informant.

(2) The complications to which extended scenarios point us include more than past decisions that impinge on present demands. There is also the complexity that they are able to convey through the diversity of considerations that come to bear on decision making. It is sometimes convenient to distinguish factors that make decisions psychologically hard from factors that make them morally difficult—when, for example, a police officer is faced with the criminality of a friend. We might of course simply say that professional responsibility trumps personal attachment and, in the abstract, that may be true. But real cases can be more nuanced than that. Supt Sutton not only thinks well of ACC Jackson's professionalism, but he has also developed a trust in his integrity and overall moral probity. Nevertheless, he cannot simply dismiss what he has heard from Ch Insp Smythe. There is an intertwining of the personal and professional here that cannot be easily disentangled, and though he might have a keen sense of the demands of professionalism, he cannot simply put aside the personal dimensions of his position. He is ACC Jackson's trusted Staff Officer, and even if he investigates and puts to rest the apparent 'information' about ACC Jackson's affair, he will be doing something that would very likely be perceived by Jackson as evidencing a lack of trust, if not a betrayal. The point is not to suggest that this should be determinative, but it illustrates how a general claim, such as 'professional responsibility trumps personal attachment' becomes much more problematic or at least nuanced when the rubber hits the road.

(3) There is a further way in which scenarios alert decision makers to the complexity of situations. A police officer is not confronted simply with someone who, say, has apparently violated a law, but a human being with such-and-such

characteristics who appears to have violated a law in such-and-such circumstances and for whom a particular response is likely to have such-and-such consequences. A partial analogy can be drawn with medical decision making. A physician confronted with a patient is not dealing only with a distressed body for which a particular treatment might be indicated, but a person with a particular emotional make-up, and economic, religious, and other personal circumstances, all of which might enter into a decision about how best to proceed. It is only a partial analogy, of course, because part of the moral role of a police officer is to discount certain features of the person's situation when deciding what to do. It is why we seek informed consent in cases of medical decision making and not in law enforcement decision making. Nevertheless, one of the reasons—albeit not the only one—that we grant police officers discretion is to enable them to make nuanced decisions when these are called for. A police officer who pulls over a speeding driver does not necessarily make a bad decision in issuing a warning rather than a ticket if the driver appears contrite or was trying to respond to an emergency (say, getting to the hospital where her child has just been taken). We might wonder whether Ch Insp Roberts should have allowed his relationship to Mr Py Ken to develop in the way it did or to the extent that it did. On the other hand, Roberts is very conscious of the suspicion of police that Mr Py Ken has acquired from his homeland and of the conventions of hospitality that exist within Mr Py Ken's culture. The use of discretion is a potent yet risky prerogative, critical to the police role. It is not learned algorithmically or by means of mnemonics, but through the exercise of judgement in complex situations. For the most part, it belongs to police wisdom rather than the application of a code or rule. No doubt, there is value in reminders—such as: as the risk of serious harm increases the scope of discretion decreases—or even in continuums of force that police departments often promulgate—but in the end the wise use of discretion will require practiced engagement with the kind of complexity to which extended scenarios can draw attention.

(4) Extended scenarios also encourage students to think for themselves and to develop reasons for their thinking. The particularity of scenarios usually puts them beyond a formulaic response. Even if there are policies, regulations, and laws that can be appealed to as part of a response, why the policy, regulation, or law is relevant and how it is to be interpreted and applied is likely to be a matter about which there can be some debate and about which students will have to make decisions of their own for reasons that they will have to formulate. The point of such debates is not to convey the idea that there are 'no right answers' or that 'it is just a matter of opinion', but that 'reasonable people may sometimes disagree' and that 'some answers are better than others'. Closed scenarios are designed to show students how, despite the complexity of a situation, a particular decision should have been made or outcome sought. Such scenarios can be good exercises in the identification and prioritisation of morally relevant considerations. Open-ended scenarios, such as those in this volume are often intended to be open as well, allowing for reasonable disagreement, albeit not ruling out the

possibility that some options could be considered better than others. In 'Public Order (Nuclear Power Plant)', for example, although Deputy ACC Andrewski has primary responsibility for public order, and must be concerned not only about the potential for panic that the militants' activities will have but also about the fact that the organisers of the 'Climate Camp' have refused to comply with legal and other requirements, he is also aware that an even larger public order threat looms in the background—created by an unsafe nuclear plant. Should he try to do a deal with the CC organisers to head off the militants? Should he try to undermine the plan of the militants by leaking it to the newspapers? Should he try to assert the authority of law by cracking down on all the protesters? How should he factor in what he has learned about the ageing nuclear plant?...

(5) There is some empirical evidence to suggest that students whose training includes a significant engagement with scenarios will not only develop better critical thinking and decision-making skills but also retain course content more effectively.[13] That, of course, presumes that the case-based teaching is well managed. It stands to reason though, that if content is contextualised, as it is in scenario-based teaching, it will gain a firmer foothold in consciousness.

(6) Because extended scenarios are usually dealt with in a group context, there is a significant likelihood that students will encounter responses and perspectives that they would not otherwise have needed to consider. Not only may this broaden their horizons and perhaps challenge their preconceptions and even prejudices, but it should also prepare them for perspectives that they will encounter in the larger social world in which they will have to make their decisions. Where scenarios are integrated into activities such as role playing, they also provide opportunities for practitioners to take the point of view of those about whom decisions are being made, and thus provide opportunities for empathy that might otherwise be filtered out of decision making. Platitudes about the acceptance (or non-acceptance) of gratuities are challenged by the situation initially faced by Ch Insp Roberts as he seeks to develop relations with Mr Py Ken's growing community.

Even if police are occupationally more inclined than others to be rule oriented, it is to be expected that in any cohort of students some will be more situationally oriented and therefore less likely to decide simply according to the rules. And so there may be those whose focus in 'Community Negotiation' will be on how Supt Wiltshire will be able to implement or extend her tolerationist agenda in a potentially disruptive situation rather than on invoking provisions of the Public Order Act. Should she now invoke the Act to maintain social control rather than, as previously appears to have been the case, invoked it for tolerationist ends? In 'Public Order', ACC Andrewski also has legal weapons he may use and which some may believe he should use; others, however, may see his public order skills

[13] See, eg, Sudzina (1997); Major and Palmer (2001); Beers (2005); Gijbels, Dochy, van den Bossche, and Segers, (2005); Gossman, Stewart, Jaspers, and Chapman (2007).

as requiring the use of more nuanced strategies that will allow the protests to take place while minimising the potential for public panic.

(7) Although there is no guarantee, one of the benefits of complex and extended cases is that students are encouraged to distinguish between morally relevant and morally irrelevant considerations. Many factors that could bear on how a decision might be made or what decision ought to be made—say, what 'everyone else does' or 'how we do things round here' or 'this is what you can get away with' or 'what the law allows'—have a questionable or at least controversial place in ethically acceptable decision making. The benefits of learning how to distinguish that which is morally relevant from that which is not will then be transferable to other cases. Students will need to consider whether Mr Py Ken's ethnic background in 'The Free Cup of Coffee Problem' or ACC Jackson's colour in 'Compromised Senior Officer' should have any relevance to the ways in which their cases should be handled. If so, they will need to determine how ethnicity and colour might come to be morally relevant—not, perhaps, by virtue of any *in se* relevance they have, but via the social meanings that they are accorded. And they will need to consider how such social meanings are to be factored in. Ch Supt Dalrymple needs to consider the moral weight—if any—to be accorded to the intense pressure that she and her unit are under to make headway in the hate killing of Byron Smart. Sure, she and her unit—and the police generally—are answerable to the public and they have an obligation to act where they have reasonable suspicion; but does the pressure they are under make what seems to be a weak case any stronger? Does the need to appear to be doing something count as a morally relevant reason for taking increased investigative risks?

(8) In the case of police work, although decisions are sometimes made in isolation, many if not most decisions are made as part of a group—sometimes just partners, but often as part of a larger team or squad that has some hierarchical differentiation within it. Group-based scenario teaching can provide an environment in which joint decision-making skills can be encouraged and developed. In 'Intelligence', for example, although Det Ch Insp Bhat and Ch Supt Dalrymple both have to make some decisions on their own, it might be considered advisable that, regarding the raid that is contemplated, Det Ch Insp Bhat discusses it with Ch Supt Dalrymple, disclosing enough information to enable Ch Supt Dalrymple's decision to be based on the fullest available intelligence.

One of the unspoken values of scenario-based teaching is that it encourages more collaborative decision making in police work. Even if we are individually accountable for the decisions we make, those decisions are often better made and more defensibly articulated if habits of shared reflection are developed. For example, is Supt Sutton in 'Compromised Senior Officer' limited to obtaining hearsay information about ACC Jackson, or might he and Ch Insp Smythe engage in a discussion about the ethical as well as practical ramifications of the various options that must now be confronted? Have Supt Wiltshire and Ch Insp Roberts got no one else with whom they have been discussing developments or can now share them? Admittedly, the hierarchical nature of much police work as well as the chain of responsibility implicit in it may inhibit collaborative reflection, but if nothing else the experience of scenario-based teaching ought to carry an important lesson about the value of joint reflection or at least of listening to others' reflections.

(9) More remotely, but not unimportantly, practitioners who have a sense of the complexity of moral decision making are in a better position to offer informed critiques of prevailing practices and policies within police organisations. We are not told about the rules under which Ch Insp Roberts or Det Ch Insp Bhat are expected to operate—what, for example, the rules are concerning the acceptance of gratuities or the handling of informers—but one of the virtues of extended scenarios is that they reveal the shortcomings of oversimplified approaches to decision making and offer the hope that with a better informed leadership more enlightened management and better articulated policies will be developed. Not only will that counter some of the minimalism that is encouraged by heavy handed and oversimplified policies but also contribute to police–public relations that are more easily characterised as 'by consent'.

(10) Finally, implicit in scenario-based teaching of the kind we are considering is a recognition of the moral standing of the students themselves. If the so-called 'jug to mug' style of teaching carries the subtle message that the teacher knows everything and the students know nothing (admittedly something of an exaggeration), scenario-based teaching acknowledges the moral capacities of students and seeks to harness and refine them. But their organisation and improvement will come from a process in which the teacher functions more as *primus inter pares* than as the fount of all moral knowledge and authority. If, following Kant, we understand human dignity in terms of the human capacity for moral discernment and commitment, then, because scenario-based teaching draws on the contributions of students, it affirms the dignity of learners.

Problems with Scenario-Based Teaching

Although scenarios have an important role in ethics teaching, there are certain drawbacks to an overreliance on scenarios. Although these drawbacks do not undermine their value, they may indicate ways in which scenarios need to be supplemented or used with care.

(1) One that may disturb teachers is the relative unpredictability of where a discussion will go, in part because the teacher loses a certain type of control over the teaching situation. This is not itself a reason for shying clear of scenarios, but it indicates that scenario-based teaching makes special demands on teachers and on their acquisition of skills not as obviously required by lecture-based teaching. If scenario-based teaching is not to degenerate into a bull session or mere brainstorming, it will require considerable preparation as well as management skills. It can be hard work. Although many of the questions posed by the scenarios presented in this volume look forward to the next steps to be taken by their various

protagonists, one is also required to look back to see how the situation got to the point at which it now is and whether prior decisions might (and ought to) have been different from what they were. A teacher has to insert him- or herself into the situation without the benefit of hindsight and to engage others in an imaginative as well as deliberative exercise.

(2) Good scenario-based teaching cannot operate in a theoretical vacuum. Here it is useful to compare police officers with medical practitioners. Like police officers, the latter spend their days making individual decisions with particular patients. They are very case oriented. Yet their ability to be successfully case oriented arises in part because of what they learned during their early training. That included, though was not limited by, an understanding of generalities—anatomy, physiology, microbiology, biochemistry, and so on. Although their day-to-day decisions do not generally require that they engage in extended theoretical deliberations (about anatomy, physiology, and so on), their understanding of individual cases is nevertheless informed by the fact that they have the background knowledge they do. One might say the same for police. It is much easier to make an informed decision in a particular case if one has also had the opportunity to encounter discussions of the broader issues that will inform reflection on the particular case—whether they are discussions about ethical issues raised by conflicts of interest, corruption, the acceptance of gratuities, the use of force, or by the limits of deception.

Scenario-based teaching will work best if police students have some acquaintance with what might be termed 'middle level' ethical inquiries into, say, the limits of deception, justifications for using force, the relevant determinants of discretion, the nature and limits of loyalty, the basis for police authority, and so on. Although it will not usually be possible to derive from such discussions how particular decisions should be made in the kinds of scenarios used in this volume, such engagements will, nevertheless, enable students to see how a particular use of discretionary authority or deception is embedded in a wider framework of understanding and ongoing debate, and therefore have a particular weight as the complexities of the instant situation are addressed.

This limitation on scenarios is not a problem with scenarios as such, but involves a recognition that scenarios themselves point outwards and upwards. It might therefore be useful to have scenarios at different stages of a course so that students can see how what they are able to bring to them is augmented as the course proceeds.

(3) The strength of scenarios also points to an important weakness, though it is not one from which other teaching strategies are exempt. Those who design scenarios tend to preempt a determination of what is morally and technically relevant. That is, they include data that are deemed relevant to decision making and exclude those that are not. Sometimes that is done with great skill and, in the case of extended scenarios, little of relevance may be excluded. Yet, for the most part, real-world situations do not come circumscribed except as we circumscribe them ourselves. What we include and what we exclude is—to a considerable

extent—up to us and constitutes an element in our moral perceptiveness and sensibility. Scenario designers, to a greater or lesser degree, remove that task or burden from us. Now it is of course possible for someone reviewing a scenario to respond to it by saying: 'Now I wonder if...because if that were the case then...' Indeed. Insofar as some piece of information has been excluded from the story, the person reviewing it is denied a piece of information that might have been morally relevant. Of course, insofar as someone reflecting on the story can respond in this way, the absence of some fact or other does not constitute a barrier to ethical reflection. However, there is a tendency for those reviewing a case to be constrained by what is presented and thus have their moral imagination limited.

(4) Related to the foregoing is another weakness of scenarios. Those who design them sometimes craft them with god-like omniscience concerning the events, providing information to readers that decision makers on the ground could not have had or have had with any degree of certainty. Their insertions of material are indeed relevant to decision making but may constitute material that a decision maker could not have been expected to know at the time. Yet our judgement *of such decision makers* cannot be dependent on what they could not have reasonably known beforehand.

How serious are the foregoing drawbacks? They could be serious if students are being asked to make judgements on actual situations—if, in confronting a scenario, a student is then asked to come to a decision that will be applied to the real world. But that of course is not what is being done. Scenarios provide exercises in decision making and do not constitute real-world decisions.[14] Limited though they may be, it is not the task of scenario-based teaching to have students make decisions of actual consequence. Rather, their role is the more modest one of sensitising students to the kinds of considerations that should figure in their ethical deliberations and to how such considerations 'play off' each other. Ideally, what students get from scenario-based teaching is not a template that is then applied to real-world situations but sensitivity and skill in seeing what is relevant and how it is relevant to their ethically acceptable decision making. What are drawbacks in scenario design may not be drawbacks for what scenarios are designed to achieve. Indeed, their very drawbacks may be turned to advantage by helping to disabuse students of the idea that there is a fixed framework to their moral decision making.

(5) Realistic though scenario-based teaching/learning may be, it needs to be kept in mind that there is still a significant gap, including a moral gap, between scenarios and real-life decision making. Some of the important values of scenario-based teaching—enabling students to find their decisional feet, be exploratory,

---

[14] The possible complication here is that some scenarios are drawn directly from the real world, and so, knowing what they are provided, students may come to decisions about real-world cases that, because of the selection of data, distort them in important ways.

etc—also serve to differentiate such situations from those they will later encounter, in which decisions will be 'final', 'potent', maybe 'irrevocable', and often made under considerable pressure. They need to be aware that real-life decision making takes place under conditions of uncertainty and will draw upon a range of attributes and skills for which the scenarios themselves may not have prepared them. John Stuart Mill (1978) observed that a morally mature decision maker 'employs all his faculties. He must use observation to see, reasoning and judgement to foresee, activity to gather materials for decision, discrimination to decide, and when he has decided, firmness and self-control to hold to his deliberate decision.' The 'firmness and self-control' of which Mill speaks, though of great importance, is not likely to be greatly developed by scenario-based teaching.[15]

Placing Scenarios

Scenarios might constitute the whole of a police ethics training programme or they might be used in conjunction with other forms of teaching. They might, for example, provide initial scene-setting, by provoking reflection and thus contextualising an engagement with theoretical materials that should inform reflection on the particularities of the scenarios. Or they might supplement a general text or narrative presentations on matters such as deception or interrogation. As indicated in the previous section, my own belief is that although scenarios should constitute an important part of police ethics training, they should not constitute the whole of it. But even with that said, there may be more than one way of integrating scenarios into a syllabus.

Two approaches to medical education may provide something of an illustration. One approach—the traditional one—has students attending 'medical science' classes for, say, the first three years of their training, followed by clinical training in hospitals for two years, and then a residency.[16] A more recent approach, however, inducts students into hospitals from the beginning (as observers of patients whose medical situation is shown and described), followed by, say, lectures on the physiology, epidemiology, and biochemistry of diabetes or emphysema or whatever maladies the students have encountered. Because the links between theory and practice are more visible, those whose ambition is to be medical practitioners are probably best served by the second approach.

I believe that the second approach may also have much to be said for it in the police case, not only in the sense of providing police with some field experience, but also in helping them to grasp the complex particularities of their task via scenarios. A single, extended scenario will not only draw on a diverse range of

---

[15] The point is not to advocate a stubbornness that is resistant to reconsideration, but strength of will that follows through when a final decision has been made.

[16] In the case of students who studied under the former approach, the introduction of case studies during their transitional years was thought important to their shift from foundational to clinical studies. See, eg, Hudson and Buckley (2004: 15–22).

considerations, but those considerations will themselves be embedded in wider discussions with which students might profitably be familiar. Moreover, it is by virtue of those wider discussions that what is relevant in a particular case can be successfully transferred to other cases.

Engaging with Scenarios

Reasons are reasons. But reasons may be of different kinds and they do not exist in isolation but in juxtaposition with other reasons. Moral decision making is not algorithmic but judgemental. That is, there is no formula for teaching how to make a decision in a particular case, but a complex procedure in which reasons are advanced, weighed, traded off, and reassessed in reaching a conclusion about what, all things considered, should be done. And what, all things considered, should be done, may itself be the beginning of yet another judgemental process that will proceed in a similar way.

Reflection on scenarios will likely focus not merely on 'how do we go on from here?' (in the case of an open-ended scenario) but also on 'how we got to this point' and 'whether it should have come to this', and 'what might have been done at an earlier point to have avoided this situation?' A strong virtue of extended scenarios is that they can remove some of the inevitability of situations—they can involve 'defensive driving' as well as 'crisis management'. If occupational decision making is seen as part of a larger narrative rather than in isolation, then 'how what I am deciding now might play out in some future situation' is a relevant consideration even though the future may be unknown. Of course, given the future's unknowability, we ought not to be too fixated on its possibilities (as in the common police focus on 'covering one's ass').

As well as the narrative benefits of scenarios, they can also have an important strategic role in helping students to develop ways of thinking about ethical challenges. Again, the point is not to develop a formal algorithm for decision making, but to foster ways of being alert to the morally relevant factors to be taken into account, strategies for disentangling them from other factors that may seem to intrude themselves into the decision-making situation, and ways of juxtaposing different moral considerations.

Managing Scenarios

Although scenarios offer an important entrée to teaching police ethics, they do not 'sail by themselves'. As Kenneth Winston has pointed out, success in teaching with cases is not just a function of the case itself—the richness of its content and complexity of its design—but also requires a good hand at the helm. 'The principal challenge for a teacher is so to structure a class discussion that students are forced to reflect on and analyse the opinions they express.'[17] This may be as necessary when students are inclined to agree about a case as when they are inclined to disagree. Certain forms of group think can be as destructive of moral sensibility as unregulated and mindless opinion swapping. It is the task of a teacher to prod when a shallow consensus is reached, and to probe when little more than brainstorming and opinion exchanging seem to be involved.

In a scenario of some complexity, it will be most helpful to have a visual representation of relevant (and perhaps irrelevant) considerations—eg a listing on a white board—of the questions to be addressed, of alternatives that are open to the relevant decision makers, and of possible consequences of the alternatives, along with a tracking and analysis of other decisional points. The challenge for the teacher will be to evoke these options from the group and to represent them in ways that engender creative thinking rather than confusion.

Winston offers an important insight into the management of scenarios when he compares two Cartesian images of the development of knowledge—on the one hand, a city planned by a single hand who, because of his ability, makes sure that its various elements are crafted to form a unitary and coherent whole—Brasilia? Canberra? Washington?—and, on the other hand, an ancient town that has gradually grown through accretions into a large and somewhat unwieldy metropolis—London? Jerusalem? Rome?[18] We have been greatly attracted to the former conception of knowledge, especially since the Enlightenment, but perhaps also as part of a natural human inclination to make sense of and control the world around us. But, Winston argues, our moral knowledge is much more adequately apprehended via the latter model, something we gradually accumulate over the course of a life as we see cracks in larger structures, the dead ends in particular ways of thinking, or find we now have to accommodate new experiences and challenges. Moral knowledge is acquired through meeting and surmounting individual challenges as much as from applying some larger plan to the social world we encounter.

What is more, and this is Winston's critical pedagogical contribution, the teacher is not above but part of the constructive process. No doubt those who lead scenarios have acquired certain skills of leadership and questioning that situate them well among those who are engaged in learning police ethics. But ethically they are also inhabitants of the developing metropolis and must make their own way through the moral byways as well as highways of the scenarios they moderate. So-called moral expertise has always been problematic.[19] Teachers may know rather more about moral theory, be better trained in discerning relevance and irrelevance, and possess more sophisticated reasoning skills. But do they have greater moral sensibility and insight? Although we may hope so,

---

[17] Winston (1997: 177).

[18] Winston (1997: 161–3), referring to Descartes (1637: chap 2).

[19] For a variety of views, see, eg, Szabados (1978); McConnell (1984); Driver (2006); Cholbi (2007); Archard (2011).

it is not generally used as a criterion for teaching eligibility, and there is some question about how we would test for it. Teachers are not tour guides who know the city through and through but fellow dwellers who must find their own way through the moral complexities they address. No doubt we should learn from their experience, but that by itself does not equate with exclusive moral insight.

There is one final but critical task that teachers have—implicit in the foregoing, but occasionally lost in the task of developing the individual moral sensitivity of practitioners. That is the importance of seeing the conscientisation of practitioners as role-related and not simply as private or personal. Those who accept the role of constable, police officer, or police manager, as the main protagonists of the scenarios included in this volume have, (should) have also accepted certain moral constraints that flow from that role on what is morally relevant and how it enters into morally acceptable decision making. It is, perhaps, the special gift of an experienced teacher to be able to discern the difference between the private or personal moral responses that someone might have to, say, a nuclear power plant or gesture of hospitality, and the response that may be appropriate by virtue of one's professional role. The point is not that there are two distinct moralities—one for police officers and the other for those who are not—but that roles themselves can be defended as placing distinctive moral constraints on decision makers. Just as my role as father gives me special obligations toward and privileges with respect to my children that I do not have with respect to other children, so students considering scenarios of the kind that are included in this volume must learn how to approach them in terms of the demands placed upon them by virtue of their role. Although there may be rare cases in which the moral demands upon one *qua* human outweigh the moral demands that flow from occupancy of a socially sanctioned role, for the most part one has consented, in taking up a role, to viewing the moral demands of a work-related situation through the lens of the role.

References

Archard, David, 'Why Moral Philosophers Are Not and Should Not Be Moral Experts' (2011) 25(3) *Bioethics* 119–27.

Beers, Geri W, 'The Effect of Teaching Method on Objective Test Scores: Problem-based Learning Versus Lecture' (2005) 44(7) *Journal of Nursing Education* 305–9.

Brecher, Bob, *Torture and the Ticking Bomb* (Oxford: Blackwell, 2007).

Callahan, Joan C, 'Teaching Criminal Justice Ethics: Freestanding, Pervasive, and Combined Approaches', in John Kleinig and Margaret Leland Smith (eds), *Teaching Criminal Justice Ethics* (Cincinnati, OH: Anderson, 1997), pp 87–102.

Cholbi, Michael, 'Moral Expertise and the Credentials Problem' (2007) 10(4) *Ethical Theory and Moral Practice* 323–34.

Cliff, WH and Nesbitt Curtin, L, 'An Open or Shut Case? Contrasting Approaches to Case Study Design' (2005) 34(4) *Journal of College Science Teaching* 14–17.

Dancy, Jonathan, 'The Role of Imaginary Cases in Ethics' (1985) 66 *Pacific Philosophical Quarterly* 141–53.

Descartes, René, *Discourse on the Method of Rightly Conducting the Reason, and Seeking Truth in the Sciences* (1637), chap 2, available at: <http://www.literature.org/authors/descartes-rene/reason-discourse/>.

Driver, Julia, 'Autonomy and the Asymmetry Problem for Moral Expertise' (2006) 128 *Philosophical Studies* 619–44.

Freire, Paolo, *Education for Critical Consciousness* (New York: Seabury, 1973).

Gendler, Tamar, *Thought Experiment: On the Powers and Limits of Imaginary Cases* (NY: Garland Press, 2000).

Gijbels, David, Dochy, Filip, van den Bossche, Piet, and Segers. Mien, 'Effects of Problem-based Learning: A Meta-analysis from the Angle of Assessment' (2005) 75(1) *Review of Educational Research* 27–61.

Gossman, Peter, Stewart, Terry, Jaspers, Marlene, and Chapman, Bruce, 'Integrating Web-delivered Problem-based Learning Scenarios to the Curriculum' (2007) 8(2) *Active Learning in Higher Education* 139–53.

Heffernan, William C, 'The Aims of Criminal Justice Ethics Education', in John Kleinig and Margaret Leland Smith (eds), *Teaching Criminal Justice Ethics* (Cincinnati, OH: Anderson, 1997), pp 3–20.

Herreid, Clyde F, '"Clicker" Cases: Introducing Case Study Teaching Into Large Classrooms' (2006) 63(2) *Journal of College Science Teaching* 43–7, available at: <http://www.sciencecases.org/clicker/herreid_clicker.asp>.

Hudson, JN and Buckley, P, 'An Evaluation of Case-Based Teaching: Evidence for Continuing Benefit and Realization of Aims' (2004) 28 *Advances in Physiology Education* 15–22.

Kamm, Frances Myrna, 'Ethics, Applied Ethics, and Applying Applied Ethics', in David M Rosenthal and Fadiou Shehadi (eds), *Applied Ethics and Ethical Theory* (Salt Lake City: University of Utah Press, 1988), 162–87.

Kleinig, John, 'Teaching and Learning Police Ethics: Competing and Complementary Approaches' (1990) 18 *Journal of Criminal Justice* 1–18.

Kleinig, John, 'Response: Moral Neutrality in Criminal Justice Ethics Education', in John Kleinig and Margaret Leland Smith (eds), *Teaching Criminal Justice Ethics* (Cincinnati, OH: Anderson, 1997), pp 21–31.

Major, Claire H and Palmer, Betsy, 'Assessing the Effectiveness of Problem-Based Learning in Higher Education: Lessons from the Literature' (2001) 5(1) *Academic Exchange Quarterly* 4–9.

McConnell, TC, 'Objectivity and Moral Expertise' (1984) 14(2) *Canadian Journal of Philosophy* 193–216.

McWilliams, Victoria and Nahavandi, Afsaneh, 'Using Live Cases to Teach Ethics' (2006) 67 *Journal of Business Ethics* 421–33.

Menkel-Meadow, Carrie, 'Telling Stories in School: Using Case Studies and Stories to Teach Legal Ethics' (2000) 79 *Fordham Law Review* 787–816, available from: <http://www.scholarship.law.georgetown.edu/facpub/174/>.

Mill, John Stuart, *On Liberty*, ed. E. Rapaport (Indianapolis, IN: Hackett, 1978), p 56.

Ryle, Gilbert 'Can Virtue Be Taught?' in Robert F Dearden, Paul H Hirst, and Richard S Peters (eds), *Education and the Development of Reason* (Boston: Routledge and Kegan Paul, 1972), pp 434–47.

Sudzina, Mary, 'Case Study as a Constructivist Pedagogy for Teaching Educational Psychology' (1997) 9(2) *Educational Psychology Review* 199–218.

Szabados, Béla, 'On "Moral Expertise"' (1978) 8(1) *Canadian Journal of Philosophy* 117–29.

Walsh, Adrian, 'A Moderate Defence of the Use of Thought Experiments in Applied Ethics' (2011) 14(4) *Ethical Theory and Moral Practice* 467–81, DOI: 10.1007/s10677-010-9254-7.

Winston, Kenneth I, 'Teaching with Cases', in John Kleinig and Margaret Leland Smith (eds), *Teaching Criminal Justice Ethics* (Cincinnati, OH: Anderson, 1997), pp 161–81.

PART TWO

The Compromised
Senior Officer

3

Scenario: The Compromised Senior Officer

Superintendent Mike Sutton is Staff Officer to Assistant Chief Constable (ACC) Anthony Jackson. Mr Jackson is notable for having been the youngest officer appointed to ACPO rank and also a prominently successful ethnic minority officer. He is regarded as almost certain to be appointed as a Chief Constable and indeed has been short-listed for interview for a relatively small and largely rural force—a stepping-stone for greater things!

Supt Sutton has enjoyed an excellent working relationship with Mr Jackson leaving him with a very favourable impression of his boss. Mr Jackson is not particularly conscious of his rank or professional celebrity. He calls Supt Sutton by his first name, unlike his predecessor who was stiff and formal. Occasionally, the two men eat together at local ethnic restaurants and Mr Jackson steadfastly refuses his subordinate's offers to pay. Professionally, Supt Sutton holds Mr Jackson in high regard. Mr Jackson was on duty when there was a terrorist alert in the city centre near where the police have their headquarters. Mr Jackson immediately stepped into the Gold command role, grasping the operation with clarity and firmness as it unfolded. The strategy that he devised on-the-spot was courageous and was validated by events. He was widely congratulated for the way in which he handled this operation.

Mr Jackson is married to Melanie and has two school-age children. In interviews with the local press he has been keen to be seen as a happily married family man. He recently invited Supt Sutton and his partner to dinner, and he went to considerable lengths to make Mrs Sutton feel at ease. Melanie was charming and an excellent cook. Mr Jackson's children put in an appearance at the beginning of the evening and were cheerfully pleasant. The other guests and their respective partners were drawn from a wide spectrum of local affairs. Supt Sutton was particularly impressed by how Mr Jackson introduced him to these other guests: not as 'my Staff Officer', but as a 'colleague' and referred to his previous operational experience in command of the firearms and public order teams.

A friend of Supt Sutton is Chief Inspector Bob Smythe, who has recently been promoted and is now responsible for the 'Guns and Gangs' unit which also has responsibility for Drugs. The careers of both men have developed in parallel (but with Ch Insp Smythe lagging one step behind Supt Sutton in rank). Ch Insp Smythe has, treated Supt Sutton as a mentor as well as a friend. Supt Sutton admires him as an officer and likes him as an individual; more importantly, Supt Sutton trusts his judgement. Ch Insp Smythe has confidentially told Supt Sutton that he has been informed by officers within his department that Mr Jackson appears to be having a homosexual affair with Kevin Elsey, who is well-known to police as a drug addict. Elsey is closely connected to local organised criminals as a drug dealer within the homosexual community—trading drugs via certain pubs and clubs frequented by gay people. Supt Sutton understands that the intelligence suggests that the affair between Mr Jackson and Kevin Elsey began at least three months ago, and came to light because Elsey was under surveillance.

If the affair were to become public it would grievously damage the career prospects of Mr Jackson and pose, Supt Sutton imagines, a very serious threat to his boss's marriage and family life. However, there are other issues at stake: the most pressing is intelligence regarding the penetration of the gay, lesbian, bisexual, and transgender (LGBT) community by organised drug gangs. There is a joint operation planned by the force and HM Revenue and Customs (HMRC) investigators to intercept a large consignment of illegally imported drugs. The relationship between the force and HMRC's Investigation Branch has not been an easy one. HMRC distrust the capacity of the police to retain secrecy, whilst the police worry about the HMRC's grasp of law and procedure. Forging the relationship between these two organisations has been very lengthy and arduous. If this operation is a success, then it may be a harbinger of more to come; but if it goes awry, it is unlikely to be resurrected any time soon. Supt Sutton is aware that Mr Jackson is privy to this operation.

On the other hand, the intelligence implicating his boss with Kevin Elsey is not foolproof. Supt Sutton believes that there are those within the force who resent Mr Jackson and his high profile. Supt Sutton's assessment is that there is a barely-concealed vein of racism that is still to be found amongst some officers, especially those whose careers have not developed as they had hoped. They see Mr Jackson as someone who owes his success more to his ethnic minority status than to his talent and experience as an operational officer. When Mr Jackson was recently featured in a local newspaper, his photograph was cut out and pinned to a noticeboard with a montage of other clippings spelling 'Pass the vomit bag, I'm about to puke!' Supt Sutton suspects (and Ch Insp Smythe agrees) that some of those in the 'Guns and Gangs' unit are opposed to Mr Jackson. Both men fear that these resentful officers might either have 'put two and two together' unwittingly to arrive at the most damning conclusion regarding Mr Jackson, or have more consciously decided to exploit what little information is available to inflict deliberate damage on Mr Jackson.

If Supt Sutton takes precipitate action it may imperil the career of a man he admires; it may well de-rail the joint operation and damage the fragile relationship with HMRC. If the operation goes ahead and is a failure, especially if it comes to light that intelligence was leaked to Elsey, then the ramifications for the force will be even greater. Time is tight, the operation is imminent: teams will be assembled and briefed in a matter of days.

What should Supt Sutton do? What options are available to Supt Sutton? Which options deserve serious consideration and which of them should be excluded? On what grounds would some options be included or excluded?

What considerations should he bear in mind when deliberating on future courses of action? What are the likely possible consequences and implications? Is there anything that Supt Sutton can do to mitigate the worst of them? What could he do to encourage the most favourable outcome? What difficulties and obstacles lie in his path?

Is there anything that could have been done that would have avoided the situation in which Supt Sutton now finds himself?

Addressing the Scenario
Integrity Insights and Dangerous Liaisons[1]

Jenny Fleming[2] and Juani O'Reilly[3]

Introduction

John Kleinig reminds us that 'ethical policing' is not about whether police fudge their tax returns or, indeed, whether they cheat on their partners. It is concerned with how they act, either as individuals or organisationally, in the provision of police services; and, moreover, as Neyroud puts it (2003: 598), 'doing the right things for the right reasons'. Thus, ethical policing:

> ...will refer not so much to the morality of police officers and their institutions but to that morality as it is refracted through various roles and institutional purposes. (Kleinig, 2009: 107)

Ethical policing is, as Kleinig also notes, 'an ethic of professionalism'. In recent years, such ethics have been embodied in various forms of 'codes of conduct', as in, for example, the United States Law Enforcement Code of Ethics (International Association of Chiefs of Police) (Kleinig, 2009: 108), which is also used in some other countries. In February 2011, the European Code of Police Ethics celebrated

---

[1] Organisational arrangements reflect those of the Australian Federal Police, but are equivalent to the English context in which the scenario is couched.

[2] Institute of Criminal Justice Research, Southampton University, UK.

[3] Federal Agent, Australian Federal Police. Opinions and statements in this paper should not be considered an endorsement by the Australian Federal Police.

its tenth anniversary and in the United Kingdom various Home Office reports, reform agendas, and police units moved towards embodying the principles of ethical policing (Neyroud, 2003: 598). In Australia, a series of major police misconduct scandals and inquiries over the past two decades have stimulated reform programmes at 'the cutting edge of police integrity management practices' (Porter and Prenzler, 2012: xix). All jurisdictions, in varying degrees, have established internal police professional standards (and/or internal investigations) units with a responsibility to investigate and report on instances of misconduct, as well as enhancing the ethical and professional standards of the organisation and to promote ethical policing generally. Externally, ombudsmen, oversight agencies, corruption and crime commissions, police integrity commissions, and other jurisdiction-specific agencies are committed to promoting law enforcement integrity. Most jurisdictions through a variety of methods (legislation, memoranda of understanding, for example) have in place models for assigning cases between internal and external agencies where appropriate (Porter and Prenzler, 2012: 220). In recent years (largely prompted by high profile misconduct cases) there has been a concerted shift in Australian organisations from the traditional *reactive* organisational response to internal ethics problems to a more *proactive* and wide-ranging role of addressing ethics education and training and, in some cases, implementing early intervention systems and frameworks for following through an intervention, including support/training for local managers. Porter and Prenzler's 'stocktake' of Australia's various ethics and integrity frameworks noted the progress made in recent years and identified leadership, communication, and relevant knowledge/information as key to effective integrity system frameworks, which in turn support and enable more focused individual strategies (Porter and Prenzler, 2012: 234–7).

This chapter considers an ethical dilemma in an Australian context. That is, the officer who is central to the 'compromised senior officer' scenario is considered a Superintendent in the Australian Federal Police (AFP). The first part of this chapter provides an introduction to the AFP and explores some of the components of the AFP's integrity framework. It highlights some of the activities and strategies developed and implemented to build and maintain the confidence of its communities, its national and international partners, and the Australian government. However, ethics, integrity frameworks, and strategies do not guarantee ethical conduct at all times. Culture is important and the AFP is consistently building and striving to maintain a culture that rejects unethical behaviour. The second part of the chapter examines the compromised senior officer scenario and provides responses to the questions posed from an Australian context. It also provides points of discussion and debate. The chapter concludes that while leadership, communication, and knowledge exchange are central to strong integrity system frameworks, it is a supportive culture that will ultimately determine their success. As well, it is crucial that police organisations in their bid to further police integrity and ethical behaviour remain alert to emerging ethical issues that will require innovative and creative strategies to confront them.

The Australian Federal Police (AFP)

The AFP was established in October 1979 and is the primary law enforcement agency of the Australian government. The AFP's role is to enforce Commonwealth criminal law and to protect Commonwealth and national interests from crime in Australia and overseas. The AFP is Australia's international law enforcement and policing representative, and the government's chief source of advice on policing issues.

The AFP currently has a workforce of approximately 6,898 staff consisting of 3,217 sworn police, 1,066 sworn Protective Service Officers, and 2,615 unsworn staff (AFP, 2011a). The roles and functions within the AFP are diverse, covering investigations into counter terrorism, drugs, fraud, people smuggling, and high tech crime operations. The AFP has a presence in thirty countries around the world through the International Liaison Network. The AFP also provides a community policing role in the Australian Capital Territory (ACT), Christmas Island, the Cocos (Keeling) Islands, Norfolk Island, and Jervis Bay. The AFP's International Deployment Group has a capacity to deploy Australian police internationally and domestically in support of stability and capacity development operations and includes deployments to Sudan, Timor Leste, Afghanistan, and the Solomon Islands (AFP, 2010a). The size, complexity, geographic spread, and activities undertaken by the AFP (as with any police service) means that it operates in a high corruption-risk environment (Prenzler, 2002).

When the AFP was established, a para-military model with a rank structure that mirrored standard policing idioms in the common law world was adopted. The organisation attracted limited oversight by the Commonwealth Ombudsman, despite repeated calls for an oversight agency that would play a larger role in police corruption prevention and complaints investigation (Prenzler, 2011: 284). As this chapter shows it would be over twenty years before formal internal and external oversight mechanisms were introduced. The following section provides an overview of the AFP as an organisation and the Integrity Framework it supports.

Integrity Framework

The AFP is a values-driven organisation and these core values are articulated in the AFP Commissioner's Order on professional standards. The AFP Professional Standards Policy requires the incorporation of the AFP 'Core Values' into all policies, practices, and procedures. Most performance development agreements include a commitment to behave in accordance with the values of the organisation. In the AFP the values are: integrity, commitment, excellence, accountability, fairness, and trust (AFP, 2003). These values apply equally to sworn and unsworn staff, including contractors, and are available to the public on the AFP website (<http://www.afp.gov.au>).

The values are clearly displayed in high traffic areas within each police premise and as a screensaver on every AFP computer. The Professional Standards intra-web provides extensive information and guidance about professional behaviour. It includes a reference guide to professional standards in the AFP, ethical decision making, and case studies. There are currently three case studies presented on this site—covering sexual harassment in the workplace, inappropriate use of the AFP email system, and driving under the influence of alcohol. The case studies are from actual events involving AFP employees.

Prior to 2002, the AFP had an internal complaints and discipline system that relied heavily on pursuing charges for breaches of discipline that were then inves-tigated by a team with coercive powers, overseen by an independent review body and with a tribunal to hear and determine certain cases. The Australian Federal Police (Discipline) Regulations 1979 specified the standards of conduct for AFP employees as follows:

Improper Conduct

(1) An AFP employee or special member must not:
   (a) use the fact that he or she is an employee or special member, as the case may be, for the purpose of obtaining any personal advantage; or any advantage for another person; or
   (b) without lawful authority or excuse take, use or possess any property belonging to the Commonwealth for a purpose not connected with his or her employment or appointment; or
   (c) wilfully or negligently waste, or cause loss or damage to, any property belonging to the Commonwealth and made available to, or for the use of the employee, special member, or the Australian Federal Police; or
   (d) place himself or herself under a pecuniary obligation to a person so that there are reasonable grounds for believing that the person may be able to influence the employee or special member in the manner in which he or she is to carry out his or her duties; or
   (e) act in a manner that is prejudicial to the good order or discipline of the Australian Federal Police; or
   (f) act in a manner that brings, or is likely to bring, discredit to the reputation of the Australian Federal Police.

It was a discipline system with 'strong notions of punishment as a means of securing adequate standards of behaviour' (Fisher, 2003) and did *not* necessarily secure integrity in the workplace. The discipline regime stemmed from a com-plicated legislative framework and brought with it numerous problems, particu-larly in terms of the time and cost taken to resolve a disciplinary matter, the negative impact on the workplace of a protracted adversarial hearing, and the subsequent reduction of managerial control over the outcome (Fisher, 2003). At the time it was observed that complaint investigations were inflexible and convoluted and that minor disciplinary matters and serious offences were pursued with the same tenacity, even if it was deemed to be a minor customer service matter.

Following a review of the AFP's professional standards by Justice William Fisher AO QC in 2002, the AFP implemented substantial changes to its internal integrity arrangements. The legalistic discipline model was replaced with a managerial model (Scott, 2004) based on managerial and administrative discretion rather than relying on adversarial and punitive processes. AFP supervisors and managers now have a wide range of options available to address poor performance and inadequate professional standards. The current regime utilises managerial resolutions for minor management issues, taking less time to complete, reducing costs and providing more timely outcomes.

In 2006, external oversight was restructured and the responsibility for ethical conduct in the AFP was now shared between the Commonwealth Ombudsman (low level complaints) and the new Australian Commission for Law Enforcement Integrity (ACLEI) which had the prime responsibility for preventing and investigating corruption. The ACLEI significantly enhanced the AFP's ethical framework (Porter and Prenzler, 2012: 47). Internally, the AFP's Professional Standards Unit continued to oversee ethics and professional standards across the organisation.

The AFP's professional standards are articulated in various legislative and governance arrangements and there are several layers to its integrity infrastructure. The Commissioner's Orders set out the level of professional standards that is expected of all AFP employees in their official and private capacity and place an obligation on all AFP employees to report all breaches of professional standards including a self report should a member realise they have made such a breach. To illustrate, some personal associations may conflict with the AFP's 'Core Values' and/or Code of Conduct and could compromise a member's integrity. Some associations are deemed declarable and include relationships or activities involving, for example, AFP appointees currently suspended due to integrity issues or people suspected to be engaged in criminal activity, including 'social' drug use.

The AFP has invested significantly in its organisational integrity. From the outset this investment has been tailored to change the organisational culture around misconduct, and/or the tolerance of misconduct of any kind. There are currently seventy-one full time employees in professional standards who work in one of three business areas: prevention, detection, or response.

Ethics and professional standards training and awareness programmes are a constant theme in all training courses from recruitment/induction through to management training. There is continuous reinforcement of key messages with respect to organisational integrity at all stages and levels for AFP employees. During 2010–11, the Professional Standards Unit delivered awareness and prevention programmes to more than 3,700 AFP employees (AFP 2011a). The aim of the prevention programme is to reinforce the values and principles governing professional conduct in the AFP and to promote an organisational culture of integrity and honesty.

Organisational integrity is viewed as an important issue by the AFP senior executive. As part of further developing and consolidating an ethical culture, in 2008–09, the AFP Commissioner, the two Deputy Commissioners, and the Chief Operating Officer held staff musters and personally delivered ethics and integrity presentations to AFP employees across every AFP site in Australia. Attendance was mandatory. These education strategies are deemed by others as successful. As Porter and Prenzler (2012: 49) have observed:

> It was noted that spikes in complaints had been recorded in areas after receiving an integrity presentation, which was taken to be a positive sign that the presentation had increased reporting behaviour.

The Professional Standards model adopted focuses on early intervention to identify individuals and workplaces potentially vulnerable to misconduct and corruption issues. It also addresses the resolution of minor professional standards matters, with most minor complaints being dealt with by managers through resolution or conciliation in the workplace. This reinforces the supervisor's role in managing staff performance. Formal mediation is not at the time of writing a 'likely response to complaints in the AFP' (Porter and Prenzler, 2012: 26). All serious professional misconduct matters are thoroughly investigated and these investigations are subject to external review by the Commonwealth Ombudsman's Office which has the discretion to return the complaint for internal review. Approximately 50 per cent of complaints referred to the Ombudsman are returned to the AFP for resolution each year (Porter and Prenzler, 2012: 43).

Following the Fisher Review the role of the Commonwealth Ombudsman changed. Previously the Ombudsman reviewed each individual complaint but now its office essentially validates the AFP's complaint handling system. All corruption matters must be referred to ACLEI by the AFP Commissioner (AFP, 2006). The AFP also measures organisational integrity by means of an independent Australian university conducting a Business Satisfaction Survey which provides data for reporting against key performance indicators identified in the AFP's Portfolio Budget Statement. Participants in the survey include staff from Federal, State, and Territory government agencies; foreign governments; and law enforcement agencies in Australia and overseas that work regularly with the AFP. In 2012, the highest levels of satisfaction were reported for 'ethical standards' (97 per cent), 'respect for individual' (95 per cent), and professionalism (94 per cent) (Jamieson, 2012).

The Confidant Network

> The AFP is an agency at the forefront of most aspects of internal corruption control… While the AFP gathers information about possible corruption and

misconduct from a variety of detection methods, one useful source is the AFP's Confidant Network—a type of professional reporting, whistle-blower or internal witness program. (ACLEI, 2008)

In 1996, the AFP instigated an internal whistle-blower scheme [Confidant Network] following a recommendation from the Commonwealth Ombudsman. The Confidant Network provides support and advice for AFP members as well as representing an official reporting channel. Via the network, the AFP hopes to build a culture of accountability that is pro-disclosure and seeks to remove any stigma associated with reporting (McEvoy, 2011).

AFP Professional Standards also has a prominent role in the ongoing development and delivery of the AFP's Respectful Workplace Strategy. This strategy aims to raise awareness about behaviours that reflect respectful workplace practices and the avenues of support available to AFP employees who experience behaviour which may be perceived as inappropriate and/or unacceptable in the AFP environment (Porter and Prenzler, 2012).

The AFP has moved away from an autocratic disciplinary process to one of accepting and learning which has resulted in AFP employees being more willing to report inappropriate or corrupt behaviour by others without fear of reprisal. The 2009–10 AFP annual report revealed that 37 complaints (4.6 per cent) resulted from self-reporting and 303 complaints (37.78 per cent) were made by AFP employees about their colleagues. They are able to do this through an 'innovative and successful' Complaints and Reporting Management system which provides a networked electronic reporting capability for members (Porter and Prenzler, 2012: 48). Most complaints were incidents of failing to comply with direction or procedure or a breach of the AFP Code of Conduct. Just under two thirds of complaints came from the public. Complaints from members of the public have decreased since 2006—from 668 in 2006–2007 to 509 in 2008–2009 and 447 in 2009–2010 (Porter and Prenzler, 2012: 24).

This section has presented an overview of some of the components of the AFP's integrity framework. Other components which have not been discussed include: pre-employment screening; financial declarations; and the fraud and anti-corruption control plan. The section has also not discussed drug and alcohol testing and public hearing and reporting powers, both strategies that have been identified by academics as 'successful' integrity strategies (Porter and Prenzler, 2012: 49). In addition, the AFP established the Security Portfolio in January 2009, which ensures the integrity of AFP information, resources, people, assets, and reputation. This brings with it a great emphasis on security, particularly information security as one of the key corruption risks is the access to and unauthorised disclosure of information—a risk that the AFP currently sees as one of its potentially difficult areas to monitor. Other perceived emerging ethical issues include social networking and DNA sampling (Porter and Prenzler, 2012: 50–2).

There are challenges involved with any integrity framework but the AFP endeavours to have a suite of measures in place that match identified risks and vulnerabilities. The AFP has invested heavily and has a strong focus on integrity. Organisational integrity in the AFP is concerned with systematically reviewing, analysing, and maintaining its ability to manage and prevent breaches of integrity whilst at the same time monitoring the horizon for emerging ethical issues.

To remain legitimate, the police must assess and improve their integrity continually. What is acceptable behaviour today might not be acceptable behaviour tomorrow. What is considered the 'norm' in one country may be unacceptable in another.

It would seem that the AFP has learnt that 'maximising ethical conduct and good police-citizen relations, rather than busting bad cops' (Prenzler, 2002) is the way forward in building and sustaining a culture focused on its core values and maintaining the confidence and legitimacy of its many key stakeholders.

This discussion has demonstrated how the AFP has established a strong ethical framework that provides a broad range of education, prevention, and proactive investigation strategies, with a strong emphasis on integrity and cultural change. It has demonstrated that, as Neyroud (2003: 588) has noted, 'far from police culture being an impassable barrier, a concerted drive towards a more professional model of policing can potentially edge the service nearer a more professional occupational culture'. The rise in internal complaints in the AFP (from 19 per cent in 2006–2007 to 35 per cent in 2009–2010—with a high of 41 per cent in 2008 (Porter and Prenzler, 2012: 24) suggests in part that culture change has been relatively successful.

The remainder of this paper considers a 'Compromised Senior Officer' scenario as if the officer was employed as a Superintendent in the AFP. That is, responses to his dilemma are considered in the context of the structures, programmes, and strategies available to him as an AFP officer.

What Should Supt Sutton Do and What Options are Available to Him?

Supt Sutton needs to identify and explore the implications of all options to judge how best to address the issue based on sound reasoning within the boundaries of the AFP's integrity framework. The 'issue' in the first instance is that of the possible relationship between Deputy Commissioner (D Comm) Jackson and Kevin Elsey, an illicit drug user, closely connected to local organised criminals as a drug dealer. The tenuous and difficult relationship with the Australian Customs and Border Protection Service (Customs) is a dilemma but has to be a secondary concern for Supt Sutton at this time. Once the ethical issue surrounding D Comm Jackson is resolved (as a matter of urgency) then the problems emanating from the collaboration between Customs and the AFP can be addressed.

There are several options available to Supt Sutton; some are worthy of further consideration, whereas others should be rejected. Each of the options listed is not mutually exclusive and several of the options could be pursued concurrently. The options are not listed in chronological order as each of the options could occur at any time. In some of the options Supt Sutton has a minor advisory role, allowing others to follow through with action.

The available options are discussed in more detail later in this chapter. Supt Sutton could:

1. Ignore the information and do nothing.
2. Report a potential conflict of interest to Professional Standards.
3. Submit an integrity report to Professional Standards.
4. Advise Sergeant Smythe to remind his staff of their obligations to report such matters to Professional Standards.
5. Remind Sergeant Smythe of his own obligations to report.
6. Request Sergeant Smythe to ascertain the source of the intelligence and the credibility of the information before making a decision on an appropriate course of action.
7. Raise the issue with the Commissioner personally.
8. Raise the issue with Deputy Commissioner Jackson.
9. Raise the issue with Kevin Elsey.
10. Raise the issue with members of the Serious and Organised Crime Operations.
11. Approach a Confidant from the AFP's Confidant Network to further explore potential options.

Option One

Supt Sutton could reject the information provided by Sgt Smythe and do nothing. However, this is not an appropriate course of action. A potential conflict of interest has been identified that needs to be managed. A conflict of interest is defined in the AFP National Guideline on operational conflicts of interest as

> a situation where an appointee has a private interest matter which is also the subject of a decision or duty of the appointee. It involves an actual, perceived or potential conflict between an appointee's responsibilities in serving the public interest/AFP duties, and the appointee's private interests. A conflict of interest can arise from avoiding personal losses as well as gaining personal advantage—whether financial or otherwise.

Supt Sutton needs to adhere to this Guideline and the values it espouses. The Guideline is part of the organisation's professional standards framework and Commissioner's Order 2 is the vehicle that gives effect to the policies and guidelines. Inappropriate departures from the provisions of this instrument may constitute a breach of the AFP's Professional Standards and as a consequence, Supt Sutton may be disciplined under Part 5 of the Australian Federal Police Act 1971.

Supt Sutton is obliged to determine the risk posed by the potential conflict of interest. He needs to consider a number of issues. What influence, if any, does

Kevin Elsey have over D Comm Jackson? Could any reasonable person perceive that the potential conflict of interest might influence D Comm Jackson's proper and appropriate performance of his duties? Is it likely the potential conflict of interest will directly affect D Comm Jackson's proper and appropriate performance of his duties? Is D Comm Jackson open to blackmail? Is this an actual or perceived conflict of interest? Regardless of the answer to these questions, the conflict needs to be reported.

Option Two

The suggestion that D Comm Jackson is having a homosexual relationship with Kevin Elsey, if correct, would require D Comm Jackson to report a potential conflict of interest to professional standards. However, it is unclear how reliable the intelligence is regarding D Comm Jackson's alleged relationship with Kevin Elsey. Supt Sutton has no information about the reliability of the source of the information, or the credibility of the information. One needs to be mindful of the opposition to D Comm Jackson within Serious and Organised Crime Operations (SOCO) and it is possible, but unlikely, that Kevin Elsey could be a Human Source for D Comm Jackson. A Human Source is a person recorded on the AFP Register of Human Sources who provides information and/or assistance to the AFP and whose identity and relationship with the AFP needs to be protected.

As part of this option, Supt Sutton could ascertain if D Comm Jackson has reported a conflict of interest and whether or not Kevin Elsey is a registered Human Source with D Comm Jackson as his handler. However if Supt Sutton takes this course of action and D Comm Jackson finds out this would impact on their working relationship as D Comm Jackson may feel that his Staff Officer is basically disloyal. In addition, if it is established there is no relationship between D Comm Jackson and Kevin Elsey, or their relationship is an innocent, platonic relationship and Supt Sutton takes the action described, and D Comm Jackson finds out, a lack of trust within their working relationship may come about which could impact on Supt Jackson's future career prospects. It should be noted that if the relationship between D Comm Jackson and Kevin Elsey is only an innocent, platonic relationship, that relationship must be reported as a result of Kevin's criminal conduct.

Option Three

If Supt Sutton and Sgt Smythe ascertain that D Comm Jackson has not reported a conflict of interest pertaining to Elsey, Supt Sutton and/or Sgt Smythe should submit an integrity report to the Professional Standards Unit.

Other options available to Supt Sutton include advising Sgt Smythe to remind his staff of their obligations to report such matters to the Professional Standards Unit (Option Four).

Supt Sutton may choose to remind Sgt Smythe of his obligations to report the matter himself (Option Five) or he may request Sgt Smythe to ascertain the source of the intelligence and the credibility of the information before making a decision on an appropriate course of action (Option Six). For example, if in fact the intelligence 'came to light because Elsey was under surveillance' then it should be logged in the surveillance log and photos should have been taken. There is a possibility that the surveillance officer was mistaken in his identification of D Comm Jackson or has misunderstood the relationship.

In addition, Supt Sutton has the options of raising the issue with the Commissioner personally (Option Seven), raising it either with D Comm Jackson (Option Eight), Kevin Elsey (Option Nine), or members of SOCO (Option Ten) to establish the veracity of the information and/or to ensure it is not a vexatious report. Options Seven to Nine would more than likely impact on the working relationship (issues of trust) between Supt Sutton and D Comm Jackson. Options Seven and Nine may also not be ideal for Supt Sutton given the potential repercussions for his friend Sgt Smythe's failure to deal with the situation himself.

Supt Sutton may wish to approach a Confidant from the AFP's Confidant Network to further explore potential options (Option Eleven).

Which Options Deserve Serious Consideration and which of them should be Excluded? On what Grounds Would Some Options be Included or Excluded?

The AFP's core values provide fundamental principles to guide ethical decision making which can assist in complying with the AFP's Professional Standards. The AFP has an Ethical Decision Making model which provides assistance to its employees in relation to identifying the ethical component of a situation and making ethically sound decisions. It provides guidance when making difficult, complex decisions and the intent is to give some guidance on how to do so. The model comprises seven steps as follows:

Step 1—Matter/issue

Identify and assess the matter or issue.

- Have you recognised that there is a potential ethical issue or problem?
    - o Do you feel that you are in an ethically 'risky' situation?
    - o Do you have a 'gut feeling' that something is not quite right?
- What AFP values (ethical principles) does it relate to and why?
- Are there conflicts between the AFP's values and your personal values or between two or more of the AFP's values?
- What are the facts and circumstances of the situation?

- Who will be affected by your decision or action?
- Are other people involved in any way?
- What assumptions are you making?

Step 2—Your options

What are your options?

- What do you want to do?
- What are the desired outcomes?
- Who is the best person/area in the AFP to provide you with authoritative advice?
- Who else should you consult?
- Have you fully considered all of your options and the likely implications or consequences of each option?

Step 3—Scrutiny

Will your decision withstand scrutiny?

- Is there any conflict of interest (perceived or otherwise)?
- Would your decision stand up if it was made (and questioned) in the full light of public scrutiny by the media, community, and government—the 'sunlight test'?
- Would a reasonable person perceive your decision as honest and impartial?
- Could a reasonable person consider that you were in a position to improperly use your powers or position?
- Could it be perceived that your own personal beliefs adversely influenced your official decision?
- What will your course of action do to your character or reputation?
- How will your course of action reflect on your work mates?
- How will your course of action reflect on the AFP?
- Would you be happy if your family knew what you'd done?
- Who will you involve to check that this is an appropriate action to take?
- How will you document your action?

Step 4—Ensure compliance

Will your decision ensure compliance?

- Will it accomplish what you are trying to achieve?
- How does it relate to your duties and obligations as a public official?
- Does it involve the 'use of discretion'?
- Will the end result be congruent with the law and AFP governance including the AFP values and the Code of Conduct?

Step 5—Lawful

Is your decision lawful?

- What legislation, policies, procedures, or guidelines are relevant?
- Will your decision break the law/rules or is it inconsistent with government policy?
- Could the outcome of your decision be compromised by any unlawful actions in achieving it?
- Is your preferred action within your authority?

Step 6—Fair

Is your decision fair?

- Is it fair to all stakeholders?
- What would happen if everybody took this course of action?
- How would you feel if the action you are going to take was done to you?
- How would you feel if your actions were done to your partner, child, or parent?
- Have you considered the possibility that the ends may not justify the means?
- Can you rightly justify the decision?

Step 7—Review and learn

If you have any concerns about any of these questions seek a second opinion. Learn from your decision:

- How did it turn out for all concerned?
- If you had to do it all over again what would you do differently?

Any course of action by Supt Sutton must stand up to the 'sunlight test'—that is, his decision must withstand public scrutiny by the media, the community, and the government; unlike the phone hacking scandal that rocked the Metropolitan Police and Rupert Murdoch's media empire with the United Kingdom's most senior police officer resigning in July 2011 (BBC, 2011).

Option One—to do nothing is unacceptable and Supt Sutton would be breaching Section 8.10 of the AFP's Code of Conduct ('An AFP appointee must at all times behave in a way that upholds the AFP core values, and the integrity and good reputation of the AFP') and the integrity framework which would result in disciplinary action. This option would not pass the sunlight test and should be excluded. However, Supt Sutton may be tempted to do nothing as the present situation is personally complex and problematic. Supt Sutton may be of the view that the accusations levelled at D Comm Jackson are inconceivable based on his knowledge of and friendship with his boss and therefore decide the situation requires no further action. In addition, he may do nothing believing Sgt Smythe has reported the matter (Supt Sutton could make some enquiries to establish if Sgt Smythe has in fact reported the matter) or he may do nothing believing the surveillance officer who reported the intelligence is mistaken in his identification of D Comm Jackson (Supt Sutton could make some enquiries to determine if this is correct).

Option Two—Supt Sutton could ascertain if D Comm Jackson has reported a conflict of interest and whether or not Kevin Elsey is a registered Human Source, with D Comm Jackson as his handler. Members of the Professional Standards Unit would not disclose to Supt Sutton whether or not D Comm Jackson had submitted an integrity report with respect to the potential conflict of interest. In addition, for operational security reasons, the Human Source Management Team would not disclose if Kevin Elsey was a registered Human Source. The identities of Human Sources are protected as there is considerable risk to their safety if their identity is compromised. This option is not a viable one.

Option Three—Supt Sutton submits an integrity report to the Professional Standards Unit. This option is worthy of serious consideration and should be included. It would pass the sunlight test. If Supt Sutton submits an integrity report, he will be meeting his reporting obligations. Supt Sutton, through the submission of the report, would throw into question D Comm Jackson's integrity and if D Comm Jackson becomes aware of this, it could damage their working relationship as it may be seen (indeed, it probably would be seen) by D Comm Jackson as an attack on his integrity and dignity. This may result in a lack of support from D Comm Jackson for Supt Sutton, which could impact on his possible future career prospects. However, on the other hand, the submission of the report may be seen by the Commissioner of the AFP as courageous, resulting in increasing support by the Commissioner for Supt Sutton. Within the AFP's integrity framework, Supt Sutton should not be advantaged or disadvantaged by his course of action; however, human nature being what it is, in reality the action will have consequences. Supt Sutton could consider a transfer to another position prior to submitting the integrity report. He could inform D Comm Jackson of his decision to report the matter, acknowledging the difficult position both are facing. A transfer may reduce the stress and anxiety and is worthy of serious consideration.

Option Four—Supt Sutton could advise Sgt Smythe to remind his staff of their obligations to report and the possible consequences of not adhering to the organisation's integrity framework. This option deserves consideration; however the workplace behaviours displayed within SOCO suggests that those members do not adhere fully to the AFP values, nor the integrity framework and as such are less likely to report the matter. However, Supt Sutton could challenge members of SOCO who are gossiping about the allegation to desist and report the matter immediately. Aware of the hostility to D Comm Jackson, Supt Sutton needs to ensure that the allegation is not merely malicious.

Option Five—Noting Sgt Smythe's friendship with Supt Sutton, the Superintendent could remind Sgt Smythe of his obligations to report. This is a viable option and merits further consideration. However, Sgt Smythe might be of the view that Supt Sutton is 'throwing him to the dogs' depending on whether the allegation against D Comm Jackson is true or false. Sgt Smythe has a responsibility to act and he should be reminded of this as it is his officers who have made the allegations.

Option Six—Supt Sutton could request Sgt Smythe to identify the source of the intelligence and ascertain the credibility of the information. This option warrants consideration as it may establish the intelligence to be false and/or the report to be vexatious. However, if the intelligence is credible then Sgt Smythe should, as previously mentioned, direct the officer under his command to report the matter. If the report is vexatious, Sgt Smythe should report the matter to the Professional Standards Unit for further investigation. There is also the possibility that the subsequent investigation would reveal that the surveillance officer who reported the intelligence is new to the AFP and is mistaken in his/her identification of D Comm Jackson.

Option Seven—Supt Sutton could raise the issue with the AFP Commissioner. If the intelligence is correct, this is a serious issue involving a senior officer that could have severe ramifications for the AFP. This option deserves further consideration, since the AFP is a relatively small organisation and it is unlikely that Supt Sutton has risen to his current rank and position without previously working with most members of the senior executive team. This should be sufficient to give him confidence that their doors would be open to him and he could raise his concerns in confidence even with the Commissioner. The Commissioner is D Comm Jackson's immediate superior and he has the responsibility and authority to make D Comm Jackson accountable for his actions. This would pass the sunlight test and fulfil the Superintendent's obligation to report. If Supt Sutton did not know the Commissioner on a personal basis, this option could be a difficult one as the Commissioner should have a very good working relationship with D Comm Jackson, and Supt Sutton is just one of many Superintendents in the AFP.

Option Eight—Raise the issue with D Comm Jackson. This is worthy of further consideration, noting the excellent working and private relationship between D Comm Jackson and Supt Sutton. There could be ramifications following this discussion depending on the outcome. D Comm Jackson could be affronted, their working and personal relationship could be damaged, and there could be a breakdown in trust.

On the other hand if D Comm Jackson is innocent of the allegation and has been advised of the situation by Supt Sutton, this may in fact improve both their personal and their work relationship. D Comm Jackson may feel indebted to Supt Sutton for alerting him to the situation.

Option Nine—Raise the issue with Kevin Elsey. Mr Elsey is a known illicit drug user and drug dealer; he may also be a Human Source. He may be unreliable as a result of his drug use or he may be compromised if he is in fact a Human Source. This option should be excluded.

Option Ten—Raise the issue with members of SOCO. Not all members of SOCO may be aware of the information which alleges an affair between D Comm Jackson and Kevin Elsey. Being mindful that there are officers within SOCO who are resentful of D Comm Jackson, it would be unwise to take this course of action as this may increase the number of members who are aware of the allegation, probably resulting in the allegation becoming more widespread. This option should be excluded.

Option Eleven—Approach a Confidant. The AFP's Confidant Network is a unique referral and support option for all AFP employees and is also a formal reporting channel which fulfils the mandatory reporting requirements. Confidants provide information, options on alternative courses of action that might be taken, and support to AFP employees who are dealing with inappropriate or unethical behaviour in their workplace (AFP, 2011b). There is strong support for the Confidant Network and it has widespread acceptance. The AFP has over 200 Confidants located in Australia and overseas. Confidants deal with both criminal and non-criminal referrals and it is a very strong anti-corruption strategy. During 2009–10, the Confidant Network dealt with the 131 referrals which included twenty-three bullying matters, five harassment matters, twenty-five integrity issues, three discrimination matters, and four sexual harassment issues (AFP, 2010a).

This option is worthy of deliberation because if Supt Sutton reports this to a Confidant he may ask for, and obtain, confidentiality. A welcome scenario if he has concerns regarding potential repercussions. The Confidant Network would endeavour to keep Supt Sutton's identity from being revealed (although there are limits). In addition, this would fulfil his reporting obligations and pass the sunlight test.

What Are the Possible Consequences and Implications of Supt Sutton's Potential Courses of Action?

Supt Sutton needs to be aware that the intelligence about D Comm Jackson and Mr Elsey has not yet been confirmed. This provides him with three possibilities on which to base his actions. First, the intelligence may be false, secondly, the intelligence may be true, or thirdly, Supt Sutton will be unable to establish the veracity of the report. Each of these alternatives presents different options for consideration for potential courses of action.

Intelligence is false

If it has been established that the intelligence is false, the joint operation could proceed as planned. It would need to be established if the false intelligence was a result of an error or incompetence which may reveal systemic weakness in the intelligence function that needs addressing. Or conversely, the false intelligence may be malicious and Supt Sutton might advise D Comm Jackson accordingly so that an investigation by the Professional Standards Unit is initiated to identify the culprits and suppress any further dissemination of this false intelligence.

Intelligence is true

If it has been established that the intelligence is true, this could have far reaching ramifications to the point where it is not only embarrassing to the AFP and the Police Minister, but there could be a reduction in the confidence of the AFP partners, and the government could lose faith in the AFP.

Supt Sutton should advise the Commissioner. D Comm Jackson ought to be interviewed. During the interview it needs to be established what, if anything, has been disclosed and to whom. This may now jeopardise the conduct of the joint operation between the AFP and Customs to intercept a large consignment of illegally imported drugs and expose it to higher risks. The tactical threat and risk assessment should be re-assessed, which may result in cancellation of the joint operation or the re-planning of the joint operation (eg use of armed officers, full substitution of drugs for delivery to destination, or seizure of drugs at the border). Advice to Customs of the disclosure will not enhance the working relationship between the AFP and Customs.

D Comm Jackson's integrity is in question and he has lost all credibility. His career is ruined and his actions will impact on his relationship with his wife and children. The affair with Kevin Elsey will eventually be reported in the media and bring shame to his family, the AFP, and maybe the ethnic minority group he represents. This may result in a lack of community support and confidence in the AFP.

This would bring embarrassment to the AFP, not because D Comm Jackson was having a homosexual affair, but as a result of his connection with an illicit drug user, Kevin Elsey and his connections to local organised criminals as a drug dealer. Being a homosexual or having a private homosexual relationship is not considered a potential ethical risk within the AFP.

In years past, AFP employees would not identify as gay or lesbian for fear of notoriety, ridicule, or worse. However in recent years the AFP has supported gay and lesbian diversity in the workplace. In 2010, the AFP implemented a Workforce Diversity Strategy with the aim of attracting, recruiting, developing, and retaining people from five targeted groups (Aboriginal and Torres Strait Islander Australians; women; people from culturally and linguistically diverse communities; gay, lesbian, transsexual, and transgender people; and people with a disability) (AFP, 2010b). The AFP won a top award for its role in advocating gay and lesbian diversity in the workplace and was ranked as the top public sector organisation for the 2011 Australian Employer Quality Index award. The AFP's Gay and Lesbian Liaison Officer (GLLO) Network was also recognised and was ranked second among employee networks (AFP News, 2011). Officers wear GLLO badges to identify themselves as having had special training in this area.

D Comm Jackson's actions could potentially harm ethnic relations within the AFP; minority officers might be harassed or discriminated against by racist members of the community. The disclosures might damage the AFP's relationships with other law enforcement agencies. Law enforcement agencies that contain 'bad apples' can harm collaborative working relationships as this may raise the issue of trust.

The advice to the Commissioner may derail or improve Supt Sutton's career prospects. It may also call into question the Commissioner's management of his staff. This may have repercussions for the Commissioner, the Police Minister, and the government in power; it may impact on future funding to the AFP, and thereby its capacity to deal with threats to the Australian people.

These are some of the possible consequences and implications if the intelligence is true.

Unable to establish the veracity of the intelligence

If Supt Sutton is unable to establish the truth or otherwise of the intelligence, it is suggested that he submit an integrity report to the Professional Standards Unit. We would advocate the use of the AFP's Confidant Network in the hope his identity can be kept confidential. In the event the intelligence is determined to be false, this would then not affect his excellent working relationship with D Comm Jackson but at the same time fulfil his reporting obligations.

Is There Anything that Could Have Been Done that Would Have Avoided the Situation in which Supt Sutton Now Finds Himself?

Over the past decade the AFP has sought to put in place a strong integrity framework committed to ethical behaviour and a culture and environment that supports ethics in the workplace. However, as mentioned at the beginning of this chapter, integrity frameworks and innovative strategies do not always guarantee ethical behaviour. Even a strong organisational culture that is conducive to reporting corruption and misconduct may be challenged by individuals and/or groups whose own ethical values are not necessarily in keeping with those espoused by the ethical framework within which they may work. As a result, others who diligently strive to work within that framework may find themselves inadvertently caught up in situations and scenarios that challenge their thinking and pose potentially ethical dilemmas. Poor leadership, a lack of effective communication, and poor knowledge exchange between organisations have all contributed to this scenario and the difficult decisions Supt Sutton has to make.

Supt Sutton enjoys his role as Staff Officer to D Comm Jackson. He admires him as an officer and likes him personally. It is these facts that arguably make his ethical dilemma slightly sharper than it may have been if they had not enjoyed meals together and socialised informally at D Comm Jackson's home. We might observe that had Supt Sutton remained slightly more socially distant from his immediate supervisor he may not have experienced this ethical problem so acutely. However, it is not clear that this would have fostered a good working relation or avoided the situation in which Supt Sutton now finds himself. Clearly Sgt Smythe also finds himself in a state of indecision. His own poor leadership and communication in SOCO (reflected in the photograph on the noticeboard incident and in his seeming inability to speak seriously to his team) have resulted in Sgt Smythe seeking to shift the onus of responsibility to a friend and a senior officer whom he respects and admires. As that senior officer, Supt Sutton cannot walk away from the situation telling himself that Sgt Smythe is the senior officer in SOCO and should therefore look after it himself. He is obliged to at least submit an integrity report, although much of his dilemma emanates from the potential repercussions of doing so. His own personal feelings and professional respect for D Comm Jackson are not factors that can be swept away by frameworks and obligations. That is what makes this scenario an ethical dilemma.

Clearly there are 'issues' within SOCO and perhaps Sgt Smythe needs to get some guidance on how to lead from the front with those issues. In the first instance however, Supt Sutton needs to deal with the urgent situation relating to D Comm Jackson and the collaborative partnership between Customs and the AFP. Perhaps an issue for a later date is to initiate an investigation into the prevailing culture of SOCO and how it might be addressed productively.

How Should You Manage the Working Relationships Between the AFP and Customs (Regardless of the Outcome of the Elsey Affair)?

The working relationship between the AFP and Customs can only be described as strained. This is not necessarily unusual for there are a range of reasons why inter-agency work that involves police can be difficult. Exchange of resources, data management, privacy issues, different organisational cultures, non-complementary legislation, and policy can all combine to challenge inter-agency collaboration (Fleming, 2006: 91–102). However, there are always potential solutions. Regardless as to whether D Comm Jackson is found to have breached conflict of interest guidelines, the relationship between the AFP and Customs needs to be, if not resolved completely, at least worked on in a constructive manner.

Inter-agency distrust is not uncommon. Collaborative relationships must be based on mutual respect, trust, and a commitment to cooperate in pursuit of common goals. Each agency needs to recognise that while it has different roles, these are often complementary. Tension between the AFP and Customs may be addressed through the development and implementation of a memorandum of understanding which should include clarity around roles and functions, media releases agreed to by both parties that adequately reflect the contribution of each agency, briefs to Ministers on operational matters agreed to by both parties, development of protocols for the exchange of information, specialist training, secondments, standard operating procedures for each operation, and agreement to consult the other party on any proposed legislative changes that may have an impact on the other party.

Is the issue with respect to secrecy, perceived or real? Is it about a genuine lack of trust on the part of Customs that AFP officers are unable to remain discreet or is it about a lack of willingness on the part of the agencies to share private information? If the latter, are there legislative and/or data management issues that constrain knowledge exchange between the two agencies? If so this needs to be addressed. If the former, the issue needs to be investigated with a view to resolution, whether or not it is real or perceived.

With respect to the view that Customs lacks a good understanding of law and procedures, the AFP could provide learning opportunities by seconding officers from Customs into the AFP. This would increase the mutual understanding of respective roles in combating crime and assist both agencies to meet their respective obligations and build positive working relationships between the two agencies. In addition, the AFP may outpost officers to Customs to provide training, advice, and guidance. Furthermore, both agencies could provide a number of positions on training courses for the other agency to assist with skill and knowledge development, build rapport, and encourage good working relationships. These are all issues worthy of consideration and appropriate action.

Conclusion

This chapter has considered an ethical dilemma from the perspective of the Australian Federal Police. It has taken the compromised senior officer scenario and examined potential options to that scenario available to a Superintendent employed by the AFP confronted with such an ethical dilemma. The chapter provided some context to the development of the numerous strategies employed within the AFP's complex integrity framework and highlighted some of the innovative strategies intended to build trust and confidence both within the organisation and with its external partners. It is clear that regardless of an officer's own ethical behaviour—or indeed, the organisation's innovative and strategic integrity framework—ethical dilemmas may well confront an officer in the course of their duty. Issues of discretion, abuse of authority, compliance with due process; inappropriate relationships; confidentiality; personal conduct; and cooperation between agencies can all potentially present police officers, who may or may not be of senior rank, with numerous difficult choices in their everyday activities. Integrity frameworks, clear standards about the conduct expected of employees, high personal standards, and ethical conduct in the workplace can assist in addressing the range and complexity of often very difficult decisions. The importance of leadership, knowledge, and communication within an organisation for strong ethical and integrity frameworks was noted earlier in this chapter (Porter and Prenzler, 2012: 234–7). Effective leadership, at any level and in any organisation, is vital in promoting the core values of an organisation and leading by example. Knowledge exchange both internally and externally provides opportunities to share and exchange innovation and creativity in dealing with a problem that needs to be consistently monitored. Emerging issues in terms of ethical dilemmas can be shared and new ways of thinking can inform the development of best practice. As well, they advocate a mix of proactive and reactive strategies to detect and prevent potential misconduct issues. Some strategies may be more appropriate for a police organisation than others. The local and contextual factors are important. Good communication generally but perhaps especially with complainants may be an important and effective way of improving citizen satisfaction with police activity in this area and increased confidence in police may lead to lower levels of complaints.

Research tells us that serious misconduct and unethical behaviour observed in police organisations have a corrosive effect on how people feel about the police as an institution. It is perceived as undermining democratic authority and the rule of law, reducing legitimacy and inevitably fosters resistance to authority and noncompliance (Porter and Prenzler, 2012). Raising ethical standards in police organisations and in criminal justice institutions generally is important work. It is work that needs to be continuous and alert always to new emerging ethical issues that challenge policing and the criminal justice system generally.

References

Australian Commission for Law Enforcement Integrity, *Inquiry into whistleblowing protections within the Australian Government public sector—Submission to the House Standing Committee on Legal and Constitution Affairs* (2008). <http://www.aclei.gov.au/Documents/Reports%20submissions%20and%20speeches/whislteblower+1.pdf>. Accessed on 8 May 2013.

AFP, 2002–2003 AFP Annual Report, Commonwealth Government 2003 (2003) <http://www.afp.gov.au/~/media/afp/pdf/a/afp-annual-report-2002-2003.ashx>. Accessed on 13 July 2011.

AFP, Professional Standards: A Reference Guide to Professional Standards in the AFP (2006) <http://www.afphub.afp.le/communication/newsandpubs/booklets/profstandpubs/Documents/PRS_fullbooklet.pdf>. Accessed on 13 July 2011.

AFP, AFP Annual Report 09–10, Commonwealth of Australia 2010 (2010a) <http://www.afp.gov.au/media-centre/publications/~/media/afp/pdf/a/afp-annual-report-2009-2010.ashx>. Accessed on 13 July 2011.

AFP, Workforce Diversity Plan Commonwealth of Australia 2010 (2010b) <http://www.afp.gov.au/~/media/afp/pdf/w/workforce-diversity-plan.ashx>. Accessed on 23 July 2012.

AFP, AFP Annual Report 2010–11 Commonwealth of Australia 2011 (2011a). <http://www.afp.gov.au/media-centre/publications/~/media/afp/pdf/a/AFP_Annual_Report_Book_2010-2011.ashx>. Accessed on 23 July 2012.

AFP, National Guideline on the Confidant Network (2011b). <http://www.afphub.afp.le/GovernanceFramework/NationalGuideline/Pages/HN00067.aspx>. Accessed on 13 July 2011.

AFP News, AFP best practice inspires Pride in Diversity Conference (2011). <http://www.afphub.afp.le/afpnewsonline/ANONews/2011/Pages/AFPbestpracticeinspiresPrideinDiversityConference.aspx>. Accessed on 23 July 2012.

BBC, 'Met Police Commissioner Sir Paul Stephenson quits' (2011) <http://www.bbc.co.uk/news/uk-14180043>. Assessed on 18 July 2011.

Fisher, W, Fisher Review of Professional Standards (2003) <http://www.afphub.afp.le/professionalstandards/about/Pages/default.aspx>. Accessed on 12 September 2011.

Fleming, J, 'Working through Networks: The Challenge of Partnership Policing', in J Fleming and J Wood (eds), *Fighting Crime Together: The Challenges of Policing and Security Networks* (Sydney: University of New South Wales Press, 2006), pp 87–115.

Jamieson, L, Personal Communication with Juani O' Reilly, AFP Performance Analysis Team on 25 July 2012.

Kleinig, J, 'Ethical Policing', in A Wakefield and J Fleming (eds), *The Sage International Dictionary of Policing* (London: Sage Publications, 2009) pp 107–9.

McEvoy, A (Superintendent), Personal communication with Juani O'Reilly on 11 October 2011.

Neyroud, P, 'Policing and Ethics', in T Newburn (ed), *Handbook of Policing* (Devon: Willan Publishing, 2003), pp 578–602.

Porter, LE and Prenzler, T, *Police Integrity Management in Australia: Global Lessons for Combating Police Misconduct* (Florida, USA: CRC Press, Taylor and Francis, 2012).

Prenzler, T, 'Corruption and Reform: Global Trends and Theoretical Perspectives in T Prenzler and J Ransley (eds), *Police Reform: Building Integrity* (Sydney: Hawkins Press, 2002), pp 3–23.

Prenzler, T, 'The Evolution of Police Oversight in Australia' (2011) 21(3) *Policing and Society* 284–303.

Scott, A, 'Professional Standards—charting the way forward' (2004) 82 March *Platypus* 35–8 <http://www.afp.gov.au/~/media/afp/pdf/f/fisher-review.ashx>. Accessed on 13 July 2011.

Further Reading

Caldero, MA and Crank, JP, *Police Ethics: The Corruption of Noble Cause* (Burlington, MA: Anderson Publishing, 2010).

Davis, C, *Conflict of Interest in Policing*, Sydney Institute of Criminology Series (Annandale, NSW: Federation Press, 2008).

Murray, J, *Leadership and Integrity in Policing: The March away from Militarism,* 'Presentation at the Third Police Leadership Conference' Managing Change through Principled Leadership; 10–12 April (Vancouver, BC, Canada, 2002).

Neyroud, PW and Beckley, A, *Policing, Ethics and Human Rights* (Devon: Willan Publishing, 2001).

Porter, L and Prenzler, T, 'A National Stocktake of Police Integrity Strategies' (ARC Centre for Excellence in Policing and Security, Griffith University, 2011).

Prenzler, T, *Ethics and Accountability in Criminal Justice* (Bowen Hills, Qld: Australian Academic Press, 2009).

Prenzler, T and Ransley, J (eds), *Police Reform: Building Integrity* (Sydney, NSW: Federation Press, 2002).

Victoria Police, *Organised Crime Strategy 2005–2009* (2005) <http://www.police.vic.gov.au/retrievemedia.asp?Media_ID=2544> Accessed 6 February 2013.

Westmarland, L, 'Police Ethics and Integrity: Breaking the Blue Code of Silence (2005) 15(2) *Policing and Society* 145–65.

Whiddett, A, 'Directions in the Australian Federal Police: Recent Past to Near Future', in B Ellem (ed), *Beyond Catching and Keeping: Police, corrections and the community* (Centre for Police and Justice Studies, Monash University, Caulfield East, Victoria, 1995), pp 24–38.

Addressing the Scenario
A Socratic Police Dialogue

Peter Neyroud and Colin Paine

Introduction

The 'compromised officer' scenario is a complex one and we have chosen to present our response in the form of a dialogue between the two authors. The setting is, therefore, akin to a mentoring meeting at which we play our past and present real life roles—Chief Constable and Chief Inspector. We aim both to bring out the ethical issues in the scenario and illustrate how the issues can look when viewed from different standpoints in the organisation.

The Opening: Colin Paine

This is a very difficult and complex set of circumstances. The scenario presents a classic ethical dilemma or 'Catch 22'. That is, doing the right thing may well bring about bad consequences. In this case, the obvious course, taking action to initiate an investigation into Assistant Chief Constable (ACC) Jackson (to prove or disprove misconduct), could result in damage to the organisation's reputation, might destroy the ACC's promising career and give succour to the bigots who resent his position, might damage his family life and, finally, could undermine the forthcoming operation.

This dilemma is made more acute, in my opinion, by three main factors; the friendship between Superintendent Sutton and ACC Jackson; the potential for damage to the fragile relationship between the Police and Her Majesty's Revenue and Customs (HMRC); the information suggesting that ACC Jackson is having a homosexual affair with a known drug-addict is uncertain or potentially even a malicious fabrication.

The fact that Supt Sutton holds ACC Jackson in such high professional regard accentuates the issue of loyalty. The theme of loyalty runs through the scenario— from one perspective how can Supt Sutton be disloyal to his boss (to whom he does indeed owe a debt of loyalty) when acting purely on the intelligence from those in the 'Guns and Gangs' unit, whom he suspects may have an axe to grind? However, I would argue that his loyalty to ACC Jackson is trumped by his loyalty to the organisation, and further, by his loyalty to the impartial administration of the law. The oath of office provides a higher form of loyalty than the bonds of friendship.

For Supt Sutton there are real tests of character here, particularly in terms of his personal courage and attitude to personal risk. It would be easy to discount the intelligence about the ACC as unsubstantiated speculation, conjecture, and lacking in substance and therefore that there is no requirement to act on it. However, such a conclusion could probably only be arrived at as a result of a motivation to protect oneself. If Supt Sutton lacked personal courage he could even make a case that it is Ch Insp Smythe's responsibility to report the matter as the senior leader of the 'Guns and Gangs' unit. However, such an approach would ignore his senior rank and betray a lack of personal responsibility for the information now in his possession. An assessment of the personal risks to Supt Sutton would indicate that taking any form of action or, indeed, lapsing into inaction, carries considerable risks. If Supt Sutton reports the matter and any subsequent investigation does not bear out the allegation then ACC Jackson has the capability to cause significant and irreparable damage to Supt Sutton's career and reputation. Equally, a failure to report could leave him exposed for a neglect of duty. Bravery in the context of policing is often discussed as a matter of physical bravery, but the moral bravery required in this case is probably as great as any officer will ever face in the course of their career.

A further dimension of the scenario is the way that it brings the personal life of ACC Jackson into the public sphere. The fact that his suspected affair is homosexual in nature is undoubtedly a red herring. However, I would argue that the fact that ACC Jackson may be having an affair (regardless of who it is with) *is* ethically relevant on two fronts. Firstly, as a friend of ACC Jackson Supt Sutton should seek to shield or advise him from taking any action that might cause him significant personal harm. Secondly, at this rank the distinction between professional and private life becomes blurred; particularly if the affair were subsequently to result in a messy divorce or be brought to light within the public eye. Police officers—particularly senior police officers—know that on or off duty they remain a warranted officer and their actions can affect public confidence in the police.

This, in turn, raises an important issue about rank and status. Regardless of the position or status of ACC Jackson, is it not the case that if any person in a position of great trust and authority is suspected of being involved in criminal activity to a greater or lesser degree an investigation should be commenced? That would certainly be the right thing to do if the same intelligence were available regarding a police constable in the organisation. The reasons for hesitation here seem to be the much greater consequences rather than the nature of the behaviour itself.

It seems to me that we need a reference point to guide our judgements regarding our duty in such circumstances. The best one we have is the Code of Conduct that all police officers know and by which they have to abide. At its simplest the Code of Conduct for Police Officers states 'any conduct which could, if proved, bring discredit on the police service should be investigated'. For this reason, as well as those previously listed, I believe the right course of action is for Supt Sutton personally to inform the head of Professional Standards for the force of the intelligence and allow them to investigate the matter to prove or disprove the allegation.

However, I do not believe that his duty stops there. The duty to the organisation may be complete, but his duty to his friend is not. Personal loyalty should also lead Supt Sutton to inform ACC Jackson that he has informed Professional Standards once he has permission to do so from the head of the department. If ACC Jackson is an honest and decent character then, although feelings may be hurt, he will understand the reasoning. If not then Supt Sutton will be at great risk through this process. Anonymously informing Professional Standards may appear the most expedient course of action, but to do so would lack the personal loyalty that is owed to ACC Jackson.

Two other options are initially appealing, but both should be promptly discounted. For Supt Sutton to either seek to bottom out the intelligence himself or to discuss the intelligence with ACC Jackson in person may seem intuitively appealing. After all, it might be that this is all down to an innocent misunderstanding. However, to take this course of action would implicate Supt Sutton in the investigation and potentially tip off ACC Jackson if the intelligence is well founded, thereby frustrating any future investigation. It would be best to allow Professional Standards to initiate an impartial and independent investigation that will either exonerate or condemn ACC Jackson.

Peter Neyroud's Response

Colin, there are a lot of issues in this scenario, but I want to start with the wider context. The events are particularly significant because they are happening in a police force. As a chief I know how important reputation is for police service, but I can also look at the research evidence and find that the perceptions of fairness and integrity in the way police operate are a critical part of the public's preparedness to cooperate with the police and, potentially, to keep the law.[1] Secondly, the police are a powerful organisation entrusted with powers to use force and deprive people of

---

[1] Tyler and Huo (2002).

their liberty. The police define 'on a daily basis, the real law of the land'[2] and thus the importance of the police both obeying the law and setting high standards is greater than in other organisational contexts. I start from the presumption, therefore, that the organisational need for action to tackle potentially corrupt behaviour is likely to prevail over other considerations. I think we agree on that point.

However, that need for action to investigate will need to be balanced with fairness towards ACC Jackson. As you have identified, there is a risk here that the information suggesting a homosexual affair with an active criminal is conjecture driven by prejudice and dislike of the ACC by the Unit undertaking the surveillance. If that were to prove to be the case and the investigation were handled badly and perceived to be unfair, then the resultant damage to the force's reputation and legitimacy—particularly with ethnic minority communities—could be substantial. There is already a strong perception in Black and Asian communities and amongst Black and Asian officers that ethnic minority officers are disproportionately targeted by discipline enquiries.[3] That is not a reason not to enquire, but does dictate care and forethought in the decision to investigate and the approach taken, particularly if this matter entered the public arena.

The other key issue is to be clear whether any criminal offences have been or are likely to be committed on the information provided. It would seem from the information that the only likely offences would be the potential perversion of the course of justice (or misconduct in a public office) that might result from the leaking of information about the operation to the drug dealer. However, there is neither evidence nor reasonable suspicion that this crime is about to be committed, merely a risk or supposition that this is a possible outcome if the affair is, indeed, happening.

However, if we follow the intelligence through by steps, then we are left with a number of logical steps that would be appropriate whether Jackson is an ACC or a police constable. The first inference of the intelligence is that Jackson has a strong association at least and possibly a sexually intimate relationship with Elsey, the drug dealer. That relationship alone would be highly problematic for the force, given Elsey's criminal activities. It might well amount, as you suggest, to 'conduct likely to bring discredit on the force', leaving aside the personal morality of the affair in the context of Jackson's marriage (which I will return to). As Jackson is not just a police officer, but also a very senior officer, this alone would justify an investigation, with or without the up and coming drugs operation.

If the circumstances justify an investigation, then, what sort of investigation, conducted by and overseen by whom and how? You have suggested that Supt Sutton should be speaking to his Professional Standards Department. Whilst this is perfectly sound, I wonder whether it is the right course of action. Jackson is an Assistant Chief Constable. His accountability as a Chief Officer is to his Chief and to the Police Authority.

---

[2] Sherman (1974: preface).
[3] MacVean and Neyroud (2012).

Colin Paine

How would that change once the directly elected Police and Crime Commissioners (PCC) are in place from November 2012 in England and Wales?

Peter Neyroud

Your question highlights the importance of context and also why there is a very real difference of substance between this set of circumstances applied to a police constable and an ACC. From November 2012 the Chief Constable will be directly accountable to the PCC and that accountability will undoubtedly stretch to cover the way that the Chief Constable manages the team of Chief Officers. There is a real issue here of the confidence of the elected PCC in the Chief Constable if an issue of such sensitivity relating to a Chief Officer is not handled effectively. O'Hara, in his study of why law enforcement organisations fail, demonstrates that 'oversight failure' is a major cause of organisational failure in police forces.[4] He specifically mentions failures to tackle allegations of corruption against powerful individuals or groups in the force. I would argue that mishandling of this case would be a strong and justifiable reason for any PCC to dispense with the Chief.

Hence, I would argue that any investigation has to be initiated with the full involvement of the Chief Constable. After all, it is the Chief who will personally have to handle the outcome. If Jackson is completely exonerated, it will be much better for Jackson and Sutton if the decision to initiate the investigation has been taken by the Chief. Secondly, if Jackson has formed a relationship with Elsey, it will be the Chief who will need to judge the nature of the relationship and the risks that it poses and, therefore, the action, non-disciplinary, disciplinary, or even criminal, that needs to be taken as a result.

Colin Paine

It is a big step for a police officer, even at Superintendent level, to seek a meeting with the Chief about the conduct of one of the ACCs. To do so would require significant moral courage and real self-belief.

Peter Neyroud

I can assure you, as a Chief, that I would much rather hear about this issue direct from the Superintendent, rather than indirectly via the Professional Standards Department. There are two reasons for this: the direct approach would tell me

---

4 O'Hara (2005).

that I was leading the force in the way that people felt confident not only to approach me but also that I would deal with the issues raised; secondly, it would give me the option to deal very confidentially with the case, which might be a better way of dealing with it. How many people in the force do you think would be aware of the case if Sutton informed Professional Standards and they carried out the investigation?

Colin Paine

There are already a number of officers in the 'Gangs and Guns' unit and then there would be a team in Professional Standards. I see your point. It is highly unlikely that the case could be kept confidential. But why is that important?

Peter Neyroud

The fewer people that are aware before an effective investigation has been concluded the more chance there is, if the investigation exonerates Jackson, for him to recover with his reputation intact. Given his very imminent potential to be a very significant leader within the police service, that is important beyond the individual concerned. If the Chief could ensure a rapid, independent investigation, then it would not only be better for Jackson but it would have a major benefit for public confidence and potentially the confidence of the HMRC, if they pick up the rumours about Jackson (as seems quite possible).

Colin Paine

That makes sense. However, investigating a PC for suspected misconduct is one thing, but how should the investigation into an ACC be approached?

Peter Neyroud

We have both established that an ACC is in a different position because of his seniority. The impact of a police constable associating with Elsey would be significant, but an ACC not only has access to much greater information, but also represents the most senior management of the force. Not only because of his seniority but also because of the need for transparency, I would very rarely consider investigating someone as senior as Jackson using the internal investigation team.

However, bringing in the outside investigation team is one thing, setting a policy for investigation is another. How do you get the right balance between an effective investigation and fairness for Jackson? In short, how do you ensure an ethical approach to such a sensitive investigation?

I have always liked the analysis developed by Gary Marx in his study of covert policing.[5] He set out a series of criteria that should be considered:

- Seriousness: particularly the harm you are seeking to prevent.
- Alternatives: are there less intrusive or non-deceptive alternatives?
- Democratic decision making: in this case is it clear that whatever means we opt for are publicly set out as options available to police (for example is there a force policy on pre-emptive investigation in cases of suspected corruption)?
- Spirit of the law.
- Prosecution: is the outcome you seek a criminal justice one and, therefore, are your suspicions going to be tested in public?
- Clarity of definition: are you clear what sort of criminal behaviour you are targeting and is it clear that the target knows it is criminal too?
- Crime occurrence: can you be sure that the unintended consequences of your actions are not a further crime?
- Grounds for suspicion: I have discussed this already, but this question is designed to discourage fishing expeditions where no crime has occurred or is likely to occur.
- Prevention: will the operation prevent a crime taking place?

Colin Paine

These questions are not far from the sort of questions which the European Convention on Human Rights forces you to ask. They are probing the necessity of your action, the proportionality, legality, and the overall fairness of the process. In this case, the potential harms—a possibly corrupt relationship between a senior officer and an active criminal—do seem to meet Marx's seriousness test. That seems to rule out inaction and whilst it would be possible to deal with the case by simply confronting ACC Jackson, this, in the absence of some independent corroboration, would be easily denied and could undermine any subsequent investigation. Worse, such a direct challenge unsupported by evidence could be perceived as motivated by prejudice and if publicised could seriously damage the force's reputation. This would seem to permit an initial covert approach.

As I remember, such a 'pre-monitory' or proactive approach is described in Sherman's study of corruption.[6] It should be in every force's Professional Standards policy these days. It would also be consistent with the legal framework created by the Regulation of Investigatory Powers Act 2001, the Code of Practice, and national guidelines on covert policing.

On the questions relating to the nature of the crimes or potential crimes, it would be very clear to such a senior officer as Jackson that associating with an active criminal would be a serious conduct issue. However, it is possible that he is

---

[5] Marx (1988: 105).
[6] Sherman (1974).

in the relationship, but does not know that Elsey is an active criminal, but this still leaves open the possibility that Elsey is aware that Jackson is a senior police officer and is seeking to use the affair to compromise and blackmail Jackson. The only real weaknesses of a covert approach are the concerns about the motivation and accuracy of the intelligence. However, Sutton does trust Ch Insp Smythe and this seems a sufficient basis for, at least, 'rational' suspicion, even if the legal test of 'reasonable suspicion' is not yet established.

Peter Neyroud

I agree with this reasoning. I think that a particularly strong question in Marx's list is the challenge to consider alternatives. In this case, given the potential harm to reputation and operations, it is difficult to argue for passivity. Once you have ruled out inaction, it seems to me that you are left with either overt action—to confront Jackson, with the likely consequences that you have suggested—or covert action to provide further corroboration or to refute the allegations.

On balance, I would certainly be considering a covert investigation at this stage, because, whilst you have suspicions of a potentially serious misconduct, you don't have enough proven information to move forward one way or another.

When considering what sort of operation, Marx[7] posed a further set of questions:

- Autonomy: is the target free to choose?
- Degree of deception: is the intrusion proposed minimal?
- Bad lessons: does the approach provide a bad moral lesson itself?
- Privacy and expression: will the approach show respect for private life?
- Collateral harm: are there any third parties or unintended consequences?
- Equitable target selection: is the selection of the target equitable? I have touched on this issue when discussing the potential disproportionality in misconduct investigations.
- Realism: is any deception realistic (or is it entrapment)?
- Relevance of charges: are the crimes pursued directly connected to a criminal harm?

We have to remember, as both Marx and Bok[8] remind us, that covert approaches are deceptive and, as you have identified, there are issues about loyalty and relationships in this case, which could be irreparably damaged by an ill-considered operation, and which could appear to focus on proving a wrong rather than seeking the truth. The key is to ensure that at each stage of the investigation the subject is making their own choices not being set up by the police. However, one advantage of an outside team is that their judgement is unlikely to be compromised by the personal loyalty issues and they are also more likely to be perceived as independent.

---

[7] Marx (1988: 105–6).
[8] Marx (1988) and Bok (1978).

Colin Paine

From your reasoning and this set of questions, you seem to be encouraging a careful and deliberate strategy in stages. This suggests a covert operation that starts with techniques like extracting Jackson's communications data—telephone, email, and social media traffic—and analysing it for contact with Elsey before moving on to more significant intrusion such as physical or technical surveillance.

Peter Neyroud

Agreed. The investigation can start at the outset by analysing communications data, which may not be able to disprove the suspicions, but, if any traffic between Elsey and Jackson appears, can certainly provide further corroboration of some form of relationship. Such an approach does not remove the possibility of difficult decisions later. After all, it is quite possible that Jackson is either wholly innocent or criminally involved and is careful enough to use a pay-as-you-go phone and a separate webmail account for any communication with Elsey, making it more difficult to find the trail of evidence that you are seeking. The key, at each stage, is to go back to Marx's questions and reconsider the proportionality and purpose of the investigation. There have been a number of high profile investigations in policing where an initial suspicion has been followed by a large-scale investigation that was not justified by the first steps of the investigation.

Colin Paine

Who would take those decisions and would you, as the Chief, inform the Police and Crime Commissioner (PCC) or anyone else about the investigation?

Peter Neyroud

I think that the responsibility for this investigation lies fairly and squarely with the Chief Constable—the Assistant Chief Constable is a member of the Chief Constable's management board. This is still the case, even though we have decided to use another force. I would not, at this stage, tell the Police and Crime Commissioner. I would want to have the initial intelligence investigation completed and I would have that done by an outside force. If that investigation and a conversation with Jackson satisfied me that the allegations were wholly unfounded, I don't think the matter needs to go any further. As we said earlier, in these circumstances, the fewer people who know the better.

If, however, I had any firming up of the suspicions, then I think the PCC needs to know that there is a potentially serious problem with the integrity of a Chief Officer. I suspect that the PCC would want me to suspend Jackson. I would be resistant to arguments to suspend Jackson until I was fairly confident that the covert investigation had gathered as much evidence as possible. There is probably only one chance to gather the evidence and I would be keen to ensure that the investigation was able to prove or disprove culpability and its extent rather than leave us with lingering suspicion.

The other person that I am going to tell is the Chief Inspector of Constabulary (HMCIC). As soon as the initial intelligence operation has started to suggest that there is some substance to the allegations, I am going to need to hand the investigation over to another Chief Constable to secure the highest possible independence. This would be helpful in my conversation with the PCC as well, because it helps to insulate the PCC and myself from allegations of a cover-up and provides a higher level of transparency. Moreover, at some point, I am also going to be having a conversation with the Independent Police Complaints Commission (IPCC)—probably after the conversation with HMCIC. I would expect the IPCC to want to take on the oversight of the investigation at this point.

Colin Paine

What about the Home Secretary? Surely Ministers have some interest in the matter if a potential Chief Constable is likely to be shown to be involved in corrupt activity?

Peter Neyroud

With the advent of the PCC, Ministers have consciously chosen to take a back seat and devolve responsibility for policing to the PCC. However, I think you would be a very unwise Chief Constable not to make sure that the Home Secretary is briefed. Even in the new regime, the Home Secretary retains a duty to secure an efficient and effective police service and would justifiably see that they have an interest in corruption allegations at senior level being dealt with effectively. The difference between the pre and post PCC world of accountability is that I would probably tell the PCC that I was proposing to brief the Home Secretary. The PCC is likely to be sensitive to such issues being shared with the Home Secretary. If they are of the same political party then problems for the PCC on their local watch might impact their standing in the party. If they are from an opposition party, then the PCC will suspect that the Home Secretary might seek some political advantage. Either way, the conversation with the PCC seems likely to be tricky.

Colin Paine

There are a lot of people and organisations with an interest in this case. Would you tell the head of HMRC that the investigation might be compromised?

Peter Neyroud

If I knew them personally and trusted them, then I would probably tell them. This would have the advantage of reinforcing trust and would, if the allegations turned out to be untrue, demonstrate a commitment to cooperation. If the allegations are true, it would help a bit, but I suspect that no personal relationship would overcome the adverse fall out.

Colin Paine

But the scenario suggests that the operation is in mid-flight and about to go live. Is there an option to delay long enough to find out sufficient information to know whether there is a serious problem?

Peter Neyroud

It would definitely be worth considering—but I think that the Chief would need a very good relationship with the Head of HMRC to be able to persuade them to do that. It would be a question of weighing the relative benefits of delay over the risks that the operation would be compromised. The problem at the moment is that you don't appear to have information to balance those benefits and risks with any degree of accuracy.

Colin Paine

What about the media? The hacking scandal exposed some serious problems in the police relationship with the media. Is it at least possible that a malicious officer in the 'Gangs and Guns' unit would leak the information to a journalist?

Peter Neyroud

This is entirely possible and it is a distinct risk of a covert investigation where it would not be apparent that an investigation was active. The officer could, in these circumstances, seek to portray him- or herself as a whistleblower and leak the information. This highlights one reason why it should have been Ch Insp Smythe who came forward rather than Supt Sutton. Smythe would then have known that an investigation was being undertaken and might have been able to head off any disaffected officers in his unit.

You would clearly be sensible to have a well thought through media strategy. Moreover, making sure that you have briefed the PCC, HMCIC, IPCC, and Home Secretary is also crucial so that if and when the story breaks, you have other allies helping you (you hope!).

Colin Paine

Meanwhile, what about Jackson? A week ago he was waiting for a board for Chief Constable. Now, he may be tarnished by allegations of corruption and his career may be over. How do you deal with him?

Peter Neyroud

If there is any truth to the allegations about a relationship with Elsey, he would frankly deserve what is coming. He was either naïve, in which case he shouldn't be supported for Chief Constable's jobs, or discreditable or corrupt, in which case he shouldn't be in his current role. Given his very overt presentation of himself as a happily married man, he would have lost a great deal of his moral standing in my eyes even if he was merely naïve. Moreover, even in this case, he would almost certainly have lost a considerable amount of his legitimacy as a leader with his subordinates, including, I suspect, Sutton. Porter and Nohria's work[9] on senior executives has shown that moral congruity is a key component of trust and legitimacy at the most senior levels.

On a personal level, Jackson has probably presented himself to me, as he did to Sutton, as a happily married man. There is nothing in the narrative to suggest that he has shared problems in the marriage with his Chief. I would feel very badly let down by Jackson and quite unable to trust him.

Colin Paine

I suspect that the same loss of trust would be felt across the organisation. You seem to be suggesting that this situation is unlikely to end well. Moreover, what about the consequences for the relationship with HMRC—how would you mitigate the damage to that?

Peter Neyroud

I think that you would have to be very lucky to bring this scenario to a positive conclusion. The allegations against Jackson are potentially serious and, even if they are dealt with expeditiously and transparently, are likely to damage the reputation of the police force if there is any substance to them. If they were proven to be malicious then there would be an equally difficult investigation that would have to follow into the source of the allegations and their possible motivation. Either way, the reputation of the force would be affected.

---

[9] Porter and Nohria (2010).

However, if we go back to the beginning and reflect on the consequences of inaction, they are far worse. Inaction would suggest that the force was prepared to tolerate corruption and ignore racism. No citizen could feel confident in such a police force and any PCC would be justified in removing a Chief Constable who went down this path. In policing, it is better to take risks to maintain integrity than risk integrity by inaction.

I think that approach is also the saving of the relationship with the HMRC. The Chief would have to take some risks and be open with the HMRC at senior level as early as possible. This might still not be enough to repair the damage, but it would be a great deal better than trying to cover up the problem and keep HMRC in the dark. That is no basis for a partnership between two law enforcement organisations.

Peter Neyroud and Colin Paine: Our Conclusions

This is a tough scenario in which potential corruption, police legitimacy, and personal loyalty are all in play. As we worked through the approach in our dialogue, we appear to have followed a somewhat consequentialist line: the right decision being driven by the consequences of something worse that might happen. This is a natural sequitur of the way we debated the issue, but not, in conclusion, the prime way that we would argue that ethical policing should be nurtured. Delattre,[10] drawing on Aristotelian ethics of virtue, argued that the key driver of ethical policing lies in the moral character of those in positions of power in policing. As the police service moves to a professional status,[11] the police service will need its own version of the Hippocratic oath and systems and processes to bolster its implementation, but it will also, as Delattre argued, need professionals with the moral courage to make the right decisions for the right reasons, despite the threat of personally adverse consequences. We conclude, therefore, with a passage from Delattre:

> Living up to the oath inevitably involves some assignments that are odious and some situations that are dangerous. Police should be forewarned of this fact of life in policing when they apply to become recruits and when they are being trained. (p 317)

References

Bok, S, *Lying: Moral Choices in Public and Private Life* (New York: Pantheon, 1978).

Delattre, E, *Character and Cops: Ethics in policing* (Washington, DC: AEI Press, 1996).

MacVean, A and Neyroud, PW, *Policing, Ethics and Values* (London: Sage Publications, Learning Matters, 2012).

---

[10] Delattre (1996).
[11] Neyroud (2011).

Marx, GT, *Undercover: Police Surveillance in America* (Berkeley: University of California Press, 1988).

Neyroud, PW, *A Review of Police Leadership and Training* (London: Home Office, 2011).

O'Hara, P, *Why Law Enforcement Organisations Fail* (Durham, NC: Carolina Academic Press, 2005).

Porter, M and Nohria, N, What is Leadership? The CEO's role in large, complex organisations, in N Nohria and R Khurana (eds), *The Handbook of Leadership Theory and Practice* (Boston, MA: Harvard Business Press, 2010).

Sherman, LW (ed), *Police Corruption: a Sociological Perspective* (New York: Anchor Books, 1974).

Tyler, T and Huo, YJ, *Trust in the Law: Encouraging public cooperation with the police and courts* (New York: Russell Sage Foundation, 2002).

Editor's Commentary

PAJ Waddington

This commentary is unusual since we are fortunate enough to have two analyses and prescriptions quite distinct from each other in the perspective adopted and recommendations made. As such, they are complementary: enabling us to consider the issues from different angles. It also reveals how scenarios pose difficult issues that provoke debate and discussion. In this commentary, I wish to adopt a third stance!

Fleming and Reilly in their contribution and Paine in his role within the second contribution both commence their consideration of the case from the same standpoint—viewing the situation from a position of a subordinate toiling with an accusation made against his boss, Jackson; whereas, Neyroud regards the situation from the more elevated position of a former Chief Constable. Also, we can view the same scenario through the lens of two very different policing systems: England and Wales, on the one hand, and the Australian Federal Police (AFP), on the other. The AFP is particularly interesting, first, because it is the federal police of *Australia* and Australia—or rather New South Wales—was the location for Janet Chan's research (Chan, 1999, 1996, 2003) upon which I rested so heavily in my introduction. What Chan argued was that the origins of the supposed *police* culture lay not inside the police organisation, but in the society it policed—post-colonial Australia. Presumably, this is much the same for the AFP, albeit that its reach is Australia-wide and stretches beyond Australia's frontier to provide international assistance. The good fortune to have a scenario set in the AFP is increased by the fact that the AFP itself is in a post-scandal phase of development, during which it has gone to considerable lengths to articulate its values and a code of conduct, reminding officers of this emphasis through prominently placed notices and the screensavers on official computers. They have also been imaginative: introducing a 'confidante' scheme, which enables officers to discuss in confidence difficult ethical situations that they face. This institutionalises what John Kleinig (point '8', pp 33–4) advocates as good practice: not to confront difficult dilemmas of this nature alone. Ethical dilemmas are best discussed with others who are less directly involved and have the necessary emotional distance to afford them the luxury of objectivity. The AFP has also been pro-active, emphasising the importance of ethical behaviour throughout the training of officers. For an officer confronting such a dilemma, there is probably no better place to do so than in the AFP.

In other respects this scenario is anything but unusual; indeed, it involves a classic corruption scenario: a senior officer who might have become compromised by a relationship with someone of dubious character and who might be in position to interfere with a serious criminal investigation. To add complexity to the problem, this criminal investigation involves another agency with whom the police enjoy somewhat strained relations. Moreover, Jackson is an officer of minority ethnic heritage and has acquired a public profile as such and there is more than a whiff of personal hostility, perhaps racism, lurking around his accusers. What Jackson is accused of is immorality—a homosexual affair—which, as O'Reilly and Fleming note, is not in itself 'considered a potential ethical risk within the AFP'. However, the web is so tangled that, as Neyroud and Paine remark, this is unlikely to end well for any of the participants—Jackson, Sutton, perhaps Smythe too, and certainly the police organisation is in danger of sustaining severe reputational damage. One wonders what would be worse: that Jackson is guilty of becoming involved in an intimate relationship with a known criminal, or that officers in the 'Guns and Gangs'/Serious Organised Crime unit are found to have been motivated by malice? Either way it hardly enhances the reputation of the force and, as Neyroud remarks, reputation is vitally important to the everyday work of ordinary officers. One can only imagine what youths standing on street corners would yell to passing police patrols, or what confidence potential witnesses would have in the integrity of the force. Yet to do nothing would be far worse. However bad it seems to get, covering up suspected wrongdoing is always more damaging if it is revealed. Therefore, as all our contributors conclude, 'doing nothing' is not a viable option for Sutton.

Values, Rules, and Procedures

O'Reilly and Fleming, and Paine all commence their deliberations in terms of the values, rules, and procedures of the particular force. All are agreed that this is a task for Professional Standards officers to investigate. They are also agreed that if Sutton takes that course of action he is risking his professional and personal relationship with Jackson. This is precisely the type of situation where it seems to me that formal rules and procedures fail to connect with real-life dilemmas. If, as O'Reilly and Fleming observe, '[b]eing a homosexual or having a private homosexual relationship is not considered a potential ethical risk within the AFP' (this volume, p 64), then what is the problem that Jackson's alleged behaviour poses? They answer that question by arguing that as a 'result of his connection with an illicit drug user, Kevin Elsey and his connections to local organised criminals as a drug dealer' (this volume, p 64) are the real threat. Yet, it seems to me that this glosses too readily over five uncertainties: first, 'having a private affair' *is* 'a potential ethical risk', not because it is *homosexual* but because it is extra-marital and Jackson has been publicly flouting his home life which in turn leaves him vulnerable to blackmail and the charge of being a hypocrite. It could be even more threatening than that, for it is commonly believed by officers of my acquaintance that organised criminals deliberately seek to compromise serving personnel, so as to gain illicit access to police information. From this point of view, it is conceivable that Elsey has discovered Jackson's covert homosexual preferences, enticed him into an indiscreet liaison, and is now blackmailing him by threats of exposure to the media. Such a prospect would surely be a 'potential ethical risk' to any police force. However, unless Elsey is aware of the surveillance operation, there is no reason to suppose that Jackson has been enticed into a liaison with Elsey in order to de-rail the forthcoming joint operation with Revenue and Customs; it could easily be that the relationship is a coincidence. Even if it is coincidental, it may not be perceived as such. Secondly, whilst the officers engaged in the surveillance operation might recognise Kevin Elsey as a drug dealer associated with organised crime, it is not clear that Jackson realises this, although perhaps he should, given the intimate nature of their alleged relationship. Thirdly, whilst Jackson is privy to the joint operation it is not clear that he is in a position to interfere with it. It is likely that his elevated position would allow interference, but it cannot be assumed. Fourthly, as O'Reilly and Fleming point out, we cannot even be sure that the accusation is not the result of a genuine mistake on the part of a, perhaps inexperienced, surveillance officer. Jackson's relationship with Elsey might be 'innocent' and 'platonic' (this volume p 57). Jackson might conceivably be employing Elsey as a covert intelligence source. Finally, what is more firmly suspected is that there is hostility towards Jackson amongst those most closely associated with the accusation. In other words, the scenario is suffused with uncertainties and ambiguities.

These uncertainties could be resolved by a thorough investigation. Yet, this would be warranted *only* if the accusation is credible. All contributors accept that if Sutton passes the allegation to Professional Standards, Jackson would correctly infer that Sutton must have considered it credible, and, if so, this would destroy the mutually trusting and supportive relationship the two men have enjoyed so far. Integrity procedures that require, as they inevitably do, that *potential* wrongdoing is reported, are designed (even if they abstain from avowing it) to create a climate of mistrust. Even if Jackson is exonerated, suspicion will cling to him— 'no smoke without fire'. Moreover, even if Jackson has not acted wrongfully, but merely unwisely, then this would blight his career. Neyroud mentions, as a Chief Constable, that he would feel 'badly let down' by a senior colleague who had deceived him into believing that he is happily married whilst conducting an extra-marital affair. On the other hand, if the allegation is found to be baseless, then what does this mean for the surveillance officers in the 'Guns and Gangs

Unit' who reported their suspicions? Integrity procedures often emphasise the necessity of protecting 'whistleblowers'. However, a prior investigation that has the purpose of establishing the credibility of the allegation might very well be experienced by the surveillance officers and others as implicitly casting doubt on their integrity: because some officers are hostile to Jackson does not mean that this accusation is tainted by the whiff of racism. To investigate those making the accusation is likely to send a signal to other officers that they are risking their careers if they do 'blow the whistle' on superiors. The Morris Report (Morris et al, 2004) drew attention to the perversity resulting from supervising officers dealing with minor disciplinary issues made against non-white officers more formally than they dealt with similar complaints against white officers *in order to ensure that they were compliant with disciplinary procedures*. On the other hand, the long-running saga of suspicions and complaints regarding one of the highest-profile non-white officers, Commander Ali Dizaei (IPCC, 2010), shows how corrupt officers will use their own ethnicity to shield themselves from accusations of wrongdoing by repelling accusations as mere racism. This, it seems, is how official values, rules, and procedures can conspire to make difficult dilemmas almost impossible to resolve.[1]

Suspicion, Uncertainty, and the Prospect of Undeserved Damage

It was never the intention of this scenario to raise wider issues about the nature of policing as such, but it does so nonetheless. All contributors recognise the impact that even conducting an investigation is likely to have on Jackson's career and home life, because it is not crystal clear that he has done anything wrong. Hitherto, he has demonstrated that he is a decent man (kindly in his relationship with Sutton) and an effective police officer, who could deal with a major terrorist emergency; not to mention a prominent icon in the struggle for ethnic equality within the police. Even a suspicion of wrongdoing could cast a cloud over Jackson. But how distinctive is such a scenario from other incidents that officers may become involved in? Police officers are routinely obliged to take action on the basis of equally uncertain suspicions, the investigation of which might possibly cause undeserved damage to those they investigate. Because Jackson is a police officer, other police officers can empathise with his plight and worry about the consequences this accusation could have, even if it proves to be baseless. However, if Jackson was a public figure in another public service, would officers be quite so concerned about the prospects of undeserved

---

[1] It is also interesting that Fleming and O'Reilly's 'Option Two' (this volume p 61) is frustrated by the rules and procedures governing surveillance operations and the identity of covert human intelligence sources that prevent Sutton acquiring information that would exonerate Jackson, or lend greater credence to the accusations.

damage being caused? Police officers habitually stop and search people, arrest them, and investigate them on suspicions of wrongdoing that more often than not prove to be insufficient to warrant further investigation. The characteristic feature of criminal justice systems is case 'attrition': that is, at all stages of the process a substantial proportion of cases are dropped (President's Commission on Law Enforcement and Administration of Justice, 1967; Chambers and Millar, 1983). In the meanwhile, a person's career could be de-railed, marriage wrecked, future blighted, and so forth. For instance, Chris Jefferies was arrested on suspicion of the murder of Joanna Yeates in 2010. He was held for three days during which a media frenzy amounting to 'vilification' (in the words of the Lord Chief Justice) engulfed him. In due course, Vincent Tabak was convicted of the murder and Chris Jefferies successfully recovered damages from various media organisations for libel and gave evidence to the Leveson Inquiry into the press. The police did nothing improper, and yet Chris Jefferies found the experience 'absolutely devastating'.[2] Is Jackson any different? Perhaps the real and unintended value of this scenario is that it should bring home to police officers the implications of their actions for those whom they suspect *whoever they may be*. This might encourage all officers to recognise explicitly that suspicion is very different from established truth and that 'suspects' are likely to be proven to be innocent and therefore deserving of respect. Even a youth suspected of theft becomes transformed into a minor public figure once they are stopped and searched in a public place.

Loyalty, Trust, and Mistrust

The reason that officers express more concern for Jackson than they would for someone routinely stopped and searched in a public place, is loyalty to one's colleagues. No matter what our profession, we assume that our colleagues are decent, honourable, and competent. Loyalty is surely a virtue and is essential to organisational efficiency and effectiveness in any enterprise. It is because there is mistrust between Customs and Excise, on the one hand, and the police, on the other, that the forthcoming joint operation to interdict an illicit drugs shipment is so fraught. The abandonment of the joint operation, especially if accompanied by accusations of corruption, would fuel the suspicions that Customs and Excise harbour about the police, which would in turn impede future investigations. Mistrust is corrosive and there is mistrust about the squad whose officers have made the accusation against Jackson. Yet, excessive loyalty too can prove corrosive, for it can camouflage wrongdoing. It is difficult for colleagues to be disinterested and objective when investigating colleagues. Hence, Neyroud's suggestion is to remove collegiality by involving officers from another force to conduct a speedy, but covert, investigation, for

---

[2] <http://www.bbc.co.uk/programmes/b006qj9z>.

instance by checking Jackson's phone records. If Jackson emerges unscathed then his character will remain unsullied. However, as Neyroud acknowledges, many of the lines of the inquiry would be likely to arrive at asymmetric conclusions: that is, they might unequivocally confirm Jackson's association with Elsey, *or be inconclusive*. For instance, a clean phone record would not demonstrate innocence, but could simply reflect the possibility that Jackson had covered his tracks very well. Hence, *incriminating* evidence will speed the resolution of the inquiry, but inconclusive evidence (which perversely is the more likely outcome of an inquiry that exonerates Jackson) would simply require that more evidence was needed and that would take time. The longer the investigation continues the more likely it is that it will find its way into the public domain with damaging consequences for all concerned.

Security

Whichever way the police now turn, security becomes problematic. As more people become involved, the likelihood that secrecy will be lost grows exponentially. In Neyroud's view the force's own Professional Standards department could not be relied upon to maintain confidentiality. Hence, he proposes employing officers from another force to do so. This is a sensible move, but is it sufficient? These officers from another force may also be aware of Jackson, because of his high profile. This may have prompted admiration amongst some of them, but resentment amongst others. Another worry is that powerful figures will need to be kept informed—not even Chief Constables can act autonomously. In England and Wales, we have entered a new era in police governance with the election of Police and Crime Commissioners with the power to hire and fire Chief Constables. Such a figure would need to be told, but what the Commissioner does with the information is a matter for him or her. One hopes that Commissioners will be honourable people, but election does not confer virtue and it could be electorally to the advantage of the Commissioner to use the information for narrow partisan ends and the same goes for the Home Secretary. These political figures operate within a framework of adversarial politics and their opponents would have even more vested interests in exploiting the situation for partisan advantage. They also have staff who may disagree profoundly with a proposed course of action and leak their misgivings to the press. The Independent Police Complaints Commission also has a staff and there have been occasions where quite junior clerical personnel have been privy to sensitive and damaging information that they have leaked to the news media because they felt that the truth as they understood it was being kept from the public. Her Majesty's Inspectorate of Constabulary also has its own professional agenda and is supported by staff who would become privy to this information. With each extension of the circle of those who possess confidential information, security becomes less reliable.

Operational Security

Just as pressing is the imminence of the joint drugs interdiction operation with Revenue and Customs. Because a full investigation of the allegations will take time, especially if the allegations are baseless, it is almost bound to overlap with this interdiction, since Elsey is involved in both. How much does Jackson know about the operation? Sutton is aware that Jackson is 'privy' to it, but does he have or could he obtain access to operational details? Is Jackson in a position to influence the course of the investigation? Jackson is a member of the senior management team and could be expected to be generally aware, but if it was not his particular portfolio he may be unaware of the details. For security reasons information about such operations would normally be distributed on a 'need to know' basis. If Jackson is likely to know little or nothing about the joint operation, part of the response to the accusations made against Jackson could be to incorporate ways of insulating him from any sensitive information. If need be, this could be justified as a general tightening of security with the imminence of the interdiction. If Jackson does know or could have found out about operational details then any corrupt association with Elsey becomes far more serious. However, opportunities as well as dangers beckon. Although it becomes a high-risk enterprise, Jackson could be deliberately misled about the operation, for instance he could be told that the interdiction would be made in one location at a specific time, whereas it could be made earlier, elsewhere. If Jackson is corrupt then his corruption could make the task of the interdiction easier. Ideally, this misinformation should be contrived so that criminals in possession of it would act in a distinctive manner. If Jackson was corrupt and the misinformation was passed to Elsey then the criminal behaviour would incriminate Jackson.

This is not a tactic with which police officers are unfamiliar, but obviously it is fraught with danger. One such danger would be the obligation to disclose these operational details to the defence during the course of any subsequent prosecution. Jackson may be incriminated by such a 'sting' and his position in the police might become untenable, but the evidence may not reach a level of provenance to be admissible in a criminal court. Nevertheless, it would be likely to be disclosed during cross-examination, since the defence might be tempted to raise the spectre of what in American courts is known as 'entrapment'. It could become very messy!

Protecting the Innocent

In considering the damage limitation strategy it is interesting that the one figure whose welfare is not expressly considered is that of Sutton himself—the officer at the heart of this dilemma and who is suffering it most acutely. All organisations tend to treat their whistle-blowers poorly, but if Sutton does take Neyroud's advice and reports the matter directly to the Chief, then what obligations does the Chief now owe Sutton? It would be, as Paine notes, a very big step for Sutton to take and if police organisations wish to encourage officers to act on their suspicions of corrupt behaviour, then how the Chief deals with this would be a demonstration of how wise it would be for others to follow the same or a similar path. Part of Sutton's problem is the personal loyalty he owes to his current 'boss'. Fleming and O'Neill suggest that Sutton should pre-emptively seek an alternative posting away from Jackson, but should this be a decision for Sutton to make? Perhaps it would be appropriate for Sutton to be removed, or better still promoted or given a prestigious responsibility, on the instructions of the Chief Constable/Commissioner on some pretext or another with a different post well away from Jackson and told to sever any friendship ties he might have with him. Doing something like this would remove volition from Sutton and place authority for his actions in the hands of his superiors.

Time

Finally, all of this needs to be decided and accomplished 'on the hurry up'. This has been a reflective exercise that has lasted through many months of deliberation, drafting, re-drafting, discussion, and final drafting. The actors in this scenario would not have that luxury, not least because of the imminence of the drugs interdiction operation, which may only be days away. This is also a reality of policing generally: hours of tedium, interrupted by moments of blind panic! Nevertheless, it is a constraint of which all those who contemplate and comment upon such matters should be aware.

References

Chambers, G and Millar, A, *Investigating Sexual Assault* (Edinburgh: HMSO, 1983).

Chan, J, 'Changing police culture' (1996) 36(1) *British Journal of Criminology* 109–34.

Chan, J, 'Police culture', in D Dixon, ed, *A Culture of Corruption* (Annadale, NSW: Hawkins Press, 1999), pp 98–137.

Chan, JBL, *Fair Cop: Learning the Art of Policing* (Toronto: University of Toronto Press, 2003).

IPCC, 'Final Report Concerning the Actions of Commander Jamshid Ali Dizaei and his Involvement in the Arrest of Waad Al-Baghdadi on 18 July 2008' (London: Independent Police Complaints Commission, 2010).

Morris, SW, Burden, SA, and Weekes, A, 'The Case for Change: People in the Metropolitan Police Service. The Report of the Morris Inquiry. An Independent Inquiry into Professional Standards and Employment Matters in the Metropolitan Police Service' (London: Metropolitan Police Authority, 2004).

President's Commission on Law Enforcement and Administration of Justice, *Task Force Report: 'The Police'* (Washington DC: US Government Printing Office, 1967).

Part Three

The 'Free Cup of Coffee Problem'

Scenario: The 'Free Cup of Coffee Problem'

Chief Inspector Mark Roberts' responsibility in the force area is 'community rela-tions'; a task at which he has proven very successful. In this multi-ethnic area of religious pluralism that has suffered in the past sporadic but violent and destruc-tive episodes of conflict between different communities, he has succeeded in establishing a forum which all those communities attend and at which they discuss common problems. He has also successfully mediated various incipient conflicts that were beginning to surface and brokered rapprochement before rela-tionships were soured beyond repair. His greatest success has been to promote the police as a fair, impartial, and effective service to all communities in the area. Complaints made against officers, particularly those relating to racism and ethnic discrimination, have declined considerably during his tenure of the post. It has been hard painstaking work, often involving meetings late into the evening and attendance at ceremonies and festivals hosted by one group or another. He has recently formally been notified of his promotion and it has been indicated to him that he will be posted to a position that he has long coveted as a reward for his successful occupancy of this community relations post. As an eager environmen-talist Ch Insp Roberts is keen to take command of a small unit of officers targeting illegal pollution and other environmental crimes.

Amongst Ch Insp Roberts' many contacts in various communities is 'Mr Py Ken', who belongs to an ethnic minority whose numbers in the area have been steadily increasing because of civil war in their small country in the Far East. At first, Mr Py Ken had been reluctant to reciprocate Ch Insp Roberts' overtures of friendship, since his experience of policing in his native land was that they were brutal and corrupt. It had taken considerable persistence on Ch Insp Roberts' part to break down his suspicions, but the breakthrough came when Mr Py Ken invited him to 'take tea' with him. It was altogether a different experience to the many cups of tea that someone in Ch Insp Roberts' role feels compelled to drink with prominent members of many of the communities in the area! It was quite a significant affair in which Ch Insp Roberts was seated with Mr Py Ken whilst his wife and daughter served an endless supply of thick sweet brown liquid of a kind Ch Insp Roberts had never tasted before and Mr Py Ken pressed him to eat one delicacy after another. It was worth it: following that occasion Ch Insp Roberts had been treated as an honoured guest whenever he visited Mr Py Ken's home. Gradually, Mr Py Ken had introduced him to other leading figures amongst his ethnic group who became a rich and useful source of intelligence. Ch Insp Roberts helped them with various problems being experienced by their community; began to mediate between them and various official bodies with whom they came into conflict (often around issues connected with immigration); and Ch Insp Roberts had been enlisted in counselling some of the younger members of the community who were thought by their elders to be coming off the rails. The only downside was the unstinting hospitality with which Ch Insp Roberts was greeted, especially by Mr Py Ken. Ch Insp Roberts discovered via the internet that it was incumbent upon hosts to offer their guests lavish hospitality and a grave insult by the guest not only to refuse it, but even to partake with restraint. So, it was gallons of the sweet brown liquid (that he had come to tolerate, if not to enjoy with any enthusiasm!) and mountains of the very fattening delicacies that accompanied the 'tea'.

Over the period that Ch Insp Roberts had been developing his relationship with Mr Py Ken he had grown to admire Mr Py Ken's capacity for hard work which had seen his business as a private hire car service grow until he ran several cars, all of which were driven by members of his flourishing extended family! Ch Insp Roberts was aware that he committed minor transgressions in connection with his business, but found it easy to keep quiet because Mr Py Ken was such a likeable person and he had been unstinting in helping Ch Insp Roberts and his community. For instance, it seemed to Ch Insp Roberts that his extended family allowed services to be rendered and reciprocated that perhaps should be incorporated into his business accounts for tax purposes, but he is not an accountant and frankly his own tax affairs were more than enough for him to worry about! Anyhow, Ch Insp Roberts knew that if he reported Mr Py Ken to HMRC he could not trust their investigators to keep his name out of it and if he was exposed as the source of any incriminating information he would be instantly ostracised from the community as a result—all his hard work and tea drinking would have been for nought! It also seemed to Ch Insp Roberts that practices that no doubt were commonplace in Mr Py Ken's native land might be violations of health and safety legislation in this country. Yet, Mr Py Ken's business was conducted almost entirely within his own ethnic community and Ch Insp Roberts figured that most of his customers were well aware of the conditions under which the services that Mr Py Ken offered were provided. If he didn't provide those services, it is unlikely that anyone else would and certainly not at a price that members of this community could afford. On balance, Ch Insp Roberts thought it was better not to inquire too closely.

One feature of the community of which Mr Py Ken is a prominent member is their hypochondria; the merest sniffle elicits pills and potions galore! Ch Insp Roberts felt sufficiently secure in his relationship with Mr Py Ken to tease him gently on the matter and Mr Py Ken reciprocated by seeing the funny side. This prompted Mr Py Ken to show Ch Insp Roberts his rich collection of traditional remedies. He is particularly proud of an aphrodisiac derived from the testicles of an exceedingly rare species of sloth that lives only in Mr Py Ken's native land. It is immediately apparent to Ch Insp Roberts that the importation of this and other potions in Mr Py Ken's medicine cupboard violates the Convention on International Trade in Endangered Species of Wild Flora and Fauna. The more Mr Py Ken talked, the more apparent it became that he has become the sole supplier of such medicines to his community and that he is importing all these commodities illegally. Rare species are being sacrificed for the sake of superstition.

What should Ch Insp Roberts do? What options are available to him? Which of them deserve serious consideration? On what grounds are some included and others excluded from such consideration?

What considerations should he bear in mind when deliberating on future courses of action? What are the likely possible outcomes, not only as an immediate response to any enforcement action taken against Mr Py Ken, but also in the longer term? Is there anything that Ch Insp Roberts can do mitigate the worst consequences and encourage the most positive outcome?

Is there anything that could have been done that would have avoided the situation in which Ch Insp Roberts now finds himself?

8

Addressing the Scenario
Ethical Policing Practice in Community Policing

Sarah Stewart

Community Policing

Community Oriented Policing is an operating strategy used by many police forces the world over. In this model the problems of the community are the highest priority and the police are only as effective as the community allows. There is also a greater level of accountability to the community, not just to the police organisation and government. The community provides legitimacy and support for any actions taken by police and the nature of *public value* is at the core of all decision making. In order to be successful within this environment, members of the community must have 'trust and confidence' in *their* police force. So essential is this that most police organisations have trust and confidence as one of the key goals in their respective Strategic Plans. Trust and confidence is gained through strong relationships that are formed within a framework of transparency and ethical practice that is expected by, and of, the policing organisation in using the authority and powers it has been given. Lack of transparency and poor ethical practice can lead to corruption or a perception of corruption by an individual or sections within the organisation. It is possible that community policing itself brings with it certain 'corruption proneness'—the possibility that corrupt practices may be facilitated and will flourish unless particular vigilance is exercised (Lusher, 1981).

The potential for corruption either actual or perceived is evident in the scenario at hand.

The Problem

The problem emerges perversely out of a foundation of positive community inter-action, strong relationships, and interventions that have been initiated by Chief Inspector Roberts. His current role is in community relations in a multi-ethnic community of religious pluralism that has suffered episodes of conflict between different communities. He has promoted the police as being fair, impartial, and an effective service to all communities and has established a forum for communities to attend and discuss common problems. Roberts has also been successful in mediating emerging conflicts. In order to do this he has attended numerous ceremonies, festivals, and meetings, with various community groups, often until late in the evening. Roberts has been recognised for his success in this post by being offered a promotion which will see him move to a position commanding a team targeting illegal pollution and other environmental crimes.

The problem arises out of his relationship with Mr Py Ken who belongs to an ethnic minority whose numbers have been increasing because of a civil war in their small country in the Far East. Mr Py Ken was initially resistant to the Chief Inspector's attempts to build a relationship. This is likely to be due to his experience of policing in his home land which was brutal and corrupt. How-ever Mr Py Ken eventually invited the Chief Inspector to 'take tea' with him which is a ceremonial activity with the Chief Inspector being treated as an honoured guest. In Mr Py Ken's home country it was incumbent on the host to offer guests lavish hospitality and a grave insult for the guest to refuse this hospitality or even to partake with restraint. Gradually Mr Py Ken introduced the Chief Inspector to other prominent members of the community who became a rich source of intelligence. Roberts was then able to assist with various problems members of the community were experiencing and mediate between them and the various official bodies they came in contact with (often around issues connected with immigration). He was also enlisted in counselling younger members of the community who the elders felt were 'coming off the rails'.

There are a number of ethical dilemmas for Ch Insp Roberts: first, Mr Py Ken's taxi business has flourished. All of his vehicles are being driven by members of his extended family. Ch Insp Roberts was aware of the minor transgressions in con-nection with this business such as possible breaches of the tax law. Roberts 'knows' that if he reports this to HM Revenue and Customs he cannot trust their investigators to keep his name out of it and therefore he will be ostracised from the community as a result. It is unclear how he 'knows' this. Are his concerns based on previous experiences or from an assumption? I will return to this later. Secondly, Roberts has also noticed a number of violations of the health and safety legislation. Mr Py Ken's business is conducted within his own ethnic community and most customers would be aware of conditions in which those services were provided as they were likely to be commonplace in their native land. It is also unlikely that anyone else would provide those services at a price the community could afford. Roberts decided that it was best on balance not to inquire too closely. As I will discuss later, this forms part of the decision making environment for Roberts. Part of this is to look at the wider picture of what he is trying to achieve in a community policing context. But also it is to look at how his actions or lack thereof will be perceived. I will discuss whether it is acceptable in a community policing context to tolerate or 'turn a blind eye' to minor transgressions, if it will in turn assist in meeting a more strategic goal.

Mr Py Ken is the sole supplier of traditional medicines and remedies to the community. To do this he is illegally importing potions and pills made from the products of rare species. This is in violation of the Convention on International Trade in Endangered Species of Wild Flora and Fauna. As stated Roberts is about to take up a promotion in a role that targets environmental crime. This issue is therefore personally and professionally fundamental and his decision and approach in dealing with these violations will have an effect on his future career.

What Should Ch Insp Roberts Do?

Roberts' relationship with this community hinges on the trust he has built up with Mr Py Ken. This has opened doors to the rest of the community and led to his being in a position where he has successfully resolved disputes and conflicts. This relationship is also allowing him to focus on crime prevention by putting in place measures that could reduce more serious offending and prevent a breakdown in the police relationship with this group. He has the option of doing what he is now, effectively nothing. By turning a blind eye to the offending, Roberts is able to continue the good work he is doing and continue to strengthen his relationships with this community. As his promotion is based on his effectiveness in the community, to damage this now may affect his ability to occupy his new position effectively. But do the risks of doing nothing outweigh the risks of reporting the breaches and illegal activity?

Police officers have discretion and regularly use this in order to weigh up appropriate legal charges based on the cost or benefit of these to the individual or community. This discretion has to be based on a number of factors: what are the department guidelines; what are the risks to the individual and the organisation; and what is the risk of further offending or current offending going unchecked?

Herein lies the crux of the problem. Roberts has a higher level strategic aim which is to assist the minority ethnic groups to be a part of the wider community so that they have a place in the society they have chosen to live within, to quell violence and disorder, and to work with young people at risk. However if in order to do this he has to dismiss the very principles of community policing, those of transparency and ethical practice, this could then damage any trust and confidence other groups may have had in him and the police organisation as a whole. Does the fact that Mr Py Ken is so influential mean that it is acceptable to treat him differently from other community members? What must be considered is that if Mr Py Ken and his community become alienated then does this foster the conditions in which crime, inter-communal violent disorder, or even 'home grown terrorism' is created or encouraged, all of which pose a threat to the wider public. Even if the most dire consequences did not come to pass, the fact that a police officer failed to take action might adversely affect the reputation of the police in the area and beyond, if it became known. In the face of these and other eventualities, would this course of action still be worthwhile?

Roberts' second option is to report the offending to the appropriate agencies either covertly or overtly. If he reports the offending overtly this would have the benefit of showing other communities (who may already be aware of Mr Py Ken's offending, and Roberts' relationship with him) that the police are transparent; regardless of relationships, offending of any type will not be tolerated. It is also likely to have the effect of ending the relationship with Mr Py Ken and his community. He could report the matters covertly which may have the opposite effect, with the wider community continuing to believe he is engaging in an unethical and potentially corrupt relationship. However if his name is not associated with any action taken by other agencies against Mr Py Ken, Roberts may still retain this relationship and also his interactions with the community as a whole.

Roberts' final option is to discuss the breaches with Mr Py Ken, to outline Mr Py Ken's options to both rectify the situation and ensure he is not breaking the laws of the country he is now living in and Roberts can also explain why in this country none of these breaches is acceptable. The result for Roberts will depend on what Mr Py Ken does and whether he accedes and changes his practices or whether he disagrees with Roberts. If he accepts that the breaches have occurred and changes his practice this would be a successful result. However Mr Py Ken could also see this as Roberts giving him a warning which would allow him time to get rid of evidence and therefore damage any future prosecution. It may be seen as Roberts providing a favour, which may have to be repaid and the cycle of potential corruption begins.

What Considerations Should Roberts Bear in Mind when Deliberating on Future Courses of Action?

The dilemma Roberts is faced with is the value of the relationship with one member and one community versus the relationships with other groups within his policing area. The danger here is that each community may feel that other communities are receiving a 'better deal' than the police are providing for itself. If they came to know, or suspect, that Ch Insp Roberts was tolerating Mr Py Ken's wrongdoing, then this would fuel suspicion and damage police–community relations amongst surrounding communities in the wider area. An essential factor in building strong community relationships is equity. Does each community group or member feel as though they are getting an equal service from the police? If not it can create division and a break down in the relationship. Transparency is also important, because inter-communal hostility breeds mutual suspicion. If it became known, or suspected, that Roberts was 'turning a blind eye' to criminal practices, he is likely to be seen as being unethical and corrupt, therefore denying him an effective role in working with other communities in this area.

Community policing is not just about individual relationships. It is about how those relationships are seen by members of the community and how they function to either support, enhance, or detract from possible relationships with other minority communities. It is essential that Roberts considers how his actions are viewed by others. This is particularly true if those communities are distrustful of and hostile towards Mr Py Ken's community.

On the other hand what is the risk of damaging the relationship with Mr Py Ken? At one end of the scale the risk could be extreme. Community policing has a hand to play in counter terrorism. 'Home grown terrorism' (which was and remains the most common form of radical political violence) occurs when alienated young people become radicalised through either associations with other radicalised individuals or in recent years through interactions with content on the internet. We know that home grown terrorism is a significant risk and that one way to help prevent this is by identifying and working with disaffected young people in minority communities who are at risk of becoming involved in crime and/or falling under the influence of radical ideologues. Community and ethnic liaison officers are often best placed to do this and therefore can have a significant role in preventing home grown terrorism. The counselling that Roberts has been doing with the youth in this community is likely to have played a part in this and therefore the risk of damaging the relationship with Mr Py Ken and consequently his access to and the trust of the community's youth could be catastrophic.

Roberts received his promotion based on the relationships formed within the community. However his new role is in an area where potentially he could be working against the illegal importation of endangered animals and therefore if his ethics are compromised in any way his new role is also in jeopardy. So too, is his own self-esteem: this is no longer a matter of mere 'law enforcement', but touches Roberts personally.

Ethical Codes

What is his organisation's code of conduct or code of ethics? What are its organisational values? These are usually clearly stated and are aspirational, outlining what all officers should aspire to be and how they should behave. Do these offer any guidelines to Roberts for the actions he should take? Do his actions thus far stand up to the Code of Conduct? Roberts must operate within the norms of the policing organisation's culture and if his practices sit outside this then it is likely that he is breaching the ethical code set by his organisation.

The New Zealand Police, for instance, have documented a set of core values: Integrity, Professionalism, Respect and finally (a value which is specific to our indigenous group)—commitment to Maori and the Treaty. Each of these has a listed set of desirable and undesirable behaviours. Officers are expected to display these desirable behaviours in their everyday activities and any breaches could result in performance management interventions or disciplinary procedures. All New Zealand Police are expected to apply a 'SELF' test to all ethical decisions. The test has four questions that officers are expected to ask themselves in considering any decision:

Would your decision withstand *Scrutiny*?
Will your decision *Ensure compliance*?
Is your decision *Lawful*?
Is your decision *Fair*?

These questions would be useful for Roberts to use responding to this challenging ethical dilemma. I will come back to them at the end of this essay.

The core values and the 'SELF' test are introduced and discussed at recruit training and also feature within the training calendar where they are reinforced with all staff. The 'SELF' test is also displayed in a poster format throughout police stations. Therefore all staff are conversant with and aware of the New Zealand Police values, our ethical code, and how we are expected to challenge any dilemmas. In essence by having an ethical police service we are trying to avoid corruption and it is therefore appropriate to consider what the definition of corruption is.

Codes of practice are not restricted to parochial standards in particular police forces in different countries, but are also imposed by international agreements and treaties. For instance, Article 2 of Interpol's Global Standards to Combat Corruption in Police Forces/Services defines Police Corruption as:

> The solicitation or acceptance (directly or indirectly) by police personnel of any money, article of value, gift, favour, promise, reward or advantage, whether for himself/herself or for any person, group or entity, in return for any act or omission (failure to act) already done or omitted to be done or omitted in the future in or in connection with performance of any function of or connected to police work. (Interpol Group of Experts on Corruption, 2002)

Roberts must consider his options in light of this not only objectively but also subjectively. What would the members of other communities think of his actions or inactions? How would his organisation perceive this?

It must be remembered that ethical breaches can arise from acts of both commission and omission. Acts of commission are those which usually greet us in the headlines, allegations of bribery, abuse of power, and assault. These are 'visible' breaches and often part of a criminal and internal investigation. Acts of omission are more difficult to 'see' and are those which are the most difficult to resolve and also to prevent. This is why a subjective/objective test, such as the 'SELF' test described earlier, should be taught to all police to help them in making decisions when faced with these ethical challenges.

What Difficulties and Obstacles Lie in Ch Insp Roberts' Path?

There are at least three prime difficulties that now confront Chief Inspector Roberts. First, if he decides to do nothing there is the potential for Mr Py Ken and his community to believe that Roberts accepts the breaches of law and therefore this acceptance could mean support for their actions and behaviour. This could lead to further infractions and then: where does it stop? At what point is Roberts at risk of being exposed by the community itself. He is putting himself in a position where his 'blind eye' approach puts him at risk of being threatened to be 'outed' by the community unless he turns a blind eye to more serious offending.

Secondly there is also a risk to his successor: for if the successor's practice and approach is radically different from Roberts, then this could prove disastrous to community relations. Maintaining reasonable consistency in the actions of police officers is why police organisations and the individual officers must abide by a code of ethics and there must be robust systems in place to ensure that this situation does not occur.

Thirdly, by overtly reporting Mr Py Ken's offending to other enforcement agencies Roberts could succeed in driving Mr Py Ken's community underground and if they no longer trust police then it may be impossible to re-establish any connection with them. This could provide the opportunity for greater offending and even contribute to home grown terrorism and community based violence.

Police are continually faced with having to balance action with risk and choices with consequences. This is crucial when the risks are significant or catastrophic. The possibility that the risk may justify the action is one that is never more true than when dealing with, investigating, or being involved in activities of counter terrorism as the risks and consequences of failure are so high.

Roberts believes that he cannot report the matters to the other organisations (with the expectation that his name will be held in confidence and that he will not be exposed as the informant). How does he know this? Is this based on his knowledge, his own experience, or is it a misinformed belief? There are mechanisms in every government department for confidential information to be supplied and shared. In the New Zealand Police, memorandums of understanding are entered into with different organisations for just this purpose and there are interagency taskforces and groups such as the British SOCA (Serious Organised Crime Agency) that are set up specifically to engender cross-agency cooperation and operations. However at the lower end of the offending scale, it is probable that this level of cooperation, and the interaction and levels of security required, are likely to be taken less seriously. Therefore perhaps Roberts' concerns are valid and this may not be an option for him.

There are significant risks in discussing the breaches with Mr Py Ken. Firstly Mr Py Ken might interpret the discussion with Roberts as a warning and rather than stopping the offending and righting the breaches, use that warning to destroy incriminating evidence and thereby frustrate any future prosecution. In addition, it could confirm for Mr Py Ken that Roberts has more than turned a blind eye, he has accepted the favours of the relationship and omitted to report the matters thereby opening the door for greater levels of corruption. However, this would be to assume that Mr Py Ken knows that what he is doing is illegal in his new country of abode, and that Roberts is abstaining from informing other agencies.

Thirdly, Roberts must also consider what the wider community's reaction is to his response. Already many will be aware of Roberts' relationship. On its own it is no secret and on the face of it is a positive situation, no different from the relationships with other community leaders. However if any others become aware of Mr Py Ken's breaches of various laws, the implications of this are potentially significant. They could interpret Roberts' inaction as favouritism or otherwise unethical and possibly corrupt—has Roberts been bought off by some inducement? All of the hard work carried out by Roberts could be negated and lead to a rise in complaints against police and even a return to inter-communal violence. This is particularly important when dealing with different community groups (as part of an individual's community policing role) who are mutually suspicious or hostile towards each other. The groups may have historic conflicts that can be generations old and therefore rooted in strongly held beliefs that friends of the opposing group are no friends of their own community. This is an extremely difficult situation for an officer to deal with and will only be exacerbated by any perceived corrupt or unethical practices.

How Should Ch Insp Roberts Deal with these Difficulties?

The difficulties outlined can be resolved depending on which of the three options he selects. I would suggest that the solution is twofold. First to discuss the breaches of these various regulations with the relevant government departments and as the breaches are at the lower end of offending, gain an undertaking with them to work with Mr Py Ken to resolve the offending and rectify his practices. This approach is on the understanding the Mr Py Ken may not be aware of the fact that he has breached the laws in this country. This is supported by the fact that he is willing to tell and show these activities to a police officer who is by all accounts seen as an honest member. Roberts can then continue further work with Mr Py Ken to ensure he understands the law and brings his practices into line with this. Roberts has already helped members of the community in their dealings with official bodies, especially in connection with immigration matters. This approach would represent no more than an extension of this role.

There are a number of cultural differences and practices that will need to be worked through for each of the three breaches and it may be that this will be an ongoing process which could be facilitated through the community forum and would provide an opportunity for other members to learn from this. However if Roberts suspects that Mr Py Ken knows that his actions are breaching the law then the only ethical solution for Roberts is to report the matters to the various government departments and then, once the departments have taken action, Roberts could discuss with Mr Py Ken how he can avoid the attentions of these services in future. If the risks of ending the relationship are too great to do this overtly then confidential information supply is an option. This however does not address the transparency of Roberts' actions.

Is There Anything that Could Have Been Done that Would Have Avoided the Situation in which the Chief Inspector Now Finds Himself?

The New Zealand Police teach staff a four-step process to apply when beginning relationships that have the potential to cause ethical dilemmas or challenges:

Model behaviour

This encompasses the officer demonstrating the behaviour that the officer expects from those he or she is interacting with in relation to both communication and actions.

Define 'off limits'

By defining what is and is not acceptable in the relationship for both the officer and the participants the officer is able to set limits which should prevent situations where the officer's ethics could be called into question.

Challenge assumptions

It is important that the officer challenges his or her own assumptions as to why the community members are behaving in a certain way but also that the community have the opportunity to challenge their assumptions of the officer and the police. This will only be possible when the relationship has been built to a level of trust that allows open communication.

Discuss issues

Roberts has created a forum where this is possible; however, he does not appear to have used it effectively to discuss early on the issues he is now facing. I wonder why he did not do this? The importance of the last point is highlighted in Lord Acton's quote '...nothing is safe that does not show it can bear discussion and publicity' (Gasquet, 1906).

If Roberts had begun this relationship with clear boundaries being set (such as outlined in the process just discussed) he may not have found himself in this situation. He knew that Mr Py Ken's experience with police in his home country is that they are corrupt. Mr Py Ken's understanding of what is corrupt or unethical is derived from his experiences in his war-torn native land and therefore his expectations of police ethics are possibly different from others who do not share his background and his tolerance for corruption may be higher. He may be surprised to learn his breaches of the law may not be acceptable and also that the 'taking of tea' on multiple occasions can be seen as inappropriate. Part of beginning this relationship could have involved discussing these expectations on both sides to gain a mutual understanding of each other's position. By explaining that any breaches of any law will result in the officer taking action Roberts could have circumvented the dilemma that he now faces.

It appears that there are neither any other members of the police working with this community nor that there is a cultural or ethnic liaison officer. These positions should be established for each and every community group. By having police members who have a specific understanding of a community's culture, values, and beliefs they are able to provide an insight into how police actions will be perceived and often intervene before problems arise. This of course requires a recruiting policy that aims to recruit members who reflect the community and has benefits in raising trust and confidence. However it also brings the risk that those members may find themselves faced with an even greater clash of values as the expectations on them to accept common practices within their own community would be greater.

However I have seen examples of this work successfully when posted to the Solomon Islands. In this Melanesian culture the 'Wantok' means 'one talk' or those who speak the same language. The Wantok system places great importance on supporting, taking care of, or looking out for your family which includes the wider circles of village and community. At its best the Wantok system provides for individuals to support each other in time of need such as when one family is short of food supplies or is in need of support with employment or in carrying out daily duties. At its worst members of familial groups are expected, without question, to assist others and this can involve corrupt or illegal activity. This social contract is one that challenges Solomon Island police officers daily in their duties when dealing with members of their Wantok. During ethnic tensions many officers followed the Wantok system and took sides in the conflict which has resulted in significant mistrust in the police force. However this was not always the case and following RAMSI (Regional Assistance Mission to the Solomon Islands) corrupt officers have been investigated and removed and trust and confidence in the police has begun to be restored.

Officers who navigate this challenge successfully have a very clear understanding of, and pride in their role as a police officer. They explain that the Wantok system did not apply to officers in carrying out their duties and that the uniform meant that they followed the code of their organisation, not the cultural system, when dealing with matters relating to the law and justice. These officers operate at an extremely high level and are able to interact safely (ie without the risk of exposing themselves to potential corruption) and effectively with members from both ethnic communities despite the continued conflict between these communities.

I question whether Roberts needed to have such an in-depth relationship with Mr Py Ken in order to achieve his objectives. Was there an opportunity before this time to ensure there was appropriate professional distance so that this situation and the decisions required were not as difficult? I would recommend that the organisation have a stronger support network for officers involved in community policing who have ethical dilemmas. Such a structure should include regular debriefing of members and an oversight committee that can provide support and guidance in these roles. This is similar to how covert informant relationships are managed to ensure that objective testing is carried out so that all practice meets the ethical conduct expectations of the organisation and the communities.

Summary

Roberts has manoeuvred himself into a situation that is extremely difficult to resolve. As discussed, there are a number of measures that could have been implemented that would have prevented this. There is no rule book on how to conduct relationships within the community but officers should be guided by the code of conduct or ethics of their home organisation. As a leader in his organisation it is crucial that Roberts should be a role model, demonstrating the highest ethical standards, as without this a corrupt culture could be seen as acceptable. However this is not always easy and each and every situation needs to be challenged with, as mentioned early in this essay, a subjective and objective test applied: Would your decision withstand *Scrutiny*? Will your decision *Ensure* compliance? Is your decision *Lawful*? Is your decision *Fair*?

> We judge ourselves by our best intentions and our most noble acts, but we are judged by others by our last worst act. (Josephson)

References

Gasquet, F, *Lord Acton and his Circle* (London: Burns and Oates, 1906).

Interpol Group of Experts on Corruption. (2002). Global Standards to combat corruption in Police forces/services. Retrieved June 2012 from <http://www.interpol.int/Crime-areas/Corruption/INTERPOL-Group-of-Experts-on-Corruption>.

Josephson, M (nd). Josephson Institute. Retrieved 12 June 2012 from <http://josephsoninstitute.org/policing/>.

Lusher, A, Report of the Commission of Inquiry into the New South Wales Police Administration (Sydney: NSW Government Printer, 1981).

9

Editor's Commentary

PAJ Waddington

The editors are particularly grateful to Sarah Stewart for so eagerly standing in and taking responsibility for tackling this scenario on the shortest of deadlines after another contributor was unable to complete the task. Perhaps the short deadline elicited a more immediate, less deliberative response. In which case, it is even more to her credit that she is able to chart a path through a tortuous ethical dilemma that MacIntyre and Penzler (1999) identified as the 'free cup of coffee problem'. In that article they remark that in community policing, officers are encouraged to engage in activities previously forbidden by formal rules of conduct. The response of an earlier generation of officers to those formal rules was to subvert them by finding locations where they might have been able to relax and enjoy a cup of tea or coffee without the danger that they would be caught by their sergeant—what were known as 'tea holes' (Cain, 1973). The punitive approach may have been ham-fisted and ultimately self-defeating, but was motivated by a genuine problem: if police officers come to develop closer *personal* relationships with some members of the public and not others, there is the danger that they will exhibit favouritism towards those with whom they enjoy that close personal relationship, which undermines the very foundations of equal justice.

In this scenario, Chief Inspector Roberts is motivated not by self-interest (to relieve the boredom of police patrol), but on the contrary by the highest values—to serve the community, reduce conflict, prevent crime and disorder. He sees in Mr Py Ken an influential figure in his community, through whom he can begin to exert influence. Cultivating this relationship has led Roberts to repeatedly calculate the costs and benefits of allowing to continue a course of behaviour that the law, if strictly applied, would forbid. The problem is that the breaches of the law have now reached a threshold that can no longer be tolerated. Sarah Stewart suggests that Roberts should never have found himself in such a position. That he should have established boundaries at the outset. But where should those boundaries be set? It is an abiding problem of police discretion that if police were fully to enforce the law, society would rapidly grind to a halt. In the past, when American cops flexed their industrial muscle, they sometimes did so through 'ticket blizzards'—handing out tickets for any and all offences committed. They were often successful in bringing cities to a shuddering halt. As with informants (to which we will return later in this volume), police are duty bound to calculate which is the greater danger—a minor regulatory transgression, or the prospect of crime and disorder.

However, Sarah Stewart rightly points to an oft-neglected aspect of discretionary tolerance shown towards minor offending. First, that the person whose minor transgressions are tolerated may interpret such tolerance not as the judicious exercise of discretion, but as a sign of weakness or even corruption. She points out that someone in Mr Py Ken's situation might inveigle an officer into tolerating illicit conduct and then spring the trap with the threat of 'outing' the officer if he dares to interfere with more serious offending. As Sarah Stewart reminds us, Mr Py Ken's view of policing is influenced, possibly quite profoundly, by his experience of corrupt policing in his native land. A well-worn strategy for dealing with corrupt officialdom is to 'get something on 'em!' and perhaps it would come easily to Mr Py Ken to 'get something on' Ch Insp Roberts.

Secondly, she asks how this might appear to others. Research in London (FitzGerald et al, 2002) showed that in this increasingly multicultural city different communities viewed each other with distrust and hostility, demanding that the police use their powers aggressively towards other communities, whilst being tolerant of offending amongst their own community. One can easily imagine how evidence of apparent favouritism towards one community (that of Mr Py Ken's hypothetical ethnicity) would feed the antagonism of surrounding communities. The danger of developing such close relationships is that they are inevitably selective: it just is not possible to enjoy equally close relationships with all communities in the highly diverse societies in which many people live.

So, the fundamental issue is how police officers should exercise discretion and do so without exposing themselves to the threat of becoming or being seen as corrupt. In discussing discretion, there is, it seems to me, a danger that a false opposition is often drawn between enforcing the law and *doing nothing*. There is another option, which is to *do something* without relying on enforcing the law. When Roberts becomes aware that Mr Py Ken (and perhaps others in this community) are committing minor transgressions, he could do something other than enforce the law that would actually win the favour of the community. Presumably, few in that community want the tax authorities or health and safety inspectors imposing penalties upon them. Roberts could take the opportunity to offer assistance to the community, by providing education and guidance to members of this community, to enable them to avoid inadvertently contravening the laws of their adopted land. This need not jeopardise his relationship with Mr Py Ken by focusing exclusively on Mr Py Ken's own offending. Roberts could present the initiative as addressing a general need. He could enlist the help of advisory services, both those provided by the state and by the voluntary sector.

This would send a two-pronged signal: first, such offending can no longer be considered genuinely inadvertent, and, secondly, it will not be tolerated in future. Now that the threshold has been crossed, Roberts could initiate such a strategy from the relative security of his established relationship with Mr Py Ken, presenting it as something to benefit the whole community. After all, the strategic goal is surely to prevent the continuation of such offending, rather than prosecute those who commit these offences.

There is another issue that I wish to consider: why is this breach of the 'Convention on Endangered Species...' the *threshold* at all? Roberts is a keen environmentalist and will shortly take command of a unit devoted to countering environmental crime. Does he draw the threshold of his tolerance at the point when his own personal values are offended? He has knowingly tolerated questionable health and safety practices in the conduct of Mr Py Ken's private hire service, and not inquired too closely into his tax affairs. Why now does Ch Insp Roberts draw the line? He is a keen environmentalist who has long coveted the command of a small unit dealing with environmental crime. Not only is his *duty* engaged, but so too is his personal morality. Is it self-evident that crime such as pollution of the environment is any more serious than breaching health and safety or tax laws? Health and safety legislation receives a poor press in Britain for promoting ludicrous restrictions on otherwise innocuous activities, but as Tombs (2007, 2010) reminds us, breaches of health and safety continue to inflict a significant toll on the lives of those afflicted by industrially acquired diseases, as well as those injured or killed in 'accidents' at work. Taxation attracts few defenders, but without raising income governments cannot provide valuable public services.

Perhaps this too draws attention to the dangers of developing too close a *personal* relationship with members of the community. For personal relationships are just that—'personal'—and nothing touches our sense of our own 'personhood' more than our personal morality. The SELF checklist is, perhaps, most valuable in acting as a restraint on excessive personal indulgence and maintaining what Sarah Stewart rightly describes as 'professional distance'.

References

Cain, M, *Society and the Policeman's Role* (London: Routledge & Kegan Paul, 1973).

FitzGerald, M, Hough, M, Joseph, I, and Qureshi, T, *Policing for London* (Cullompton, Devon: Willan, 2002).

MacIntyre, S and Prenzler, T (1999), 'The influence of gratuities and personal relationships on police use of discretion' (1999) 9(2) *Policing and Society* 181–201.

Tombs, S, '"Violence", safety crimes and criminology' (2007) 47(4) *British Journal of Criminology* 531–50.

Tombs, S, 'Corporate violence and harm', in F Brookman, M Maguire, H Pierpoint, and T Bennett (eds), *Handbook on Crime* (Cullompton: Willan, 2010), pp 884–903.

Community Negotiation

Scenario: Community Negotiation

Superintendent Jenny Wiltshire is commander of a police area that contains a significant Muslim minority. She was selected for this position because she has acquired considerable expertise in diversity-related matters, previously having been in command of a 'hate crime' unit within the force that proved very energetic and successful in bringing prosecutions against those who committed a range of such offences. She personally commanded a very lengthy and difficult case of racist murder, during which she was vilified by certain local free newspapers who alleged that she 'saw racism' where none existed. Because the investigation lasted more than two years, she repeatedly found it necessary to fight to retain the resources committed to it, battles in which she was victorious. Eventually, she was vindicated by the conviction of four young men for the murder, which they had contrived to appear to have been suicide. The judge in the case personally commended her and her team of officers and the local council held a high-profile ceremony at which she and all of her team of investigators were publicly celebrated for their pugnacity in the face of adversity. She also won the praise of police officers for her insistence that all members of the investigation team should share in the praise that was bestowed, even the dog-handler whose dog had uncovered a piece of crucial evidence.

Many Muslims in the area are devout, but there is no hint of radicalisation amongst them. Relations between the Imams and other Muslim leaders, and the police are favourable and Jenny has been working hard to address issues brought to her attention. For instance, at her instigation a march by far-right activists that was due to take place in the principal shopping area of the division was banned under the Public Order Act. Jenny has also convened an Independent Advisory Group (IAG) comprising leaders of all ethnic and religious communities in the area, which has proven particularly successful. As a result of meetings in this group, representatives of the Muslim, Hindu, Sikh, and most Christian churches have set up their own inter-faith organisation to promote common understanding.

Supt Wiltshire is not only concerned to foster good relations with ethnic and religious communities, but has been anxious also to establish good working relationships with other minority groups in the area, especially gay, lesbian, bi-sexual, and transgender (LGBT) groups. She prides herself that whilst in command of the 'hate crimes' unit, her officers were able to halt the disturbing increase in 'hate crimes' towards LGBT people. Since taking command of the division, she has been leading a problem-oriented strategy, identifying the source of these hate crimes and devising solutions in collaboration with representatives in an Independent Advisory Group (IAG) that focuses on hate crimes committed in relation to sexual orientation. A by-product of this activity has been to improve the general relationship between LGBT people and the police. She has responded to some concerns voiced at the IAG regarding custody arrangements, by designating a separate cell for the exclusive use of LGBT suspects. This has been achieved despite opposition from officers who believe that it has added significantly to the congestion experienced in the cells during busy periods. Officers working in the custody suite have also been required to attend an LGBT awareness training programme to alert them to the sensitivities of those with diverse sexualities, especially regarding search procedures. Only those officers who have attended this course are allowed to search those claiming LGBT status. This too has provoked some opposition from certain members of the lower ranks, but Supt Wiltshire believes that this opposition is a small price to pay for improved relationships with this section of the local population.

A prominent member of the LBGT community who has been a positive figure on the Hate Crime IAG is Danny Perkins. He plans to open an explicitly gay bar that will occupy currently vacant premises on the High Street. His proposed name for the bar is 'Queers!' and the outside colour scheme will be shocking pink designed to stand out amongst the increasingly drab collection of charity shops in that part of the High Street. Entertainment at the bar will take the form of striptease and other sex acts employing LGBT performers. The 'business case' that the proprietor has openly discussed at the Hate Crime IAG envisages that the bar will attract LGBT people, not only in the immediate area, but from much wider afield. This causes Supt Wiltshire some concerns, because she fears that it will also become a magnet for homophobes and pose a potential for increased 'hate crime' in the area. She has discussed this with senior colleagues at the Policy Group and, whilst it is regarded as a manageable problem, it will require the deployment of additional resources from neighbouring areas. This has not been welcomed by those in command of the neighbouring areas who will be required to supply additional officers at times of high demand to police her area and it has been suggested by some that she is not fully in control of her division. In addition, Supt Wiltshire has begun planning a major public order operation to handle the celebrations that are intended by the LGBT community to accompany the opening of 'Queers!' This will amount to a local 'Gay Pride!' event to which LGBT people from afar will be invited. LGBT police officers have also made it known that they would wish to parade in uniform at this event, which Supt Wiltshire and the Chief Constable both welcome as a public declaration that the police is an LGBT-friendly employer, even if it does mean that the number of officers available for policing duties on the day will be depleted.

Plans for opening 'Queers!' have been leaked to members of the inter-faith group and this has provoked outrage particularly amongst fundamentalist Christian churches and Muslim groups, not least because of the close physical proximity of the bar to their respective places of worship. They complain that members of their communities will be deterred from using the High Street, which is particularly problematic because it is the terminus for many of the local bus routes. For their adherents, the church leaders and Imams complain, it will necessitate lengthy detours to avoid passing the premises on their way to and from worship. The area in the vicinity of the nearby mosque already has problems connected with the use of vehicles to attend Friday prayers and this looks likely to be exacerbated if, in order to avoid passing 'Queers!', worshippers travel by car rather than using buses or walking.

Contact with Muslim leaders indicates that there is a strong groundswell of outrage in the community since the existence of the bar offends not only Muslim attitudes to alcohol, but also their abhorrence towards homosexuality. They say that more radical elements within the Muslim community have seized upon the bar as a cause célèbre to mobilise oppositional sentiment and plan to march in protest in a couple of weeks.

More recently opposition to the bar has begun to be voiced in the local newspaper and LGBT representatives have suggested to police that the upsurge in hate crime attacks may have been sparked by the agitation and that young Muslim men are committing at least some of the offences. There has been a recent increase in 'hate crimes' reported, but this may be due to the sudden increase in publicity regarding the dispute surrounding 'Queers!' In any case, levels of 'hate crime' in the area are thankfully now so low that a few attacks immediately stand out as a 'spike', but Supt Wiltshire is not complacent. Community intelligence indicates that the upsurge in hate crime may have more to do with far-right activism sparked by the controversy surrounding the banning of their march.

What should Supt Wiltshire do? What options are available to her? Which of them should she include and exclude from further consideration? On what grounds would inclusion or exclusion be made? Which option do you think Supt Wiltshire should favour and why?

What difficulties and obstacles lie in Supt Wiltshire's path? Does the situation offer any positive opportunities? What do you imagine will be the consequences of pursuing any of the options selected for serious consideration? How should these consequences be dealt with?

Is there anything that could have been done that would have avoided the situation in which Supt Wiltshire now finds herself?

Addressing the Scenario

Mutual Respect, Complexity, and Community Dialogue: Charting a New Path

Vern Neufeld Redekop

Superintendent Jenny Wiltshire has a complex situation on her hands in which an array of parties in a web of relational systems could potentially see themselves getting into a spiral of escalating conflict. Beneath the surface are latent resentments on the part of the far-right community and many in the police rank and file. Supt Wiltshire has some significant social capital, which she must use wisely. I will identify some of the complex dynamics, resentments, and social capital before introducing some theoretical and ethical concepts along with a process that could help sort out the issues. The analysis and conceptual framework will then be used to suggest some courses of action that could be taken.

A Complex Web of Conflicted Relational Systems

A relational system is defined as something that brings individuals or groups into contact with one another such that the actions of each have an impact on the others (Redekop, 2002). Any given relational system may be friendly or antagonistic in orientation. In this case, the significant relational systems involve the following groups: the police service under the command of Supt Wiltshire, the other police services in the area, the LGBT community, the Muslim community, the far-right activists, the Christian fundamentalists, and the members of other faith communities. Two composite groups are the Hate Crime Independent Advisory Group (IAG) and the spin-off Inter-Faith Council (IFC). Key individuals who are part of relational systems with these groups are Supt Wiltshire and Danny Perkins, the prominent member of the LGBT community who wishes to establish 'Queers!'

There are different degrees of conflict associated with some of the relational systems. The most intense social conflicts involve Danny and the LGBT community on the one hand, and some of the Muslims, fundamentalist Christians, and the far-right activists. Less intense are conflicts between Supt Wiltshire, on one hand, and the far-right activists, members under her command, and neighbouring police, respectively. The more intense conflicts are deep-rooted and intractable. Given the strong feelings, it would seem that the Muslims, fundamentalist Christians, and activists all hate the LGBT for transgressing some deeply held values. The less intense conflicts are at the level of resentments over actions that were found to be bothersome or potentially could be so.

On the positive side, a number of relational systems are marked by conviviality and mutual trust, resulting in considerable social capital. Supt Jenny Wiltshire has positive relationships with the IAG and all of the religious minority groups, except for the fundamentalist Christians; even in that case negativity could only be associated with those fundamentalists who were also part of the far-right activist group.

Conceptual Framework

I will start by introducing concepts that can help identify the dynamics of deep-rooted conflict, then propose a Mutual Respect paradigm for public order policing. The characteristics of complex adaptive systems and an ethical vision are concepts that can help guide the formulation of action plans. Finally the community dialogue process will be presented as a tool that Supt Wiltshire and various groups could use to address the conflict challenges.

Mimetic structures of violence and of blessing

Mimetic structures are patterns of orientation and behaviour that continue through time within relational systems (Redekop, 2002). They are mimetic in that parties *imitate* one another through reciprocal actions and attitudes (Girard, 1976). Within mimetic structures of blessing, parties treat each other in ways that are mutually empowering and life-enhancing. On the other hand, mimetic structures of violence are marked by mutual harm and actions that diminish the sense of worth and capacity of the parties involved. Deep-rooted conflicts have a tendency to intensify mimetic structures of violence whereas reconciliation is a process of transformation out of mimetic structures of violence and into mimetic structures of blessing (Redekop, 2002). Based on the analysis discussed, we can say that Supt Wiltshire has cultivated mimetic structures of blessing in relational systems involving inter-faith groups and between the police and the LGBT community. Mimetic structures of violence are emerging in the relational systems involving the LGBT community and sub-groups of Muslims, fundamentalist Christians, and right-wing activists.

One aspect of mimetic structures of violence is scapegoating. This is a process by which frustrated people are united through a focus on a common enemy upon whom they project their frustrations and negative feelings (Girard, 1977, 1987, 1989). Scapegoats tend to be different, illegitimate, powerful enough to cause the frustrations, yet vulnerable (Redekop, 2002). In this case, Danny and the LGBT community are potential scapegoats, uniting Muslims and fundamentalist Christians and perhaps right-wing activists against them. Less obvious is the potential for Supt Wiltshire to become a scapegoat within the police service if she does not succeed in managing the looming crisis over 'Queers!' If members of the regional police service and her own disgruntled police start grumbling to one another, she could face some serious problems. If they become sufficiently frustrated, they could unite against her.

Mutual respect approach

In the early 1800s, Peel's principles revolutionised policing as they stressed police membership in and respect for communities. This translated into public order policing marked by a minimum use of force. Since the 1960s, paramilitary police organisation coupled with the use of less than lethal weapons has meant an emphasis on crowd control. Coming out of this has been a crowd management approach in which police have used discursive means to make certain that crowd activities have been within the boundaries of acceptable (to the police) behaviour (Waddington, 1998). Drawing on participatory action research with protesters and police, a Mutual Respect Approach was developed during the first decade of this millennium. Key elements of the Mutual Respect Approach are the following:

- Crowds welcomed as essential component of civil society and generator of creative options for society.
- Crowds, security, and possibly targets collaborate on strategy for the event.
- Information is shared openly all around; identities and roles are transparent.
- Security is derived from trusting relationships based on mutual dignity and respect.
- Uses open processes to imagine new and mutually beneficial ways of dealing with conflicts.
- Tries to understand reasons for extreme emotions and passions.
- Periodic facilitated workshops to reflect on the nature and role of organised protest.
- Targets see crowds as a sign that some things need to change; as a source of key information about the world.
  (excerpts from a chart from *Beyond Control*, Redekop and Paré, 2010: 149–50)

While the Mutual Respect Approach was developed first and foremost to deal with the protest crowd–police relational system, in this case it applies primarily to Danny and the LGBT community and the Muslim–Christian–Far Right relational system with the police in a middle role. From a policing perspective, this is a case of community policing practice being engaged in problem-solving.

Complex adaptive systems

Complexity scientists have identified a number of characteristics of complex adaptive systems. As complexity increases, there is a tendency for the system to move in the direction of chaos. At the edge of chaos, when the time is right, there may be a bifurcation point at which one relatively small change can produce cascading results such that a new order is created. This new order may involve the emergence of something that is qualitatively different to what went before (Kauffman, 2008). This qualitatively new entity or condition is not reducible to what existed before; however, after it emerges the links become clear. The optimum conditions for something new to emerge are a function of the number of elements within the system and the variety of ways they can be combined. Too much of either and there is chaos; too few and there is rigidity.

In this case, there are a number of distinct players and a context in which various groups can come together. Something creatively new could emerge or the situation could deteriorate into reciprocated and escalating violence. There is evidence that some strikingly new alliances and hence relationships are possible, particularly between Muslims and conservative Christians.

Ethical vision

An ethical vision is a normative statement regarding a desired future horizon of possibilities (Ricoeur, 1984, 1992). It provides overall direction to actions and decisions. From an ethical vision can be derived a mission statement or broad goals which can be translated into strategies and eventually into tactics.

In this case an ethical vision statement could be the following:

> The actions of the police in general and Supt Wiltshire in particular should not make matters worse; rather they should contribute to mutual understanding among the parties and a plan of action that will enhance the well-being of all parties.

What this suggests is that the processes developed to deal with the potential crisis should be inclusive and future oriented. It also suggests that care be exercised to do no harm; in other words, any intervention on the part of the police needs to be carefully balanced so as to not make matters worse. Something small that might sort itself out could be exaggerated through a heavy-handed response. On the other hand, a crisis might be averted with a relatively small, discrete intervention. From this ethical vision can emerge strategies, action plans, and tactics that will contribute to this becoming a reality.

Community dialogue process

The Canadian Institute for Conflict Resolution developed community dialogue processes in the 1990s. Typically, eighty to 120 people would be gathered from diverse sub-groups within a community. After some opening remarks to situate the dialogue, they would be randomly divided into groups of sixteen such that each small group would be diverse. A facilitator would work with each group in a process of information gathering that involved groups of four with periodic rotations. This information would be flip-charted and posted during a break so everyone could read each other's ideas. After the break, each group of sixteen would be divided in half to address an open-ended question through brainstorming with a facilitator. The question generally was 'How can we develop a conflict-resolving community?' Near the end of the time, they would use a synthesis process to identify the most important ideas they had generated. Each group would then share their ideas with the entire group. These dialogues resulted in some significant new initiatives including a Cops and Kids program whereby all Ottawa Police recruits received two days of conflict resolution training with youth.

This community dialogue process has been adapted for community transformation in contexts of severe conflict, either post-violent conflict (Bosnia and Herzegovina) or a post-colonial (aboriginal people) situation. The adapted version lasts for three days and uses a framework to guide the questioning. Participants are divided into small groups for facilitated dialogues after which they report to the larger groups.

In this case, the Mutual Respect Approach Seminar would last three days and the community dialogues half a day.

Potential Actions

Given the multiple potentials for scapegoating and escalating conflict, Supt Wiltshire has to work carefully and delicately. In the past, her firmness of purpose and tenacity have served her well as she has worked for the benefit of a variety of minority groups. Now the very minority groups she has supported are at odds with one another. Her first action is to find a trusted friend or coach who will walk the journey with her and not hold back when it comes to critical feedback. Jenny (note that since I am now thinking about her as a person rather than simply as someone in a position, I will use her first name) must make it clear to her mentor that she needs to develop her shadow side—working sensitively and delicately—and she needs help in doing that. Even as a person she must make decisions from within her role as a Super, but her style might have to become more nuanced.

Action Plan 1: police relationships

Jenny will start with a commitment to applying the Mutual Respect Approach to this situation. To do this, there will need to be a three-day seminar with all of the stakeholder groups represented.[1] As a first step, she will talk with the Chair of the Police Services Board (or whatever might be the civilian oversight body to the police) about securing some resources for community–police seminars. She would then convene a meeting of community leaders with whom she has worked through the years to get their support. She would approach a neutral body— either a university or a community mediation organisation—about hosting and leading the Mutual Respect seminars. As part of the seminars, which would include representatives of all the key groups in the relational systems described, along with local political leaders and media representatives, small representative groups would be presented with a potential scenario and be asked to develop action plans to deal with the situation. Some surprising new possibilities could open up.[2]

In preparation for the Mutual Respect seminar, Jenny would convene a meeting with the public order unit of the police. After emphasising how she needed the group, how they were a team, and how each was valued, she would have a facilitator lead an open brainstorming session on what are the strengths of the unit and what concerns they might have. She would then provide an analysis of the community situation along with her vision of a tolerant community and strategy for how to achieve it. She would then ask for suggestions from the unit. She would also ask who else within the police service would need a similar briefing. She would follow up with similar briefings with other groups within her own police service. Similarly, she would convene a meeting of her counterparts from the police services of the surrounding communities. She would brief them on the situation and ask them to each designate a participant for the Mutual Respect seminar.

At the end of the Mutual Respect Approach seminar, participants would agree on which of their suggestions could be broadly shared. These would be circulated within the various police services and within the different community groups. As an added feature, they could have a public meeting, hosted by a commonly respected local political figure, such as the Mayor of the town or city, at which they would present the potential scenarios and make their recommendations.

Action Plan 2: Develop a hate protest policy

Jenny needs to appreciate that the far-right activist group, whose protest she shut down, might have some residual resentments. They might not have understood what aspects of their planned protest were objectionable and they might even

---

[1] For a description of what would happen during the three days and how it might be organised see Redekop and Paré (2010: 233–6).

[2] During one of the original seminars with protesters and police, sub-groups worked on a scenario in which a large crowd was to be dealt with in a manner that would not allow for the use of less-than-lethal weapons. One of the groups suggested that the police host a reception for protesters the night before and serve hors d'oeuvres on their shields—a surprising suggestion for everyone.

think that Supt Wiltshire has a dual standard such that she uses her position to look out for her friends.

It is important that there be a clear policy around protest with a clear definition of what it means to cross the line into expressions of or incitements to hate.

Jenny starts to realise that the expression of dissent is important even if there is disagreement about the dissenting message. She realises that unless there is criminal activity or hate speech involved it is important for police to facilitate dissenting protest. It may become apparent that she has not had clear objective criteria for identifying what is hate speech and hence grounds to stop a protest. She should arrange to meet with the head of the far-right protesters and clarify the grounds for her action. If it turns out that there was a miscommunication about intentions and that the planned protest would not have incited hatred, she could apologise for prematurely judging the former protest and shutting it down. If there were reasonable grounds for shutting it down, but with some ambiguity, she should ask if the leaders of the group would be willing to join a sub-committee of the IAG to draft a set of defining criteria that would identify a potential protest as constituting a hate action and hence one that the police would shut down at the outset. This set of criteria and subsequent policy would make it clear to everyone what the rules would be for everyone. It would also provide the grounds for limiting particularly contentious protest in the ensuing months.

Action Plan 3: Work with the owner of 'Queers!'

Jenny will approach the developer of 'Queers!' with whom she has a positive relationship in the course of which Jenny has accumulated social capital. She will explain to him that it is in everyone's interest, including his, to be able to move ahead without an escalation of conflict. She will point out the following:

1. There are several aspects of the proposed 'Queers!' that various factions in the community find objectionable: the colour scheme, the sexual minority orientation, the serving of alcohol, and the exhibition of nudity.
2. If some of these items could be put on hold, the degree of outrage would be reduced.
3. Stereotypic thought can result in de-humanisation, something of which the LGBT community has been a victim. The challenge is to re-humanise this community in the eyes of the particular groups that are alarmed.

In the light of all this, perhaps he could agree to do the interior renovations first, before re-doing the outside.

He could then invite the IAG, of which he is a member, to have a meeting in the new facility before stocking the bar. Some upstanding members of the LGBT community, including gay police officers, could be invited to the meeting. The purpose of the meeting would be to discuss how all groups within the wider community could collaborate to make the community work for everyone. By meeting inside the facility, it would lose some of its nefarious mystique.

One suggestion they could consider would be to have a wider half-day Community Dialogue to which each representative on the IAG would invite five to ten members of their own community. It would be desirable to have this Community Dialogue in the mosque. The question could be: 'How can communities with strongly held and divergent values co-exist with relative harmony?' Members of the police service would also be invited to attend to contribute their ideas. The ideas from the Community Dialogue could well point the way to further constructive actions by the various parties. Members of the LGBT community would start to see the Muslims in their own environment and become attentive to some of their concerns.

It could also be possible to consider a range of solutions, such as

- finding a different location for 'Queers!'—this could help with the parking situation and would avoid people from different faith communities having to walk by it;
- deciding on a plan to spruce up the entire street by painting all of the buildings—in this way the front of 'Queers!' could still be distinctive but not stick out as a building out of place;
- making certain that there were thick enough curtains that those walking by the building would not see what was going on;
- relocating bus stops so buses would go directly to the mosque, particularly on Friday;
- encouraging some other entrepreneur to buy the building beside 'Queers!' and start a restaurant called Straights! to symbolically show how LGBT members and straight members of society could live side by side in harmony;
- initiating an IAG series of public education evening gatherings with the following themes: What is it like to be a Muslim in Britain? What is it like to be an Evangelical Christian in Britain? What is it like to be gay, lesbian, bi-sexual, or transgendered in Britain? The evenings would focus on personal stories;
- researching the profile of bars within the region—were it to be found that there were other bars with nudity as part of the programme, a case could be made that the same principles could apply to everyone; this could reframe the problem, showing that 'Queers!' had every right to include all of the aspects of their programme that they planned;
- challenging Danny to set up a foundation to support charitable causes dear to the hearts of people in the community.

If mutually agreeable solutions would not be found, it might be important for the dissident communities to still conduct their protests. In this case, given the understanding about the hate crime policies and the Mutual Respect Approach, it would be possible for the protests to proceed with minimum negative personal impact. Practically it might be important to set up surveillance cameras in front of 'Queers!' and make it clear that anyone breaking windows or causing damage would be held accountable. It would also be important to establish a restorative justice programme so that accountability could include actually repairing the windows.

125

Back to complexity

According to complexity theory, it is impossible to predict in advance which action would make a difference when at the edge of chaos. The range of actions just discussed brings the situation as a whole into the realm of criticality, in which the potential for a creative solution emerges. There are many new creatively emergent possibilities. For instance, through these encounters, Muslim youth who happened to be gay and suicidal because of their lack of acceptance might seek out adult gay role models who could give them wise counsel. This, in turn, might lead to some changes of attitude over the long term. Various Muslim–Christian dialogue groups could emerge and meet on a regular basis. If it were to turn out that the far-right activist group was based on white supremacy and neo-Nazi ideology, it could be that some criminal activity would be traced back to them and they could be charged. Alternatively, if they were to participate in Community Dialogues, they could start to change their attitudes as they would get to know members of communities they officially held in contempt.

With the combination of the ethical vision and an understanding of the Mutual Respect Approach, police would be inclined to treat everyone—including those arrested—with dignity and respect. This would ultimately provide the police with the moral authority needed to deal with crowds with a minimum use of force.

References

Girard, R, *Deceit, Desire, and the Novel: Self and other in literary structure* (Y Freccero, trans) (Baltimore, MD: Johns Hopkins University Press, 1976).

Girard, R, *Violence and the Sacred* (P Gregory, trans) (Baltimore, MD: Johns Hopkins University Press, 1977).

Girard, R, *Things Hidden since the Foundation of the World* (S Bann, trans) (Stanford, CA: Stanford University Press, 1987).

Girard, R, *The Scapegoat* (Y Freccero, trans) (Baltimore, MD: Johns Hopkins University Press, 1989).

Kauffman, SA, *Reinventing the Sacred: A new view of science, reason, and religion* (New York, NY: Basic Books, 2008).

Redekop, VN, *From Violence to Blessing: How an understanding of deep-rooted conflict opens paths to reconciliation* (Ottawa, Ontario: Novalis, 2002).

Redekop, VN, and Paré, S, *Beyond Control: A mutual respect approach to protest crowd–police relations* (London: Bloomsbury Academic, 2010).

Ricoeur, P, 'L'idéologie et l'utopie: deux expressions de l'imaginaire sociale' (1984) 2 (Eté) *Autres temps* 53–64.

Ricoeur, P, *Oneself as Another* (Chicago: University of Chicago Press, 1992).

Waddington, PAJ, 'Controlling Protest in Contemporary Historical and Comparative Perspective', in HDR della Porta (ed), *Policing Protest: The control of mass demonstrations in western democracies* (Minneapolis: University of Minnesota Press, 1998).

Editor's Commentary

PAJ Waddington

Negotiation is not a concept that many associate with the police. Egon Bittner, in his pioneering research on routine police work (compiled in Bittner, 1990), emphasises how police impose *non-negotiable* solutions to everyday problems and 'brook no opposition'. All of this is true, but recourse to coercion is actually very rare. Another pioneer of police research (Reiss, 1971) pointed out that the only consistent feature of police officers' duty-time is that an arrest was not made, which is not to say that officers do nothing. It is to say, rather, that more often than not they deal with situations by means other than arrest. More recently, Terrill and Paoline (2007) have confirmed what many other researchers have found over the years, namely that even when ample grounds exist to justify an arrest in law, officers overwhelmingly abstain from doing so. What are police officers doing if they are not making arrests when they are empowered to do so? They deal with situations informally, very often by *negotiation*. However, officers receive very little training in negotiating, since it is often deemed to be simply a matter of 'common sense'. Negotiating is, in any case, difficult to teach because it entails using inter-personal skills rather than intellectual knowledge. Intellectuals, in my experience, make poor negotiators because they become too preoccupied with abstract 'principles' and what can or cannot be rationally justified. It is one reason why universities are notoriously poorly managed! Nevertheless, the best negotiators I have witnessed were the police officers in the Metropolitan Police's public order fraternity, some of whom had acquired their formidable reputations for their prowess in dealing with situations of intense conflict, even riot. I watched them intently for three years as they negotiated their way through thickets of all kinds of public order operations, including protest demonstrations promoting all manner of causes. Interestingly, their response to my ethnographic description of what they did (Waddington, 1994) was one of amazement—they were unaware of the subtle ploys they used and personal resources they employed when negotiating with those wishing to stage some event or other. Vern Redekop is not a police officer, but an academic who has promoted a style of engagement with protesters that emphasises negotiation. He has acted as a consultant, advising and supporting the negotiations between police and protesters. He is a craftsman too and, like other crafts, negotiation relies on *doing* rather than simply *knowing*. Hence, it is difficult to capture the elements of negotiation that will emerge in the course of a process. What he does in this contribution is to set out a framework and emphasise the importance of *mutual respect* to the success of that process.

Mutual respect is vital if people are to agree, because agreement very often entails compromise on profoundly held values. It has become popular in recent decades to recognise explicitly the extent to which modern societies are plural in their composition and to emphasise the value of such pluralisation. There is, however, a danger that 'identity politics' can create mutual distrust and hostility. Inquiries into community tensions and disorders in the northern 'mill towns' of England (Cantle, 2001; Ritchie, 2001; Clark, 2002) concluded that towns segregated by ethnicity lacked cohesion and that prompted distrust and hostility. This is not pluralisation, so much as symptomatic of social divisiveness. Of course, the tragic by-word for inter-communal strife in the British Isles has been Northern Ireland, riven by ethno-religious division. Such division is avoided when individuals possess a variety of identities that they share with those in different groups; for instance, people may have an ethnicity that links them with one group, but identities based on age, gender, occupation, politics, pastimes, and hobbies, that inter-link with quite different groups. Early research on voting (Berelson et al, 1954; Converse, 1976) emphasised how the 'floating vote' that determined elections relied heavily on the 'cross pressures' that influenced voters. For instance, in an American context ethnicity might encourage voting for one candidate, but class and age might prompt support for the opposing candidate.

In this scenario, we encounter divisions that threaten community cohesion, albeit on a small scale. How, then, can one build a community that is both 'cohesive' and 'plural'? Redekop suggests that there needs to be a clear enunciation of an overarching value structure, an 'ethical vision'. I'm inclined to the view that, whilst valuable, indeed necessary, such a vision must emerge from the negotiations rather than initiate them. The danger is that conflicts of the kind described here are 'symbolic' rather than 'instrumental'. Northern Ireland is a very good, albeit tragic, example of the power of symbols to divide and generate hostility and violence. Parades along particular streets became causes célèbres which pitted one religious community against another in violent confrontations. The point about the influence of 'cross pressures' on voting is that division and conflict cannot easily be avoided in modern societies, or indeed should not be avoided. People are entitled to disagree and conformity can be as harmful as dissension. What is dangerous are situations in which people find that divisions are repeatedly drawn along the same fault lines that preclude them from finding themselves in alliance with some groups on one issue and others on another issue—that is they are *not* 'cross pressured'.

A close affiliate of 'symbolic' division is 'essentialism' (Rock, 1973), that is, to elevate some identities to a position in which an identity dominates how individuals are seen by others and themselves. The notion that one is *essentially* 'Catholic' or 'Protestant', or 'black', 'Asian', or 'white', cements divisions and corrodes 'cross pressures'. 'Essentialism' is also associated with deviancy: as David Matza observed long ago (Matza, 1969) one *becomes* 'a delinquent' when one ceases to be a young person who has (incidentally) committed a minor criminal offence and is regarded instead as *essentially* a 'juvenile delinquent'. Tellingly, John Scott (Scott, 1981) found that the same occurred with the blind who are transformed as their sight deteriorates with age from being 'a sighted person with *impaired vision*' into 'a blind person with *residual sight*' because their sight has passed an ophthalmic threshold even though their visual acuity has barely deteriorated at all. Once this had occurred, those labelled as 'essentially blind' adopted the habits and characteristics of the blind, even though what was considered characteristic of the blind differed markedly in America, Britain, and Italy.

This scenario contains a potentially toxic mix of essentialist identities, ethnic, religious, sexuality, and political affiliation. It is unlikely that Jenny Wiltshire will be able to forge commitment to some over-arching values that will unite these disparate groups; what she can and should engineer are cross pressures, so that people find themselves in alliance on some issues and opposed on others. In the meetings that Redekop's framework envisages, opportunities exist: gay people and ethnic minorities are equally and mutually antagonistic towards the 'far right'. The issue of 'hate crime' has currently been perceived as a 'spike' and attributed to the actions of 'young radical Muslims', but Wiltshire privately believes that neither is true. She may be correct, but it could be expedient to keep her suspicion to herself and use the (mis)perception to her advantage. 'Hate crime' is a *common threat* to all minority populations, especially LBGT and Muslims. Their belief that there has been 'a spike' would increase that sense of threat and if Superintendent Wiltshire let it be known that she suspects that recent attacks have been committed by the 'far right' (and not Muslims), this might encourage LGBT and Muslims to join together in opposing this 'far right' threat and thus become a mechanism for creating cohesion (Coser, 1956). She might also prioritise the criminal investigation of these offences, since few would object to such a priority and, if her suspicions are confirmed, it could help unite gay and Muslim interests against the 'far right' criminals. Either way, focusing on 'hate crime' would be a priority that would tend to unite rather than divide diverse minorities. Muslim hostility to homosexuality is something that already unites them with fundamentalist Christians. Already, therefore, a web of cross pressures is beginning to form. What if it backfires and young Muslims are charged with these offences? This is a genuine risk, but it could be mitigated by emphasising age, rather than ethnicity.

Other cross pressures may need to be created anew: 'Christians' are diverse and there are schisms, not least in the Church of England, over issues of gender and sexuality. Perhaps an openly gay woman priest might be willing to act as an intermediary between some Christian groups and Danny Perkins. It is unlikely that such a person would be found amongst fundamentalist denominations of Christianity, but such a priest might be someone who is least objectionable both to fundamentalist Christians and the LGBT community. Perkins is not only a gay man, but also a businessman and may well be persuaded to make concessions for business reasons. Can cross pressures be exerted on him through his business contacts? After all, there would be little commercial attraction in potential customers avoiding the High Street. If the local authority did relocate bus stops away from the High Street, to placate religious sensibilities, perhaps a quid pro quo might be the sort of regeneration that Redekop has in mind. In the meanwhile, perhaps Perkins could be prevailed upon by business people in the area to tone down the purpose of his premises and placate religious outrage by avoiding opening on days and at times that have sacred significance, for instance during Friday prayers and on religious holidays and anniversaries.

A feature of essentialist identities is that it implies uniformity amongst those who are essentialised, when the reality is often one of diversity. That diversity, once recognised, offers opportunities to accommodate some sub-groups, even if others remain opposed. Muslims are divided into a diverse array of affiliations based on doctrinal, historic, and regional differences. Perhaps Wiltshire could seek the assistance of Muslim officers representing diverse affiliations to act as intermediaries. It is also tempting to imagine that the 'far right' represents a single unified movement, but like other social movements it is a coalition of groups with differences as well as similarities of opinion. There will be amongst its membership core constituents who are vehement in their views and implacable in their hostility to opponents, but there will be many others whose allegiance is 'soft' and open to compromise. Wiltshire should try to identify those whose support is soft and seek out those who amongst such 'soft' supporters are outspoken and could act as leaders. If they could be accommodated by some concessions, then it would do much to denude support for the far right, with beneficial long-term consequences. What concessions could be offered? At the moment it is likely that Wiltshire's banning of the march has united the various groups within the 'far right' in a sense of common grievance. Perhaps, an offer of an opportunity to voice their grievances in a less provocative manner may be sufficient. This offer could first be discussed with minorities in an attempt to agree the parameters of any such offer—perhaps a meeting in a hall might be acceptable. Perhaps opponents of the 'far right' could be persuaded to studiously ignore the affront, rather than being provoked into action.

One constituency that is often omitted in such discussions, but explicitly mentioned by Redekop, is the police themselves. Officers' opinions and their affiliations also need to be accommodated. They need to understand that Wiltshire is seeking to keep local community hostilities under control, not least because that will improve the working environment of officers, keeping them safe and enabling them to fulfil their duties without additional difficulties.

All of this is daunting and would require the utmost tact and sensitivity to avoid suggestions that the police were partisan in any of the tactics they employed. The craft of 'negotiation' requires skill and a sophisticated appreciation of the other parties involved. However, a clear strategy of 'cross pressuring' wherever possible could, if successful, leave community cohesion enhanced.

References

Berelson, B, Lazarsfeld, PF, and Macphee, WN (1954), *Voting. A study of opinion formation in a presidential campaign* (Chicago: University of Chicago Press, 1954).

Bittner, E, *Aspects of Police Work* (Boston: Northeastern University Press, 1990).

Cantle, TC, *Community Cohesion: A Report of the Independent Review* (*London*: Home Office, 2001).

Clark, LT, *Report of the Burnley Task Force* (Burnley: Burnely Task Force, 2002).

Converse, PE, *The Dynamics of Party Support: Cohort-analyzing Party Identification* (Beverly Hills; London: Sage Publications, 1976).

Coser, LA, *The Functions of Social Conflict* (London: Routledge & Kegan Paul, 1956).

Matza, D, *Becoming Deviant* (Englewood Cliffs, NJ: Prentice Hall, 1969).

Reiss, AJ, *The Police and the Public* (New Haven, CN: Yale University Press, 1971).

Ritchie, D, *Oldham Independent Review: One Oldham, One Future* (Oldham: Oldham Independent Review, 2001), p 99.

Rock, P, 'Phenomenalism and essentialism in the sociology of deviance' (1973) 7(1) *Sociology* 17–29.

Scott, RA, *The Making of Blind Men: A Study of Adult Socialization* (New Brunswick: Transaction, 1981).

Terrill, W and Paoline, EA III, 'Nonarrest decision making in police–citizen encounters' (2007) 10(3) *Police Quarterly* 308–31.

Waddington, PAJ, *Liberty and Order: Policing Public Order in a Capital City* (London: UCL Press, 1994).

Author's Response

Vern Neufeld Redekop

Waddington has added useful concepts and analyses to move the discussion forward. Let me elaborate on the significance of some of these.

First, let me emphasise my indebtedness to Waddington for the distinction between negotiation as 'craft' and negotiation as a discursive means for manipulation and control. If we agree that when we use the term we are talking about an open-ended exploration of needs, interests, and positions for the purpose of finding mutually beneficial ways forward, I wholeheartedly agree that the ethical vision should be a matter of negotiation. To be more precise, the process would look more like facilitation.

Waddington's commentary raises some significant points about identity. Essentialism is the basis for stereotypes, which in turn can lead to prejudice. These then can lead to dehumanisation and even demonisation. All of this contributes to radical scapegoating that can include severe violence. Cross pressures, finding other aspects of complex identities that can allow for sub-group identity formation on the basis of age, professions, interests, etc, work against the movement toward prejudice and dehumanisation. The community dialogues and seminars that I suggest have built into them processes designed to draw out the bases for what Waddington refers to as cross pressures.

The emphasis on symbol likewise resonates with me. As Waddington correctly points out, the layers of meaning involved in Northern Ireland marches contributed greatly to the escalation of the conflict. Ironically they were inspired by the Civil Rights marches as tactics of non-violent protest; in Northern Ireland they took on the symbolic meaning of marking out and claiming territory. Lisa Schirch (Schirch, 2005) shows how symbolic actions can transcend differences in ways that are often more effective than purely cognitive processes. As Wiltshire develops a strategy, she would do well to attend to the possibility of symbolic conciliatory gestures.

Finally, we have to be aware of cultural and national contexts. As a Canadian with origins in continental Europe, I remember a time when I thought of all 'British' as English—for me this included Scottish, Welsh, Irish, and any others with roots in the British Isles. I now know that this kind of essentialism was wrong and led to various stereotypes that denied both the rich blend of historic inhabitants and the concomitant identity conflicts. Nonetheless, there is in Great Britain a sense of profound identity rootedness that those with immigrant/settler roots in the 'New World' (I choose my words carefully because the First Nations, Metis, and Inuit peoples of Canada have a similar ancient tie to the land) do not experience. There have been radical changes in the demographic make-up of the United Kingdom and these changes lie behind the scenario proposed by the editors of this volume. Cultures have never been static but have themselves been the context for emergent creativity (witness how Normans, Angles, Saxons, Celts, and others contributed to the creation of 'English' culture). Now is a unique opportunity for another level of emergent creativity to foster an amazing new cultural evolution on the Isles. Or it could foment violent conflict and ontological rifts. We can only hope it will be the former and that the police will be agents of constructive societal change.

Reference

Schirch, L, *Ritual and Symbol in Peacebuilding* (Bloomfield, CT: Kumarian Press, 2005).

PART FIVE

Intelligence

Scenario: Intelligence

Ranjit Bhat has recently been promoted to Detective Chief Inspector in the Major Investigation Pool—an elite squad of detectives who deal exclusively with the most serious investigations. Her boss is Chief Superintendent Denise Dalrymple; the pair have worked together throughout much of their service, offering mutual support in a working environment that was often hostile to successful women officers. Denise has relied on Ranjit's advice and integrity, repaying her by helping her prepare for promotion and acting as a referee.

Previously, Ch Supt Dalrymple was Ranjit's boss as Superintendent in the Counter-Terrorism Unit where DI (as she was at the time) Bhat was responsible for managing its intelligence function. Unbeknown to all but a privileged inner circle, since Ch Supt Dalrymple moved on this unit has secured a prize covert human intelligence source (CHIS)—Clive Brown. He is a career criminal with numerous convictions for dishonesty and violence, and is currently engaged in drugs and firearms importation. This would have made him a highly prized asset in any circumstances, but he now offers much more. He has become involved with an extreme right-wing neo-Nazi terrorist group about which the security authorities have become increasingly alarmed. It is feared that they plan to ex-acerbate existing racial tensions by a campaign of fire-bombings of mosques and targeted assassinations of leading Muslim personalities. The group has already committed some arson attacks that inflicted damage, but fortunately without loss of life. Clive Brown acts as 'quartermaster' for this terrorist group and through his drug dealing he helps to finance their activities.

Captured in possession of a large quantity of drugs that then led to a search uncovering numerous firearms, Clive Brown agreed to act as a 'participating informant'. That is to say that he would continue his membership of this terrorist group whilst informing police of what they are planning. It is vitally important that his identity is not revealed even to fellow police officers, because it would place his life in jeopardy. The quality of his information has already proven extremely helpful, enabling the counter-terrorist unit to intercede to prevent an assassination. This is such a sensitive issue that not even Ch Supt Dalrymple knows of Clive Brown's existence.

A murder investigation has been mounted by officers from the Major Investigation Pool. Ch Supt Dalrymple is the Senior Investigating Officer. Both women discussed the case informally when they met. The case is a particular unpleasant murder: the victim is an 18-year-old mobility-disabled man, Byron Smart, who was attacked by a group of young men after he had left a prayer meeting at a fundamentalist Christian sect to which he and his brother, Jason, belonged. The two men made their way home from the meeting. As they turned from a main thoroughfare into an ill-lit quiet suburban street, four or five young men emerged from the shadows. These men barred the passage of Byron, who was in his wheelchair, being pushed by Jason. They began abusing the brothers and said that if 'Jesus Saves', why did he not heal Byron? They jeered at the brothers and then grabbed the wheelchair and began pushing Byron in his wheelchair at speed, swerving erratically, until the wheelchair overbalanced and Byron fell out. The men surrounded Byron, punching and kicking him. With the attention of the gang focused on Byron, Jason escaped and ran screaming for help back towards the main road. People standing at the bus stop were alerted by Jason's screams and several approached him. He led them back to the site of the attack, but now all that could be seen in the gloom was the wheelchair lying on its side and the huddled figure of Byron. An ambulance was called, but Byron had died from internal bleeding caused by the attack. There was only one witness to the attack and that was Jason, but his only recollection of the attackers was that one of them was unusually tall, standing head and shoulders above others in the gang.

Byron's parents are decent middle-class people who are utterly inconsolable. Only days before he died, Byron had won a scholarship to the University of Oxford to study computer science. He was also a talented musician and had composed some of the hymns sung at prayer meetings.

The police are under intense pressure to make an arrest swiftly. Apart from his adherence to the fundamentalist Christian sect, Jason is also a well-known activist for the Disability Alliance in the area. This organisation has been campaigning for police to take firmer action against disability-related hate crime in the area—Byron's murder is now a cause célèbre in the struggle for the rights of the disabled. Through the Disability Alliance Jason has access to legal advice and lawyers have been pressing the police on the family's behalf to find the attackers. People have begun posting suggestions on the Disability Alliance website that the likely perpetrators are a group of four young men who have a local reputation for indiscriminate violence (although hitherto there has been no evidence of them being violent to disabled people specifically). The evidence in support of this accusation is weak: the young men were seen drinking in a pub in the vicinity of the attack earlier that evening, but this would not be unusual. That they are capable of violence is beyond doubt: several of them have been implicated in a number of violent attacks, but these have hitherto been associated with soccer hooligan-ism (for which two have banning orders preventing attendance at soccer matches). However, none of them would be considered unusually tall, nor would any of their associates.

Talking to Ch Supt Dalrymple, Det Ch Insp Bhat learns that the investigators are bereft of leads and are contemplating raiding the homes of the four young men for evidence. The complicating factor for Det Ch Insp Bhat is that amongst those four young men is Darren Brown, son of Clive Brown, the prize CHIS. Clive has made it abundantly clear that the 'price' of his continued cooperation as a CHIS is keeping his son—to whom he is genuinely and fiercely devoted—free from the clutches of the criminal justice system. Previously, Det Ch Insp Bhat and close colleagues in the Counter-Terrorism Unit have succeeded in discouraging investigations into modest acts of violence that could easily be traced to Darren Brown.

Det Ch Insp Bhat is conflicted: on the one hand, it is possible that Darren was involved in the vicious and unprovoked murder of an entirely innocent young man. On the other hand, if Clive Brown ceases cooperation with the Counter-Terrorism Unit, it seems highly probable that intelligence on the neo-Nazi group will dry up and they will be free to continue planning outrages. Given the exist-ing level of tension between communities, it is distinctly possible that any successful neo-Nazi attack could unleash communal violence.

It would be easy enough to deflect attention from the four youths. Ch Supt Dalrymple has asked Det Ch Insp Bhat to meet her after work for a meal at a res-taurant they frequent. Det Ch Insp Bhat could simply point to the weak evidence connecting the four suspects to the murder and the possibility that if the gang are responsible, precipitate action could be used to exclude any incriminating evi-dence that was obtained—both of which are plausible and Det Ch Insp Bhat would be failing in her duty if she did not draw them to Ch Supt Dalrymple's attention. That would give time to allow Darren Brown to speak to his father, who will advise him on how best to cover the gang's tracks.

What should Det Ch Insp Bhat do? What options does she have? Which of them should she favour and which should she exclude from further consideration? What are the grounds for inclusion and exclusion of options?

What difficulties and obstacles lie in Det Ch Insp Bhat's path? Consider the likely consequences and implications of different options? How should Det Ch Insp Bhat deal with them?

Is there anything that could have been done that would have avoided the situa-tion in which Det Ch Insp Bhat now finds herself?

Addressing the Scenario
The Dilemmas of Intelligence and Ethical Police Practice: Policing Terrorism and Managing Covert Human Sources

Steve Darroch

Ethical Police Practice

Police exercise special powers to use force and deception in pursuit of broad social goals (Kleinig, 2009). In conjunction with special powers police exercise enormous discretion in deciding what laws will be enforced and where and when enforcement will occur. Wider society expects police will operate with restraint, professionalism, and ethics when exercising these powers. The public can tolerate incompetence but in recent decades ethical failures have been severely punished. This confluence of exceptional powers, discretion, and intolerance of ethical failure has important implications for police. Police are highly scrutinised and operate under a heavy administrative burden calculated to limit opportunities for ethical lapses. In spite of this, some police decision making remains obscured from exacting and timely ethical oversight. Here we consider just such a scenario.

In an effort to encourage ethical practice amongst officers, police agencies typically employ and promote simple statements of ethical doctrine. Principles such as impartiality, transparency, and accountability are often described in codes of ethical practice. Regrettably, simple principles are often unhelpful where they come into contact with the real world. Real world policing sometimes means transparency is absent, accountabilities are unclear, and objectivity lost. Innocent mistakes or misjudgements can quickly translate into cavernous or intractable ethical problems. Loyalty and relationships can colour thinking and slow or halt efforts to address emerging ethical problems. The voracious appetite of the media for policing scandals can immobilise action or precipitate a massive overreaction by senior officers. Policing is increasingly a profession with complex ethical challenges.

A key ethical dilemma of policing (Neyroud, 2003) is balancing the needs of the individual and the needs of the wider community. How are individual human rights weighed against the needs of keeping the wider community safe? This is a deceptively simple description of ethical problems which can be much more complex. How should issues involving individual human rights, the career aspirations of individual officers, community safety, and the pursuit of justice be balanced? How can decisions be ethical in situations where dilemmas are so intertwined that all pathways are fraught and well intentioned decisions have led to seemingly intractable problems? Resolving complex ethical challenges necessitates finding practical workable solutions which satisfy a broad range of audiences. Professional policing will not function unless practical solutions can be found and shortly I will turn to the practical problem this chapter will address.

Neyroud (2003) suggests a number of living principles which may be helpful in unpacking the complex ethical challenges before us. These are the most important to our discussion:

Beneficence and non-maleficence—officers should help people without harming others.

Justice—officers must maintain respect for human rights and morally responsible laws.

Responsibility—officers need to be able to justify their actions and take personal responsibility for them.

Care—officers have a duty of care which rests on the interdependency of police officers with the individuals they deal with and the communities they serve.

Honesty—officers' honesty is central to legitimacy and the authority of individual officers.

Stewardship—trusteeship over the powerless and over police powers.

To this list I add one further principle, transparency. Decisions must be made in the most transparent way possible. Real motivations and interests must be evident and not hidden. Within practical limits, decisions and motivations must be transparent to senior managers, leaders, and external supervisory bodies. While there may be limits to transparency, particularly for covert policing, real transparency must be brought to bear on the practical ethical dilemmas police face. A failure to be transparent is invariably problematic for police.

Reviewing the Problem

The complex ethical challenges the police face are well articulated in the intelligence scenario faced by Detective Chief Inspector Ranjit Bhat. She finds herself in a difficult ethical dilemma not of her making, with no clear or simple actions available to her to resolve her dilemma. Bhat's former supervisor is Chief Superintendent Denise Dalrymple with whom she has a continuing personal, mentoring, and professional relationship. Dalrymple was Bhat's supervisor previously in the Counter-Terrorism Unit. Dalrymple is unaware of the existence of a valued covert human intelligence source (CHIS), Clive Brown, who is being operated as a participating informant. Brown is a career criminal currently engaged in drugs and firearms importation. As well as criminal intelligence he offers information on an active extreme neo-Nazi terrorist group. Brown acts as 'quartermaster' for the neo-Nazi group helping to finance its activities through drug-dealing. Information provided by Brown has been particularly useful, in one case preventing an assassination.

Against this backcloth a murder investigation has commenced. The investigation is politically charged with intense community and media pressure on police to solve the crime. The murder is complicated for Bhat by involving Brown's son as a person of interest, who needs to be eliminated as a suspect from the investigation. Dalrymple is the homicide's senior investigating officer. The evidence implicating Brown's son and the wider group is weak, but the pressure to quickly advance the investigation is substantial both in the media and from pressure groups.

Bhat and Dalrymple have discussed the investigation informally. The investigation is at a dead end. Bhat understands from Dalrymple that the next stage of the investigation is likely to be a concerted effort to eliminate or implicate Brown's son and his associates. Such an action against Brown's son will jeopardise Brown's continued cooperation as an informant. Bhat has already discouraged investigations into other minor acts of violence by Darren Brown in order to ensure Clive Brown's continued cooperation.

Bhat is unclear about what to do next. Compromising Brown's involvement as an informant may have serious implications for police, hampering their ability to prevent serious violence by the neo-Nazi terrorist group. Bhat's relationship means she could influence Dalrymple. She could point to potential damage to the murder investigation if action is taken against Brown's son and would be ethically well grounded in doing so. This might allow Brown to speak to his son, resulting in Brown's son possibly covering his offending more effectively.

At the heart of the dilemma facing Bhat is the need to balance two competing priorities; the potential good that could come from maintaining Brown as an informant and the need for justice to be served through a vigorous investigation of the homicide which may involve Darren Brown. The scenario creates an ethical quandary. Which course of action serves the greater good? This is a Catch-22. On the one hand Bhat has a duty of care to wider society having identified the threat posed by the neo-Nazi group and developing an effective course of action to minimise that threat. She can lessen the risk of potential serious harm. Against this she needs to respect the pursuit of justice and uphold morally responsible laws in the cases of both Clive and possibly Darren Brown. She needs to be honest and transparent in her decision making and take full responsibility for her actions. Finally she must approach her decision through a duty of care lens balancing the needs of the individuals involved and the wider community.

When considering her options Bhat needs to remember there are limits to the police investigative capability. Even if Darren Brown and associates are responsible for the death of Byron Smart the facts of the case could mean that they will never be held accountable, especially if they are guided in a cover up by an experienced criminal like Clive Brown. However unpalatable to the police and community, the evidence may never stack up to meet the 'beyond reasonable doubt' threshold. Both Bhat and Dalrymple know this. Bhat is under no real obligation to remind Dalrymple of these facts and the dangers of risking a successful outcome of any prosecution by taking unreasonable investigative actions. If she chooses to frustrate or divert the investigation, she is stepping into ethically questionable territory. Bhat should steer clear of using this common knowledge in a deceptive way to further interests hidden from Dalrymple. Police cannot solve all crimes.

Considering Options and Involving Others

Bhat does have options. She could reveal all to Dalrymple. She could explain Brown's role as an informant and the critical nature of the information he can provide. By taking Dalrymple, her friend and senior officer, into her confidence, she relieves herself of the responsibility for resolving the dilemma as Dalrymple should now assume responsibility. However there may be uncomfortable and career limiting consequences for Bhat if she does this. Her previous involvement in discouraging investigation into modest acts of violence that could easily be traced to Darren Brown could now be viewed seriously. However well intentioned, indulging Darren Brown's modest acts of violence could, now, be seen as part of a chain of events which concludes with the death of Byron Smart. Bhat's failure to uphold morally responsible laws and to act in an honest and transparent way about her true motives when influencing Dalrymple, are now significant issues. Despite these challenges, telling Dalrymple is an option that Bhat needs seriously to consider. Continuing to make decisions in isolation may not be helpful to Bhat at this point.

Bhat could take another more senior officer into her confidence to get a fresh perspective and offer her advice. This has the advantage of again relieving Bhat of her dilemma or lessening potential consequences. A problem shared is, in this scenario, a problem reduced, if not halved. However, like telling Dalrymple, this option only sidesteps the problem for Bhat and creates one for another, albeit more senior officer. What would the senior officer do?

Certainly the right senior officer will be better equipped to deal with the problem, even if they experience a natural reluctance to want to deal with the ethical dilemma. A senior colleague will bring more resources to bear, may be able to see other ways to deal with the problem, can think longer term, and can make better informed strategic decisions. Experienced thinking may reveal vulnerabilities in Clive Brown's position and emphasise the need to positively exclude Darren Brown from the investigation. In the end something has to give.

Introducing a senior officer has other merits. There may be information to which neither Bhat nor Dalrymple is privy. Other policing or intelligence agencies may be actively working against the neo-Nazi terrorist group and the potential cooperation of Brown may not have the value presumed by Bhat. A senior officer will likely take the decision out of Bhat's hands. Clear directions may be given to eliminate Darren Brown as a suspect and review in depth the value offered by Brown senior as an informant. The extent to which other covert human intelligence information, electronic intelligence gathering, or other enforcement techniques could minimise the value of Brown's cooperation is not known to Bhat. She cannot presume 'perfect' knowledge of the dilemma she faces. There may well be important information she lacks.

Passing responsibility up the chain of command leaves Dalrymple, or the senior officer advised of the problem, with the same fundamental dilemma faced by Bhat. How should they resolve the quandary? While a senior officer does not possess a magic wand to make the problem go away, the important point is that they should bring more resources, more experience, possibly information or access to more information, and, critically, strong leadership to the problem. While the options open to them are not fundamentally different from those open to Bhat, they are more likely to resolve the situation in an ethically sound way and in a manner much more likely to survive scrutiny should all the facts become known or public. They are able to be more objective: judgements can be made based on facts, risk assessments, and established best practice, rather than the assessment of a fairly junior officer who is somewhat ethically compromised already and whose motivations are possibly tainted by self-interest and earlier poor decision making. Involving the right senior officer has strong merits.

However, career limiting consequences for Bhat are still evident with this course of action. Transparency in decision making for police is an important principle for ethical decision making. Guiding earlier investigations away from Darren Brown, however well intentioned, may now have had serious consequences. Interfering with an investigation may be a criminal act. Small actions which may seem innocent enough can blow up unexpectedly. Bhat and her colleagues are not the sole guardians endeavouring to minimise the threat of the neo-Nazi group.

Bhat has a range of ethical obligations to discharge and by bringing the right senior manager in to help her, her decision making becomes more transparent and honest, and the final decision will be much better informed. A wider view can be taken on the right approaches to minimising the threat posed by the neo-Nazi group while balancing the need to progress the murder investigation. Whatever the consequences for Bhat in bringing an experienced and knowledgeable senior manager to the problem, someone who could salvage the situation is a suggestion that strongly recommends itself. A senior manager may also be able to minimise any damage to Bhat herself. Taking the personal relationship complications out of the scenario is a compelling argument for involving a senior officer.

Options: 'Do Nothing', 'Call the Bluff'

Bhat could do nothing. She could decide not to talk to Dalrymple and let the investigation take its natural course. She may have overestimated the implications for Darren Brown. The price for Clive Brown's services may not be as high as he claims and he may have overstated the likelihood of withdrawing his services. Clive Brown has a lot to lose himself. He benefits from police patronage in his position as a covert human intelligence source. His involvement in drugs and firearms importation and the intimate knowledge police have of his actions makes him extremely vulnerable to prosecution. The boundaries of his cooperation may be more flexible than he claims. If Darren Brown is investigated but cleared, which on the current facts seems likely, Clive Brown will almost certainly continue to act as a participating informant.

Doing nothing is a serious option for Bhat. Doing nothing is far from a passive decision on Bhat's behalf and stacks up ethically. Bhat would not be acting against the interests of justice in attempting to divert attention away from Darren Brown, although of course she has done this previously over lesser matters. Her deliberate inaction does not fail tests of reasonableness, honesty, or taking responsibility for her decisions. Her overall position does lack transparency, however, as her true motives and thinking are hidden. She has acted appropriately in respect of her duty of care, having actively considered all the implications and consequences of her actions. Ultimately the correctness or otherwise of her decision will be judged on facts as yet unknown. If she is correct in her assumption that Clive Brown is unlikely to withdraw his services, then all will be well. If however Clive Brown does withdraw his services and a disastrous terrorist attack occurs then her failure to influence Dalrymple could be judged severely. In particular some of her colleagues would judge her harshly.

Options: De-Rail the Byron Smart Investigation

Bhat could influence Dalrymple as she is contemplating. Bhat understands the influence she can exercise over Dalrymple despite the difference in rank. She is clear that taking action against Darren Brown and the other suspects now, when the case is so weak, is likely to jeopardise any prosecution against them. If incriminating evidence is uncovered but that evidence is obtained illegally or improperly it could mean the evidence is excluded. It is reasonable for her to point to these weaknesses and she may be under an obligation to do so. Slowing the investigation gives Darren Brown the chance to seek advice from his father, and if he is involved in the homicide, to cover his tracks. Bhat's actions in influencing

145

Dalrymple will likely secure the continuing services of Clive Brown and ultimately protect the wider community from violent action by the neo-Nazi group.

How does the 'influencing Dalrymple' approach stack up against our ethical principles? Clearly Bhat is discharging her duty of care to wider society by minimising the threat posed by the neo-Nazi group, as far as utilising Clive Brown's services is able to secure this. But does this decision look healthy in relation to her other ethical duties and responsibilities? The pursuit of justice is frustrated. Bhat's approach is neither honest nor transparent. Her true motivations in influencing Dalrymple are not evident to anyone, let alone Dalrymple who is Bhat's friend. It is questionable whether Bhat is balancing the needs of individuals against the needs of wider society. The death of Byron Smart has left many in the community bereft, distressed, and crying out for justice.

We cannot say with certainty what Dalrymple's response would be to Bhat's efforts to influence her. Dalrymple may ignore the suggestions offered by Bhat and make her own decision. Dalrymple has many pressures and factors she needs to consider in making up her mind. Bhat's views may or may not be influential. Should Bhat be taking on so much responsibility for a decision which is not, in the end, hers? Dalrymple ultimately has the ethical and practical responsibility for ensuring that the interests of justice and the community are served in the investigation of Byron Smart's death. If the evidence points to Darren Brown he needs to be eliminated and Dalrymple has responsibility for addressing this. On balance it is presumed Bhat will be influential, as Dalrymple has no clear direction for the investigation.

However, Bhat needs to question her assumptions. Her view that she has a responsibility to draw to Dalrymple's attention the potentially damaging consequences of taking precipitate action against Darren Brown is questionable. This belief may be self-serving. Dalrymple is an experienced officer, well aware of the law. The case Dalrymple is investigating is not Bhat's responsibility and she could easily and safely conclude that Dalrymple knows what she is doing. By taking on or supposing she has such a responsibility Bhat may be acting to find justification for an action she is already motivated to take. Her desire to protect Clive Brown may be influencing her behaviour. What obligations does Bhat have to Dalrymple? Does Bhat owe Dalrymple honesty and transparency as a loyal and valued colleague? If Bhat does dissuade Dalrymple from pursuing the investigation this is manipulation unworthy of a close professional relationship and lacks the transparency essential to ethical conduct.

Options: Prosecute Clive Brown

A course open to Bhat is to arrest and prosecute Clive Brown, removing him from the scenario as an informant. It could be that the cost of maintaining him as a covert human intelligence source is simply too high, that his involvement in serious criminal offending is too deep, and his role as quartermaster in the neo-Nazi group is too close to being a leader, to acting as an agent provocateur. Clive Brown's actions in financing the activities of the neo-Nazi group make him too involved, and removing financial support may have a crippling effect on the organisation. This allows the murder investigation to take its natural course and serves the interests of justice by prosecuting an active criminal and terrorist. As a minimum it may incapacitate the neo-Nazi group, albeit temporarily. Cutting Brown loose as an informant does not mean he will never inform again, far from it. He is compromised and needs police support, should his role as an informant ever become known to his criminal colleagues. Brown will not reveal his cooperation with the police as this becomes a massive risk to himself.

This approach opens up ethical and practical questions. What obligations do police have toward Clive Brown? Is he owed protection by police? Brown has always acted in his own interests, only providing information to help himself. Brown is not acting out of any higher moral calling. His current threats to withhold information endanger innocent citizens. Beyond the general obligation police have to protect life police are under no special obligation to protect Brown. Clive Brown's only utility is as an informant and he has no right to expect additional protection from police.

Bhat could legitimately not only prosecute Brown she could merely threaten to prosecute him. Brown will know that any prosecution could reveal his involvement as an informant. The circumstances of the prosecution will open questions about why he was not prosecuted earlier. Brown will be strongly motivated to avoid prosecution. A threat alone might be enough to bring him into line and give police space to fully investigate Darren Brown. It is difficult to judge Clive Brown's response to this scenario but both prosecution and the threat of prosecution are legitimate options open to Bhat.

Weighing Options and Understanding the Context of Decision Making

It is a truism to say there is simply no simple right or wrong answer. The difficulty with practical ethical decision making is that the correctness of any decision turns on how that decision is framed by future facts, which must remain unknown to the decision maker. So it is for Det Ch Insp Bhat. If she successfully influences Dalrymple and it transpires that Darren Brown was complicit in the murder and these facts become known, it is likely there will be devastating consequences for Bhat and her police organisation. The personal damage to her reputation and that of her police agency would be crippling, especially in the context of the furore over Byron Smart's death. Alternatively, if she does nothing and this leads to a chain of events (arising from Clive Brown refusing to cooperate further because his son is arrested) resulting in serious harm or multiple deaths through a terrorist attack which could have been averted; at a minimum she bears with her colleagues the burden of knowing they could have saved lives.

A practical, although not always helpful test police sometimes use is the 'front page test'. In other words what would the tabloid headline be if the facts were known to a muck raking journalist? What would the front page article and accompanying political and public discussion look like? Using this test Bhat is in a tricky ethical dilemma. 'Cops protect murderer' comes to mind as the headline while the details of what actually motivated Bhat, an effort to protect wider society, are buried on page 6 if they appear at all. Using this test the other options open to Bhat look more promising. It is difficult to construct a headline from doing nothing. Even if Clive Brown withdraws his services leading to a possibly preventable terrorist act against a mosque, the chain of events cannot plausibly be linked to Bhat. Seeking advice creates no headline issues. Neither does arresting Clive Brown, 'Cops arrest terrorist quartermaster' is hardly a negative for police. On this simple test the way forward seems clear.

No doubt some police officers will feel strongly that the threat from the neo-Nazi group is too serious to even contemplate compromising Clive Brown's informant status. Some officers see policing as a righteous cause and protecting society at all costs as the top priority. Informant handling and serious crime investigation is a dirty business and if ethical compromises need to be made (particularly those than can be characterised as minor) for the greater good, then so be it. The 'War on Terror' has certainly encouraged this kind of thinking.

A related and important consideration is the career enhancing effect that quality informants can have on an officer's status and career prospects. Even in the age of more systemic and organised informant handling, quality informants matter and can enhance promotional prospects. There would be a real temptation to 'hold on' to Clive Brown at all costs. The success that might flow for someone like Bhat and a small cohort of officers around her is potentially very significant. Over a number of years Brown's information might generate a large volume of high profile drug, arms, serious crime, and terrorist related apprehensions. There is a real danger that the temptation of all this future success would colour Bhat's thinking, even at an unconscious level, towards maintaining Brown as an informant at any cost.

Bhat should make her decision about which option to favour by taking a number of steps. First she should be sure that her thinking is free from motivations which might consciously or unconsciously distort her decision making. She should seriously and systematically question her own motives. She should take a highly sceptical view of her own reasoning and approach to the situation. As discussed, factors such as the temptation to use Clive Brown to build her own career, or fear of damage to her career, might shape her thinking away from the correct decision. She has a very important decision to make and needs to think critically about her motivations and circumstances.

The grounds Bhat should use to include or exclude options are relatively straightforward and will be summarised here. However it is rare for officers faced with practical ethical problems to grab a white board and pen and start ethical calculations. Police officers tend to follow instincts and to be heavily influenced by the circumstances in which they find themselves, the local culture and leadership (or lack of leadership), and their colleagues. What Bhat should do and what she will actually do in reaching a conclusion are likely to be two different things. A conciliatory approach has been taken to managing Clive Brown up to this point, an approach Bhat is likely to continue. She has a good deal invested in Brown and a lot to lose if her previous efforts in protecting Darren Brown come to light. These constraints are likely to dictate Bhat's actual actions. How might these constraints be overcome?

Decision Time

Of course Bhat should do all she can to minimise harm to the community through the potential loss of Clive Brown as an informant. But it is evident that this is far from her only consideration and a critical assessment suggests that the situation is almost certainly not as black and white as she presumes. These issues all need to be considered. Bhat should not assume too much responsibility. She should not take the weight of the world on her shoulders and presume that the only way to manage the situation is to influence Dalrymple. She is a cog in a big machine, not a crusader in a noble cause. Bhat should apply critical ethical thinking to her situation. She should examine the assumptions she has made and test whether the evidence really supports these assumptions. Clearly bringing a colleague or supervisor in to help her thinking will likely greatly assist here. She should consider the responsibilities she has, and use an approach such as applying the principles suggested by Neyroud (2003) to think through the situation and her response and options. Bhat needs to consider the interests of justice, her own career, and personal liability should the full facts become public. Most importantly Bhat needs to be honest and transparent in her decision making. She needs to balance minimising harm with her responsibilities to be transparent and honest.

Bhat should not seek covertly to influence Dalrymple. Steering Dalrymple's inquiry away from investigating the possible involvement of Darren Brown in the death of Byron Smart is fraught with problems. This approach lacks transparency and honesty, as Bhat's true motives are not apparent to Dalrymple or anyone else. If Darren Brown is involved in the death, Bhat's actions facilitate a miscarriage of justice. If he is not involved she still fails to act in the interests of open justice by hiding her true motivations. Her views on the risks of losing Clive Brown as an informant are possibly overstated, as are her concerns about risks to the community from losing Brown as an informant. This is not to say there is no risk, but the issue is clouded and not nearly as black and white as Bhat chooses to believe.

This leaves a range of options open to Bhat which she should consider in much more detail through applied critical thinking. She should consider the merits of revealing the true situation to Dalrymple, taking another senior officer into her confidence, doing nothing, consulting with a colleague, or arresting and prosecuting Brown. There may be options to eliminate Darren Brown from the investigation in a way that will not harm the relationship with Clive Brown. Bhat should not influence Dalrymple in a dishonest way. The situation is more complex and more nuanced than Bhat appreciates. She needs others to help her see the situation more clearly.

Difficulties and Obstacles

A mix of obstacles and issues lies in Bhat's path. In particular, seeking advice could bring major problems for her. These difficulties are a real obstruction likely to steer her away from seeking advice or engaging with a senior officer. If Bhat briefs Dalrymple on the true situation, advises a senior officer, or discusses the issue with a colleague, she takes on significant personal and career risks. Her lack of transparency when previously protecting Darren Brown will likely be called into question. Significant issues concerning the management of Clive Brown as an informant will be raised. How serious has Clive Brown's offending been? Should (presumably) high level drug dealing and firearms importation have been tolerated in the way that it was? Have the necessary CHIS systems of management checks and balances been put in place and are they operating effectively? How have the risks around Clive Brown been managed? How have the ethical dilemmas he poses been addressed up to this point (in particular the previous protection of Darren Brown's violent offending)? Has the information he provided been circulated to the right agencies? Are the police the right agency to manage Brown? Was the decision to use him as an informant in the first place the right one, especially in light of the serious charges he faced at the time and out of which he was able to bargain his way through offering to inform? How has Clive Brown been conducting himself as an informant? He continues to commit serious offences from which he presumably benefits financially and in many other ways. Is the relationship between Clive Brown and the police in fact asymmetrical with Brown benefiting enormously (protected from prosecution, able to conduct his criminal business comfortably and afford protection to his son and others)? All these questions become live once Bhat elects to act openly and transparently to resolve her dilemma.

Unfortunately, whatever Bhat elects to do, these issues will not disappear. Predicting the future is fraught. But it seems likely that these issues will emerge at some point. Whether Darren Brown is implicated in the death of Byron Smart or not he is a young man with a history of minor violence. He also has serious criminal connections through his father, is on the fringes of a neo-Nazi group, and has access to drugs and firearms either through his father or sources close to his father (at the very least). It was always probable that Darren Brown would become involved in serious offending at some point. The odds were stacked against him. Clive Brown's enthusiasm for protecting his son was always going to come into conflict with the ethical responsibilities of police to uphold justice and act impartially and fairly. There was inevitability about this conflict. Bhat should have considered this scenario much earlier. Her failure, alone or in combination with colleagues and supervisors, to properly assess the risk of using Clive Brown as an informant is now an obstacle to her decision making.

Of real concern is the proposal that Darren Brown should be given time to speak to his father in order to get advice on how he and his co-offenders can cover their tracks. Presuming that Darren Brown is involved in the death of Byron Smart, this is highly problematic. Even if he is not involved, the intention that he should be given the opportunity is wrong. If Bhat intends to afford Darren and Clive Brown this opportunity she is in serious ethical and legal difficulty. This is a serious impediment to Bhat resolving the issue before her.

Bhat also has the challenge of the culture and leadership environment in which she is embedded. She is part of an elite group working on serious organised crime. She is recently promoted. The eyes of her colleagues and supervisors are upon her as she navigates this first step at a new rank. She will want to impress her peers, superiors, and subordinates. Police are notoriously unforgiving of mistakes. One error can make for effective career suicide. Jealous colleagues will be looking to see if she trips up. All these issues will be putting pressure on Bhat. Bhat may also be inculcated with the bravado of the counter-terrorism unit. She may still be influenced by a culture that takes more risks than it should. The quality of leadership in the group may be questionable. Again, has more risk taking been tolerated than was acceptable? All these contextual factors will be influencing Bhat, even if she is not consciously aware of them. Without some mechanism to give her perspective on the impact of these factors she may be influenced to make an unethical decision.

There are no easy options for Bhat. There are no free lunches here. The justification that Bhat relies on, both for her proposed course of action and the management of Clive Brown as an informant, is that of preventing terrorist acts by the neo-Nazi group. She calculates that on balance the prevention of future terrorist acts outweighs the harm of possibly letting a killer go free. If we accept all the apparent facts unquestioningly then Bhat may be justified in her belief. But we cannot accept all these apparent facts on their face. If we accept the facts then we are essentially faced with the thought experiment 'save five but kill the one?' Do we follow the utilitarian argument to do the least harm (see Foot, 1967; Thomson, 1985)? Real world ethics is not that clear cut. Bhat should not presume there are no other options to prevent these acts. This is a major presumption on her part and is probably a wrong one. There will be another way to fix the problem and prevent the terrorist acts. The record of western governments in the prevention of terrorism is not perfect but it is pretty good up to this point. While Bhat cannot undo poor management or poor past decisions which may have contributed to her current dilemma, she should stop thinking like a 'Lone Ranger' and instead like part of a large state security apparatus with options and resources. While Bhat has obstacles in her path including the prospect of real career damage arising from past bad decisions, there is nothing she can do to undo what has been done.

If Bhat chooses to reveal all to Dalrymple or seek advice from a senior manager or colleague she must be prepared for the potential consequences. On the other hand she could do nothing, she could covertly influence Dalrymple as she is contemplating, or she could prosecute Clive Brown for his serious criminal offending. Pursuing these options will certainly delay any close questioning of her actions and the actions of her colleagues in relation to the management of Clive Brown. But this might only be a delay and Brown's response to arrest is unclear.

Bhat has real personal and professional interests mixed up here. Undoubtedly managing serious criminal informants is a messy and challenging business. Unfortunately what seems to have happened here is that Bhat's enthusiasm and that of her colleagues has got out of balance with the need to manage Clive Brown effectively. One could ask who is managing whom? A real practical difficulty for Bhat is the question of whether taking on Brown as an informant was ethically sound in the first place. The issue of participating informants is fraught. Compromises made along the way to secure Brown's services are now major problems. There are no easy options for Bhat.

Learning Lessons—What Could Have Been Done?

There are various ways Bhat could have avoided the situation in which she now finds herself. Indeed some serious questions need to be asked about the chain of decisions that has led to the current scenario.

Managing a high risk CHIS is inevitably problematic. In particular the balance of power in the relationship between informant source and handlers is always tricky. What starts as a healthy relationship can deteriorate and become ethically compromised. Every serious offence committed by the informant has a corrupting effect on the relationship. Has Bhat's management of Clive Brown become too compromised and complex to continue in its current state? Many informants are given too much power and their offending is ignored. Great care must be taken to ensure the relationship does not become asymmetrical. Police must maintain control and an informant's serious criminal offending can only be tolerated to the minimum necessary for that informant to maintain creditability. Arguably Clive Brown's offending is beyond that point.

Many police would be uncomfortable with a situation where a serious active criminal such as Clive Brown is able to continue offending, with police collusion and complicity. The argument in favour of allowing Brown to continue serious offending is a lesser of two evils approach or utilitarian argument. Allowing Brown to continue offending produces better outcomes for society as a whole by protecting society from more serious violent offending. Policing terrorists is a dirty business. The argument runs that ethical compromises have to be made to make society safe. The niceties of 'normal' policing fall away and tough decisions have to be made. Ethical constraints have to be lifted or people die. The needs of the many outweigh the needs of the few.

The difficulties with this argument are the unstated premises. As mentioned earlier, individual police or groups of police cannot have perfect knowledge of the situation in which they are involved. To presume there is no other way to police or prevent an anticipated evil is flawed. In the fluid world of serious criminals and terrorists where allegiances are hidden, where covert human sources will be unknown to each other, and where electronic surveillance and multi agencies may be operating independently, one officer or a small group of officers cannot say with certainty that this is the only way and we must take responsibility, we must compromise ourselves ethically to get the job done. This is in effect, noble cause corruption. We are prepared to compromise ourselves ethically in order to serve wider society, to do the 'right thing'.

Clive Brown's offending is not trivial; drug dealing, importing firearms, and acting as quartermaster for a terrorist organisation are all extremely serious offences. Major drug dealing or firearms getting into the wrong hands, these are serious risks to society. A terrorist act by the neo-Nazi group could occur spontaneously without Clive Brown's knowledge yet Brown is free to operate sanctioned by police. These are all real and serious risks to wider society facilitated and not mitigated by Brown's privileged freedom to operate.

There is a real element of moral hazard here for Bhat and her colleagues. Bhat seems willing to take on all these risks because she feels insured by Clive Brown's status as a CHIS. A further unstated premise is that Brown is a reliable and trustworthy 'informant'. Most police will recognise that this is rarely, if ever, the case. Informants have their own motivations and agendas. They frequently have personal, psychiatric, drug, alcohol, or personality problems which make them inherently unreliable and untrustworthy. For Bhat to take risks, feel comfortable, or allow serious offending solely on the basis of the value to society of her protecting an individual like this is fraught with difficulty.

A very real practical question is whether or not police are the right agency to be running Clive Brown as an informant. Tempting as it may be to utilise his senior criminal position to lock up criminals, likely prevent terrorist activities, and advance careers, serious questions need to be asked about the appropriateness of police managing Brown. Other state intelligence agencies do not have the moral framework or breadth of responsibilities police do. These agencies are not upholders of the law in the broad sense that police are. They do not have the obligations to justice, personal responsibility, transparency, honesty, and care that police do. They can act in secret and in service of political imperatives. Their actions never need be subject to review by the courts or media. They can take a very long-term view on how they position informants and utilise the information they provide. They can consider terrorism and stability as long-term issues in a way police cannot.

Unfortunately if Clive Brown was managed by an intelligence agency rather than the police the ethical problem might not be resolved and could be more acute. A likely scenario sees Clive Brown making his demands on the intelligence agency. The agency then brings pressure on police to leave Darren Brown alone. The ethical dilemma then arises at the institutional rather than individual level. The intelligence agency has no interest in the death of Byron Smart. Short-term noise from community groups and concerned citizens will be of no interest to an intelligence agency. Even if he is responsible for the murder this may not raise concerns for the agency. National security takes precedence. Keeping Clive Brown on side is the number one priority.

Whether police buckle under pressure is hard to judge. The leadership and character of individual commanders might be the determining factor. If these facts were to play out then at least the ethical problem is not left in the hands of a fairly junior officer, acting in relative isolation, under pressured circumstances, and constrained by factors not of her making. Instead presumably senior officers from two agencies will have a frank discussion. This is more ethically appealing than leaving the same decision to Bhat. I judge police as unlikely to cave in to pressure, even if armed with all the facts.

Given all these considerations, one way in which Bhat and her colleagues could have avoided the problems they now face was by not taking on Clive Brown as an informant in the first place. They could have passed him on to a more appropriate intelligence agency. Or they could have utilised his services for a limited time and then prosecuted him for his offending when it became clear the relationship was becoming compromised, in that Brown's offending was becoming too persistent and serious to justify his continued use as an informant.

The problem of Clive Brown wishing to protect his son was well known to police. These issues had raised their head before and been dealt with by diverting police away from Darren Brown's minor offending. Given his familial circumstances, age, and offending trajectory, it can hardly come as a surprise that Darren Brown is now a person of interest in a homicide investigation. It was likely on the balance of probabilities that he was always going to get involved in something serious at some point. Bhat should have seen this coming a long time ago. This scenario is far from one that could not have been foreseen.

It does not appear that the right management framework is in place to support the risky informant management practices underway. Neyroud (2003) argues that a practical management framework needs to be in place to support ethical decision making, especially where high risk covert policing is taking place. The right compliance model needs to be in place. This consists of oversight at the tactical and operational levels. Chief Officers must be clear about their strategic responsibilities to ensure ethical conduct. There must be legal and societal control systems including oversight politically and through professional standards. Neyroud (2003) also argues that performance management of professional practice and public participation forms a credible whole in guiding police through ethical conundrums such as Bhat now faces.

These kinds of protective devices are absent for Bhat. Dealing with difficult people such as Brown means constant review, discussion, and oversight of ethical decisions. At each step along the way Bhat should have been able to seek credible and practical advice about where the relationship with Brown was heading.

Conclusion

Det Ch Insp Bhat faces a difficult decision. Her situation is complicated by decisions, presumptions, and weak management up to this point. There has been a lack of critical thinking, a lack of foresight, and weak informant management. The relationship between police and informant has become unbalanced. Questions should have been raised earlier about the ethics of turning a blind eye to Clive Brown's serious criminal offending. Clive Brown's commitment to his son Darren and Darren's criminal trajectory made the current scenario likely, if not inevitable. Guiding investigations away from previous violent offending by Darren Brown was ethically unsound. The lack of transparency to senior management about the ethical decisions being made concerning Clive Brown is highly problematic. Ideally these kinds of decisions should never be made by small groups behind closed doors. The compelling psychological desire within a small group for harmony can easily override a critical evaluation of alternatives. From the start questions should have been asked about whether police were the right agency to manage Clive Brown. Other agencies are better equipped, less ethically constrained, and due to the different ethical constraints they are under can better manage an informant like Clive Brown. No clear strong management structure is in place to prevent these kinds of problems arising.

However these issues commend this scenario. These problems are real world: systems fail and judgements are made quickly under pressure with good intentions. Of necessity sometimes decisions are made behind closed doors with little or no consultation. Policing is complex and often good intentions are substituted for good oversight and process. The prize of solving one serious problem by engaging Clive Brown as a CHIS always risked future problems. Nevertheless this scenario would be seductive to many senior officers. It would be very easy for an officer under pressure to minimise or ignore potential future problems. It would be easy to think that perhaps the risks around using Clive Brown would never materialise. Perhaps police could limit his offending? Perhaps Darren Brown will not emerge as a violent offender in the future? This kind of optimistic thinking could easily shape decisions to engage Clive Brown as a CHIS, effectively substituting a short-term win for a longer term problem. Experience, critical thinking, and excellent process would have averted this approach.

An interesting 'what if?' question also arises. The facts of this problem revolve around preventing terrorist acts against mosques and assassinations of leading Muslims. What if we were not preventing terrorist acts but dealing with a violent organised criminal gang poised to carry out acts of equivalent but non-terrorist violence. Would this change our approach to the facts? There does seem to be something in the attitude and approach of terrorists which is more threatening.

Perhaps it is our inability to understand or see anything rational in their actions which makes terrorism seem more dangerous. We are able to recognise the motivations of the violent criminal. We presume they are at some level making a rational choice to act in pursuit of profit and self-interest. These motivations we understand. The terrorist acts irrationally in pursuit of religious or extreme beliefs that we barely comprehend. This dimension adds an unpredictable element to terrorism which heightens fear and seems especially threatening and evil. The fear generated by terrorism makes prevention more urgent. If the loss of Clive Brown as an informant was merely leading to serious violent crime this might weaken our concern with fully investigating Darren Brown to eliminate him as a suspect. However Bhat has to address the terrorism scenario and we now consider what she should do.

What Bhat should do and what she is likely to do may be different. Bhat should not undertake the course of action she is contemplating. The best course of action for Bhat on balance is taking a very capable, trusted, and objective senior officer into her confidence. This will relieve her of her ethical dilemma. With luck the officer will bring a mature and experienced eye to the issues, will recognise the good intentions of Bhat and her colleagues, and have the wisdom to disentangle the situation with minimal damage to the parties concerned. The senior officer will explore all the options and come to a decision. It is likely Clive Brown will be either threatened with prosecution, prosecution being likely to expose him as an informant, or actually prosecuted. If we accept the facts as presented then Brown is lost as an informant. If we accept that prosecution or the threat of it will change his views on allowing the investigation to take its natural course, then all well and good. If not then other sources, methods, agencies, or approaches will need to be focused on the neo-Nazi group. I do not presume a 'Trolley Problem' scenario in the facts of this case, where the facts completely bound the problem and consequences from action are predictable with certainty.

The evolution of this problem for Bhat is understandable and plausible. Her proposal to resolve the issue is not. She is out of her depth and needs assistance. Both the current scenario and the extant problems around Clive Brown need to be addressed. Bhat and her colleagues cannot unpick these issues alone. The need for transparency and justice demands that wiser heads prevail.

References

Foot, P, 'The Problem of Abortion and the Doctrine of the Double Effect' (1967) 5 *Oxford Review* 5–15.

Kleinig, J, 'Ethical Policing', in A Wakefield and J Fleming (eds), *The Sage Dictionary of Policing* (London: Sage, 2009).

Neyroud, P, 'Policing and ethics', in T Newburn (ed), *Handbook of Policing* (Cullompton: Willan, 2003), pp 578–602.

Thomson, JJ, 'The Trolley Problem' (1995) 94 *Yale Law Journal* 1395–415.

Editor's Commentary

PAJ Waddington

'Dirty Business'

This scenario focuses on issues that have long lurked in the 'cloak and dagger' world of police intelligence, in which officers become deeply embroiled in complex relationships with informants who for various reasons are willing to inform or can be coerced into informing the police of the activities of their criminal or terrorist associates, accomplices, and others. Under the title of 'intelligence-led policing', this has been given additional emphasis in recent years. Why? I believe it is because 'intelligence-led' gives the appearance of clinical surgical incisions that remove something unpleasant in society or the 'body politic'. Instead of officers stopping and searching people who look 'out of place' or act in ways vaguely defined as 'suspicious', which invites allegations of prejudice and discrimination, the image of 'intelligence-led policing' is that officers will have acquired surreptitiously the evidence they need to intercept criminals and terrorists, leaving the rest of us to continue with our lives without let or hindrance. It is an appealing prospect, but its appeal leads us too readily to skate over the more difficult issues of how precisely this surreptitious evidence-gathering actually occurs and who gathers it.

Here the scenario involves us in one such issue. Clive Brown is a career criminal caught red-handed in possession of a large quantity of drugs and firearms. Facing a lengthy prison sentence, he has decided to cooperate with the police and act as an informant, a so-called 'CHIS'. 'Running informants' has long been regarded as the quintessential crime-fighting tool—combatting 'real crime' involving 'real villains'. Yet, academic research has also revealed it as an ethically compromising enterprise (Marx, 1988; Maguire and John, 1995, 2004). Informants who are not themselves involved in criminality or terrorism are hardly likely to be able to offer information of value, whereas, using 'participating informants' amounts to a conspiracy to allow criminality to continue. Because of this, such activity has increasingly been hedged around with rules and procedures. Money payments to informants need to be properly accounted for and informant handlers are required to make regular reports to senior officers. Yet, what takes place in the inevitably intimate conversations between informants and their handlers is difficult to verify and control. Most difficult of all to control are non-monetary inducements—favours. In this scenario we have precisely that: if the police keep Darren Brown out of the clutches of the criminal justice process, his father, Clive, will continue to act as an informant. This 'favour' does not exist in isolation: running informants involves a set of covert practices designed to protect the informant from fellow criminals and terrorists, but also from other police officers, prosecuting lawyers, the courts, and prison. An 'informant' who is under arrest has limited value as a source of information. So, when the police raid premises to arrest those incriminated by the informant, arrangements need to be made for the informant to escape capture. If by some mischance a valuable informant is arrested, it may be imperative to extricate this person from custody, misleading fellow officers and possibly prosecutors in the process.

As Steve Darroch remarks, it is 'a dirty business' and one whose 'dirtiness' has been repeatedly excused in the name of the 'war on terror'. We should, however, recognise that the 'dirtiness' of informant handling is not *sui generis*. Policing as a whole is pretty dirty, for, as Steve Darroch observes at the outset, police exercise 'exceptional powers' of using 'force and deception' and do so with 'discretion'. Since the case against Darren Brown is weak, it would not require much of an intervention for Detective Chief Inspector Bhat to de-rail it entirely. Had she been entirely ignorant of the existence of Clive and Darren Brown, she might nevertheless have observed that her superior and friend, Detective Chief Superintendent Dalrymple, was only pursuing Darren out of desperation to alleviate the public pressure for an arrest in a murder that had horrified the public. As Steve Darroch correctly observes, albeit in a slightly different context, 'police cannot solve all crimes' and the investigation of the murder of Byron Smart might in any case have been destined to grow cold.

Good v Evil

What makes this scenario exquisitely 'dirty' are the dramatis personae, which on one side features 'a perfect victim' in Byron Smart and on the other a violent thug, Darren Brown. Public outrage is stoked by Byron Smart's undoubted innocence: he was not capable of defending himself, still less of provoking some kind of fight. He was a disabled young man, nevertheless someone with much to contribute to wider society, and a committed Christian. The attack on him was purely predatory, motivated by some perverse enjoyment in victimising his helplessness. Disability Alliance activists in Britain have drawn attention to the frequency with which disabled people appear to fall victim to such 'hate crime'. Darren is the son of a man who deals in drugs and guns, and who is prepared to sacrifice his associates in order to secure his and his son's immunity. If the police obstruct the course of justice in such a case they are most definitely accepting a Faustian pact.

Steve Darroch imaginatively hopes that with better management or a less principled agency doing the managing, this situation could have been avoided. However, we should note that other intelligence agencies may be no less principled than the police, but simply pursue different goals. It is certainly true that had Clive Brown been an informant on behalf of the Revenue and Customs authorities, or secret intelligence service, then any attempt to de-rail the investigation of Byron Smart's murder by either service would need to be quite explicit and would be dealt with at a higher level than that occupied by Det Ch Insp Bhat. By being in the position that she now occupies, she can achieve the outcome that perhaps the security authorities would prefer without formal permission being granted. By giving Dalrymple the same advice as she might otherwise have done, that would be sufficient. Of course, there is no evidence in the scenario that Clive Brown has been poorly managed. It could equally have been the case that the arrangements were approved at a very high level within the police, albeit secretly. Who is to say that it has not been approved by an elected official, perhaps even the relevant Minister or head of Government? The Abu Ghraib saga tells us that such possibilities are entirely plausible. Would it make any difference if it had been?

Friends in a Jam

In this specific case Steve Darroch joins John Kleinig in emphasising the need to share and discuss intensely difficult ethical dilemmas. Steve Darroch understands well enough the intense pressures that Det Ch Insp Bhat would feel in such a situation. She is on a knife-edge and that is not a good location from which to contemplate fateful decisions. Consulting a trusted superior is good advice: what is needed is a cool head, unencumbered by the baggage of deals done, and an objective appraisal of the risks. Much hangs on the credibility of Clive Brown's threat to withdraw cooperation, but from a disinterested perspective this threat looks more than a little threadbare. It would result in Clive Brown's immediate arrest and almost certain imprisonment, in which his status as a 'snitch' (in prison parlance) would make for a very uncomfortable way of serving a sentence. It would be spent almost certainly in near solitary confinement and whilst the authorities might make his stay in prison as secure as could be arranged, there would the perpetual danger of assassination by or on behalf of his former associates. Even more threatening is life after prison, for one can only imagine who might be waiting for Clive Brown upon his release from custody! Compared to a life spent in the shadow of threatened assassination, continuing to inform despite his son's arrest and possible conviction for murder, must be a better option.

Ethics and Power

Throughout his discussion of this very difficult dilemma, Steve Darroch keeps the issues clearly within an ethical frame of reference. However, in considering the credibility of Clive Brown's threat, he does note with some satisfaction that Clive Brown is in a perilous situation. As already noted, if Clive's status as a CHIS were to become public, say during his or Darren's trial, his life would be in danger. Might it not be possible to draw his perilous position to his attention? Perhaps he believes that he holds all the cards, whereas the police hold 'the joker'. Indeed, the worst case scenario for Clive Brown is not to be arrested, but to be cast adrift amongst those he has 'snitched' on. It is a classic 'Dirty Harry problem' as Carl Klockars described it (Klockars, 1985): the use of 'dirty means' to achieve a virtuous goal.

Would this be ethical? Probably not, but what is the ethical relationship that exists between Clive Brown and the police? Brown is not a CHIS for reasons of virtue, he is exploiting the police's dependency upon the information that he has and continues to gain from participating in serious criminal conduct that damages innocent people's lives and communities. What is more, Brown is holding to ransom those same people in order to receive favourable treatment for himself and enabling his son to escape justice. If, now, Brown finds the 'tables turned' to his disadvantage, is he not simply the author of his own misfortune? What possible ethical obligation does Det Ch Insp Bhat or any other police officer owe to Clive Brown? The danger of taking such a course is not that it would violate some supposed ethical responsibility to Brown, but that it would involve the police in undermining their own legitimacy. Suppose it works, what is to stop the police using similar methods against others, perhaps those less venal than Clive Brown? Once police embrace the use of illegitimate means of achieving desirable goals, experience teaches us that it is very difficult to cease to do so (Punch, 2009). What would Det Ch Insp Bhat do if she found subordinates engaged in similar tactics in dealing with other cases? She would have abandoned the moral high ground and with it the moral right to call others who 'push the envelope' to account.

References

Klockars, CB, 'The Dirty Harry problem', in F Elliston and M Feldberg (eds), *Moral Issues in Police Work* (Totowa, NJ: Rowman and Allanheld, 1985), pp 55–71.

Maguire, M and John, T, 'Intelligence, Surveillance and Information: Integrated Approaches', *Crime Detection and Prevention Series Paper 64* (London: Home Office, 1995).

Maguire, M and John, T, *The National Intelligence Model: Key lessons from early research: Home Office Online Report 30/04* (Home Office, 2004).

Marx, GT, *Undercover: Police Surveillance in America* (Berkeley: University of California, 1988).

Punch, M, *Police Corruption: Deviance, Accountability and Reform in Policing* (Collumpton: Willan, 2009).

Author's Response

Steve Darroch

'Pushing the Envelope'

Professor Waddington neatly sums up the challenges facing Detective Chief Inspector Bhat in his concluding comments; she is indeed 'pushing the envelope'. Unfortunately envelope pushing, corner cutting, dodging or sidestepping, trying to skirt around ethical problems, is no way to police. In reality, skirting around ethical problems may be the undoing of Det Ch Insp Bhat and cooler more reflective thinking must prevail. In fact, as I argue in my response, the current problems were always likely to emerge given the way Clive Brown has been managed. This is not to criticise the scenario. I applaud the scenario because it mirrors reality. Good intentions and smart systems do break down in the face of reality. Why would this be any different for handling participating informants? As I write this response the cover up and misdirection by police following the Hillsbrough tragedy is all over the media and internet (Hillsborough Independent Panel, 2012; see also <http://www.bbc.co.uk/news/uk-england-merseyside-19577033>). Why would we expect the 'dirty business' of CHIS management to be any less susceptible to human frailty?

I agree with Professor Waddington that 'intelligence-led policing' is a clinical term for a much messier business. This messiness is most pronounced at the heart of the police informant exchange—the favour. Clive Brown and the police are exchanging favours, information for operating space and the remission of charges. Layered onto this we add the complicating insistence from Brown that his son be left alone and a confusing backcloth of personal relationships, career dynamics, and genuine uncertainty around Darren Brown's involvement and the likely actions of police; whether nudged by Bhat or not. How wonderfully real world!

Professor Waddington argues there is no evidence that Clive Brown was poorly managed. For me this is both implied in the scenario and understandable. There would not be much to discuss if there were not issues or difficulties. Although not stated explicitly it is difficult to imagine the presented scenario without conclud-ing there have been deficiencies in the handling of Clive Brown. We see this most clearly in the dilemma itself; Det Ch Insp Bhat is wrestling with a conundrum in isolation. This is all playing out in her head—'what do I do next?' Rather than 'ideal type' participating informant management involving a well managed, properly structured, experienced police team, with appropriate visibility and apportioned accountability Bhat is on her own. Where is the senior management team that should be providing professional oversight? As I argue, the absence of transparency is the real issue and implies a lack of appropriate management to this point. My central argument is that Bhat should not be a police Lone Ranger battling in isolation to resolve a complex ethical dilemma involving a participat-ing informant. If Bhat were part of a mature team then the next steps in manag-ing Clive Brown would be deliberate and, importantly, visible to the right people. I argue that experience and visibility matter, especially in the messy world of informant management. It is not being Pollyannaish to argue for clear, experi-enced ethical supervision nor is it impossible to achieve. Even if, as this scenario highlights, it is difficult to achieve.

I completely agree that Clive Brown is likely overplaying his hand. He is much more confident of his ability to manipulate the situation than he should be. As I note, his withdrawal of cooperation brings serious personal risks into play. Police do have an opportunity to press an argument about his personal vulner-ability to Brown and think seriously about reviewing his status as a participating CHIS. There is also a good argument for Brown to be prosecuted, that the risk he poses through his own offending is too great to bear. As I argue, there is more than one way to prevent terrorism and more than one agency operating to pre-vent terrorism. Again, narrow thinking and taking too much personal responsi-bility push people into making ethical compromises.

If we accept that Brown is vulnerable then it seems hard to escape the conclu-sion that police do have a 'duty of care' towards him. Brown has done plenty to make himself liable to meet a sticky end. His career choice and associates make that a persistent threat. Living outside the law comes with risks. However, having now been brought into a relationship with police, this exponentially increases his risk profile, Police cannot, Pontius Pilate-like, wash their hands of Brown and walk away. To push the metaphor, that surely leaves blood on their hands. Police knew the risks Brown was taking on, encouraged and facilitated him, and now have both the responsibility and resources to protect Brown should he need it; protection of life being the core police accountability. Brown may be the author of his own misfortune but some responsibilities and duties are too fundamental to walk away from. Should Brown be killed after being cast adrift by police then police have a genuine crisis on their hands. They need to do all they can to pro-tect him from himself. That comes with the territory.

In the end pressure needs to be brought to bear on Clive Brown to adjust his thinking. He is at risk and his son Darren needs to be cleared in the death of Byron Smart. Brown is not in a position to back up the threats he is making. His bluff can be called. Preventing terrorism is a responsibility across multiple agencies and the community. If reliable intelligence points to an imminent terrorist threat then all resources need to be brought to bear. That done, there is a high probability of prevention. Clive Brown is one cog in a big machine and a compromised one at that. Let not the tail wag the dog.

Reference

Hillsborough Independent Panel, 'Hillsborough: The Report of the Hillsborough Independent Panel' (London: The Stationery Office, 2012).

PART SIX

Public Order

Scenario: Public Order

Assistant Chief Constable (ACC) Jason Andrewski is responsible for public order operations in his police area, a role that he greatly relishes and in which he has excelled. It was his experience and success as a public order commander that persuaded the appointments committee to appoint him as ACC. Now he faces one of his most challenging tasks.

The police area hosts one of the largest nuclear power stations in the country. Facing the prospect that existing electricity generating capacity will shortly be insufficient to satisfy demand and that there have been no replacements in electricity generation for more than a decade, creating the prospect of an imminent 'energy gap', the government has announced a programme of major renewal, especially that of nuclear-powered generation. This is regarded by many of the best informed advisors consulted by government as the least environmentally damaging. However, a nuclear-powered generation plant takes years to construct and the 'energy gap' is pressing. The government has taken several strategic decisions that are proving extremely controversial amongst environmentalists. First, they have committed themselves to the renewal and expansion of nuclear generating capacity. Environmentalists object to this on several grounds, not least of which is that the government's claim that nuclear generation has a small 'carbon footprint' is unsound. They claim that whilst nuclear-powered electricity generation produces less CO_2, this pays no heed to the carbon released into the atmosphere during the lifetime of the plant, and especially during its construction. They also point to the long-term environmental hazard arising from the need to store nuclear waste for the indefinite future. The government's proposal to create storage facilities deep underground is rejected by environmentalists who argue that it risks contamination of ground water supplies and that the area selected for storage is not as seismically stable as the government contends. Environmentalists also worry at the dangers of fissile material becoming incorporated into weapons and the dangers of terrorist attack both on the plant itself and on convoys transporting nuclear waste to the storage facility some distance away. Finally, they maintain that investment in renewable energy would be much more effective.

Secondly, fearing that controversy would hold up the development of these sites, the government has passed new planning laws designed to expedite the construction of these plants. This has further stimulated opposition to the construction of nuclear-powered electricity generation, with environmentalists being joined by a much wider constituency of campaigners who believe that an ill-considered 'dash for energy' is being forced through against the wishes of local residents.

Finally, another feature of the government's programme that has enraged its opponents is the decision to entrust the construction and operation to private capital. Opponents believe that nuclear power is so inherently dangerous that it should be under the direct control of government.

The large nuclear power plant in ACC Andrewski's area is coming to the end of its useful life. At formal lunches and dinners where he has come into contact with executives of the existing power plant, they have told him that keeping the plant operating safely is proving an increasingly daunting challenge. Privately, they confess their doubts that the existing plant will be able to remain in operation until its replacement comes on stream.

At least ACC Andrewski comforted himself with the knowledge that since a nuclear plant already existed on the selected site and many local residents were employed there, this was likely to mitigate local hostility to the plan. However, investigative journalists have uncovered documents relating to the American parent company that operates plants in the USA and other countries. These documents reveal that the US Federal authorities have been investigating the construction standards and operating practices of the company's plants throughout North America and have arrived at disturbing conclusions. Those documents show what the Federal authorities believe to be serious design flaws in the type of reactor used by the company. They also document several instances of 'safety critical failures' in the operation of one of its nine plants in the USA. These allegations have recently been broadcast in a BBC 'Panorama Special' television programme. Added to which there are further allegations of wrongdoing by the company in other ventures in the developing world; it is claimed that they have exploited the lax health and safety standards in various countries resulting in many workers suffering ill-health and workplace injuries and deaths. These revelations and accusations have united environmentalist opinion with that of proponents of 'global justice' into fiercely opposing the building of this particular plant.

Together all this has led campaigners to hold a 'Climate Camp' in the immediate vicinity of the sole entrance and exit to the plant. Police have become aware of these plans through the monitoring of internet sites. Officers, assuming false internet identities, have succeeded in obtaining access to discussions amongst the militant factions regarding their intentions. Although they are rarely explicit about the actions they intend to take, it appears on the face of it that some militants intend to scale the exterior of the 'containment' building which houses the reactor core. Once atop this spherical building the militants plan to unfurl a huge banner that they will bring with them to the site. When unfurled, the banner will depict a very realistic image of a large crack in the exterior of the containment building. This image is apparently extremely realistic and will give the appearance that the containment building has indeed been severely damaged. Credibility will be lent to this conclusion, because the unfurling of the banner will be accompanied by a pre-planned eruption of calls to local and national news outlets claiming to have heard an explosion at the site. Militants have been very clear that they will not cause any actual damage to any part of the power plant (apart from minor damage to the perimeter fence in order to gain entry). Their sister organisation in the USA pulled a similar 'stunt' a few years previously when a small group of activists scaled a huge dam serving a hydro-electric plant. They unfurled a banner depicting an immense crack in the dam's wall, again accompanied by a coordinated spike of contrived calls to news outlets falsely reporting an 'explosion'. In that case, the response was immediate: residential communities downstream of the plant fled in panic from what they thought was the imminent collapse of the dam which threatened to flood them. There was so much chaos that the state Governor declared a 'state of emergency'; there is a strong likelihood that there would be a similar panic in response to a credible suggestion that the containment building housing the reactor core had been breached. None of those involved in the American escapade were convicted of any offence, not least because they benefited from the First Amendment protection of free speech enshrined in the US Constitution. Militants involved in the current campaign in ACC Andrewski's police area appear to believe that they will receive similar protection under Articles 10 and 11 of the European Convention on Human Rights.

There are additional complications to what is already appearing to be a formidable public order challenge. The most significant of these is that the multinational corporation that will build and operate the reactor has made it clear to the government in Whitehall that any interference with its construction or operation, including the operation of the existing plant that it has taken over, will not only result in disinvestment at the particular site, but it would also cause their withdrawal from all other sites across the country. Since this corporation is by far the biggest provider, this represents a significant threat to the critical national infrastructure. At a recent meeting with local Members of Parliament, the police were confidentially told that the government felt that the corporation 'had them over a barrel' and there was no alternative but to accede to the corporation's demands. In addition, it has emerged that the corporation has employed security personnel to infiltrate the militant environmentalist groups. ACC

169

Andrewski and his ACPO colleagues are privately worried about the activities of these 'undercover' operatives. They fear that the corporation's 'undercover' personnel will act as agents provocateurs towards the militants, prompting them to cause real damage, and thereby strengthening demands by corporation executives to have the militants arrested for criminal damage, or even conspiracy to commit criminal damage, prior to them invading the site.

Even if the police feel justified in preventing militants from entering the site, they are hampered by an absence of clear identification of who the militants are. So far, much of the intelligence has been gained over the internet. Given that the militants have a well-earned reputation for being highly 'surveillance aware', it is unlikely that any of the identities they have assumed for the purpose of internet conversations will reveal their true identity. Moreover, they may suspect that the police have been infiltrating internet communications and they may have laid false trails. It is almost certain that the militants will camouflage themselves by blending with the much larger majority of concerned citizens who seem likely to descend on the power plant, but have no intention of invading the site or doing damage to it. However, since the organisers of this 'legitimate' protest have refused to comply with the notification requirements of the Public Order Act, or enter into any communication, still less negotiation, with the police, any marches or similar activity conducted as part of the protest will be unlawful.

As ACC Andrewski begins to plan the policing strategy, what options does he have? Which of them deserve serious consideration and which should be dismissed out of hand? Can you explain the grounds on which you would include or exclude options? Which is the most favoured option, and why is it favoured?

What are the likely possible consequences of different kinds of police action? How can the worst of these be mitigated? How can the most favourable consequences be encouraged? What obstacles and hazards stand in the way of achieving success and avoiding failure?

Is there anything that the police might have been able to do to avoid finding themselves in their current dilemma? If so, why would those courses of action not have been pursued at an earlier stage?

Addressing the Scenario

Nuclear Power Plant Scenario: Responding to a Complex Public Order Policing Situation

Monique Marks and Sean Tait

> *In situations where rights conflict, compromise is usually the best approach. Authoritarian societies are defined by order without liberty. Yet democratic societies can only exist with both liberty and order (Gillham and Marx, 2000: 230).*

Protests are generally difficult to manage and to police. Police engaged in public order policing generally have a number of strategic objectives. These include maintaining public order, protecting all targets of protest, enforcing laws, upholding the rights of protesters, and protecting the safety of all actors and of property. At the same time, the police in public order situations want to avoid, as far as possible, any form of 'trouble' (Waddington, 1994). While public order situations, particularly of environmental groupings, might be complex and tricky, there is always room for discretion and for choice amongst a wide range of tactics and strategies.

While the policing of public order has always been complex and somewhat paradoxical, in recent years the emergence of professional environmental protest groups has rendered protest policing even more complicated. As Button et al wrote in 2002:

> During the last 10 years there has been an intensification of protests using direct action and other campaigning methods concerning some environmental issues

that have posed new challenges to policing organisations. Typified by protests against the construction of the Newbury bypass in England during 1996, the public police and other policing agencies have been faced with the task of policing a diverse variety of protesters ranging from middle class women, concerned residents, to committed environmental protesters. The latter has led these diverse groups in developing an innovative and extensive range of tactics that have provided a new experience for policing agencies in public order policing. (2002: 18)

Policing public order was always about placing oneself between conflicting interests and needs. Unlike many other policing situations which take place in more hidden spaces, off-camera and outside of public scrutiny, public order policing is very much in the public view. ACC Andrewski is well aware of the multiple audiences that will be viewing and evaluating his leadership capacity, his positioning, and operational savvy. In situations such as the one facing ACC Andrewski, there is little margin for error but there exists an extensive range of tactical interventions and partnerships in the policing of environmental protest. The decisions ACC Andrewski and his commanders make today will have considerable consequences for the image of the police, for government and his relationship with his political masters, and for service delivery of energy to the public. These decisions are likely to be carefully monitored by a range of stakeholder groupings, both traditional and non-traditional, state and non-state. Environmental issues and the protests that emerge from determinations of government and the private sector which impact on the environment resonate with a wide range of social groupings.

Button et al (2002) make the point that what have emerged in recent decades are protesters who can best be described as 'Militant Environmental Activists' (MEAs). MEAs 'are primarily distinguished by their central pursuit of innovative "direct action" tactics, deep ecological consciousness, and a non-bureaucratic organizational structure' (Button et al, 2002: 20). They also have a very fluid membership. The environmental group discussed in the scenario provided appears to fall into the category of MEAs. This group is therefore likely to include 'professional protesters' who are very well organised, knowledgeable about protest action and the issues they are protesting about, and are governed by unwritten codes of conduct. The MEAs pose what Button et al determine to be 'the greatest challenge to policing organisations' (2002: 22).

This could mean trying to prevent any demonstrations associated with the protest from being staged in the first place. In our view, the worst possible strategy for ACC Andrewski to consider, and implement, would be to bring in as many reinforcements as he can muster, make mass arrests, and prevent protest demonstrations from taking place. Such an intervention would fly in the face of the legal right to protest, as well as international trends in public order policing in liberal democracies toward negotiated solutions/management (della Porta and Reiter, 1998). Techniques that are discursive (ie reliant on 'talk' and deliberation as a means of creating solutions) are now viewed as preferable, although international scans of recent public order events—particularly of 'new' global social movements—have demonstrated that there is a creeping hard law enforcement approach in the emerging global system (Sheptycki, 2005). ACC Andrewski would be wise to avoid situations that follow such trends that have been evidenced even in established liberal democracies such as Canada and the United States.

Resorting to 'hard' policing strategies has proven to be somewhat ineffective. Where police have used tear gas to disperse crowds, innovative protesters are often one step ahead. In the demonstrations against the World Trade Organization in Seattle, for example, protestors brought their own tear gas masks, and made use of these when the police deployed tear gas. The result was an escalation of conflict between the police and protesters, an increase in the use of force by the police, and increasing acts of civil disobedience by protesters (Gillham and Marx, 2000). Given this, it is important that a seasoned officer such as ACC Andrewski has a very clear sense of the environment that he is to police and the various audiences that will be scrutinising his responses and his planning. His profile indicates that he is a sensitive, informed, and astute police commander and that he is likely to examine the entire policing environment before deciding on a plan, or engaging with the various stakeholders.

As Sheptycki has noted, in liberal democracies, senior police and commanders, such as ACC Andrewski:

> ...scan their external environment when making decisions about policy and practice. Police officials in liberal democracies are concerned with how legal audiences (the courts and legal authorities) and occupational audiences (the police rank-and-file) will interpret and judge policies that shape policing practice 'on the ground'. They are also guided by expectations as to how policing policy will play to the public generally. It is not that all audiences are given equal weight, but all are given some weight in democratic societies. (2005: 330)

ACC Andrewski will no doubt be engaging in such a 'scan' before deciding on a particular strategy and determining the range of tactics that is available to him in policing this complex event. From all reports, one of the most important lessons that ACC Andrewski has learnt over his years of service is never overtly to take sides, never to veer from the compass which was the law, and to gather all information about the proposed or planned protests before and during the event. He will be acutely aware that whatever operational decisions are determined, tradeoffs will be made. He is probably also aware, however uncomfortable this may be, that he is bound to his political masters and that, ultimately, police in his situation engage in actions that 'tilt decisively in favour of the more powerful' (Gillham and Marx, 2000). ACC Andrewski will have to determine whether or not he bows to political masters, and how he can develop a strategy which evens out the balance of power, allowing all parties to feel that their voices are heard and that the policing responses are fair and considered.

The Dilemmas at Hand

ACC Andrewski has opted for a strategy of negotiating and managing an acceptable expression of protest. It has required him to work tirelessly in the week leading up to the event to identify and meet parties, establish short-, medium-, and long-term processes mediated by appropriate authorities, and identify the least harmful opportunities for them to express their message. However, the scenario provided is one that is likely to be extremely difficult to police for a number of reasons.

First, government will want to assert its primacy in dictating policing outcomes and strategies because it will not want its own service delivery programme to be brought into disrepute or to be disrupted. Secondly, the environmental groupings are known for engaging in a range of protest actions that are innovative, radical, well organised, and often strategised in covert ways (Holloway, 1998; Button et al, 2002). Thirdly, the community has a stake both in their own health and safety, and in basic energy provision. A wide ranging group of people in terms of class, age, and political affiliation are likely to support at least tacitly the campaign of the environmental activists. Fourthly, there is also a history of tense relations between the police and environmental groupings. Despite this, the police need to be able to treat the environmental activists in ways which are procedurally fair and tolerant. The public are likely to be divided and somewhat confused about what is an appropriate policing and political response to this dilemma.

Fifthly, the private sector companies involved are likely to assert their 'muscle' through threats of disinvestment and disengagement from existing projects. The police need to develop mechanisms for engaging with this stakeholder that demonstrate an understanding and an appreciation of their investment and the impact of implementing their programme of action should the demonstration occur. Sixthly, the stated programmatic response of the private sector is likely to antagonise organised workers who also have a vested interest in securing existing jobs and in creating new work opportunities. Seventhly, the leaders of the environmental groupings have indicated that they are not willing to negotiate with the police about the nature of the protest and this makes prior consultative planning extremely difficult. This is not surprising given that MEAs are generally characterised by non-bureaucratic structures, with no formal hierarchy or leadership strata. They tend to operate in ways that are somewhat secretive, or 'underground' (see Lee, 1995).

Eighthly, the police could come under serious criticism from 'freedom of expression' groupings should it be discovered that they have infiltrated social networks and compromised privacy given that this can seriously undermine core democratic rights and the effects of such invasions can be extremely destructive for individuals, government, and other interest groupings. Ninthly, the police have to be responsive to government while at the same time working within a legal framework and international conventions that provide for the peaceful policing of demonstration, protest, and freedom of expression.

Policing Strategies Available to ACC Andrewski

Ideally the ACC should be able to call together the key stakeholders to discuss government's plans, the involvement of the private sector, and the concerns of environmental activists. Part of this discussion would include allowing all parties to state publicly their 'logics' and to lay claim to these as peacefully and constructively as possible, allowing the police to play a role as negotiators, mediators, conflict resolution specialists, and public protectors. Unfortunately, such a coming together of interested parties is unlikely to occur because the leaders of the environmental movement are not willing to negotiate their strategies, the private sector appears to have a threatening disposition, and government is beholden to what it perceives to be the 'best interest' of the public (in regard to energy supply) and to private companies who are the suppliers.

This leaves the police in a situation where they will have to meet with government and the multinational companies separately from the environmental leaders. The starting premise of the police should be framed by national and international conventions and legal frameworks that facilitate peaceful protest, even if these are not deemed to be 'legal', or are subject to the planning requirements of the police and other relevant authorities. This framework or starting point has to be carefully explained to government and to the multinational companies. It is incumbent on the ACC to explain his role and the role of his officers to these two stakeholders—to facilitate peaceful protest, to protect life and property, to resolve conflict, to maintain public order, and to investigate crime and violence. In so doing the police commander is taking account of the needs of all stakeholders and acknowledging a conflict of interests which is difficult to work out. The ACC has demonstrated that he is a leader in reading up extensively on the use of nuclear energy and advantages and disadvantages of the route that government has chosen. The ACC has also shown that he is forward thinking through his engagement with social networks and cyber technology in trying to establish the 'mindset' and the strategic thinking of the environmental groupings that are likely to engage in protest action. This information could be shared selectively with representatives from government and the multinational company.

However, the ACC needs to ensure that all information that is gathered is obtained through legal means, and as transparently as possible. If this is not the case, it will raise the ire of environmental groupings and create legal dilemmas for the police which could limit their ability to respond as a non-aligned public service provider. Having said this, it is important to take into account that there may be very little time between the various events and meetings that seem to be scheduled by the environmental groupings. The consequence of this is that the ACC would have to ensure that there is an active network of agents and that a broad legal mandate is given for gathering intelligence through covert means. And there is always the likelihood that even a well organised network will be unable to zone in on all the communication that is taking place within the environmental social movement that is organising these events.

It would be wise for the ACC to encourage both of these parties (industry and government) to consider the concerns of the environmental activists and to engage with these in the public media. By so doing, government would demonstrate that it is equally concerned with the possible environmental impact of the use of nuclear energy and the problems with the existing sites. Such a public engagement would hopefully lead to some response from environmental activists and a constructive public debate. Members of the public should be encouraged to have their say in this debate, particularly those who live close to the proposed and existing nuclear energy sites.

None of this is likely to curtail the plans of the environmental activists. The police therefore need to continue with their attempts to infiltrate social networks to gain information about when and where and how protest action will take place. The ACC does not want to lose control, nor does he want to be caught off-guard or be faced with a situation where on the spur of the moment he has to enforce ultimate restrictions because he was ill-prepared due to a lack of intelligence. The ACC will need to be able to defend this form of 'undercover' work, in much the same way that they would have to in the case of the infiltration of gangs, drug lords, and other groupings that threaten the well-being of the broader community. This infiltration and perhaps even hacking tactic is critical given that the ACC is aware that what is 'openly' declared as plans by the environmental activists may not match the action that they take. However the ACC must ensure that such infiltration and 'undercover' intelligence gathering is done legally. Responsible courts or legal regulators must approve the use of such intelligence interventions by demonstrating the dangers of not intercepting social networks and if possible showing that something illegal is or might be communicated on social networks and in email correspondence between environmental group leaders and their followers.

Using infiltration in these circumstances is generally riskier than the infiltration of criminal groupings because environmental activists operate on the premise that their activities are in the broad public interest. If the public (particularly human rights groupings) came to know about such police tactics, they could easily denounce the activities of the police as undemocratic, despite knowing that radical environmental actions can quickly take on a criminal character. ACC Andrewski would have to develop a very clear set of legitimations for such interventions and be able to use information in selective ways ensuring that at all times the right to protest against 'weak' government planning has value but can negatively impact on the provision of public goods and public safety more broadly. The obstruction of provision (even temporarily) of energy supplies can lead to massive inconvenience and even to health and safety risks such as in the supply of emergency services.

The ACC needs to create an operational strategy that ensures that the team responsible for public order policing is easily mobilised and properly equipped to intervene at short notice, especially for undisclosed and spontaneous forms of protest. The environmental activists have stated clearly that they do not want to engage in violent forms of protest. The ACC should therefore not plan for a 'worst possible scenario'. A strong law enforcement approach, such as banning all protest demonstrations on the nuclear site or making mass arrests, is likely to antagonise the environmental activists, escalate the potential for conflict and disorder, and create further distance between the police and environmental activists. While representatives from industry and possibly even from government might suggest banning all anticipated protest demonstrations or mass arrests, such tactics are likely to be counter-productive. Mass arrests are likely to exacerbate tension between police and protesters, and possibly drive the protest underground and encourage subversion. If such a tactic was used, the police would lose the moral high ground and create the possibility for 'on the job trouble', ie risk to the safety of officers (Waddington, 2003). The police would then find themselves subjected to heightened public and media scrutiny. A possible consequence of this would be increased sympathy for the protest from a diverse set of people, as well as political fallout for police leaders (Waddington, 2003). The use of mass arrests then would bring negative publicity to the police and raise the voices of the environmental activists.

Having said this, the ACC has to think very carefully about what tactics the police will employ when the environmental activists do take action. In so doing, he has to bear in mind the warnings that have been expressed by the multinational company which has 'instructed' government (via the police) to arrest activists that try to destabilise the construction of the nuclear energy sites. The use of arrests of 'ringleaders' as a strategy might be beneficial for all parties. It is the preferred policing tactic for the multinational company, and therefore would be a good tactic for government who need to keep the company 'on-side'. It might also be a good tactic for the protesters as it would bring extensive attention to their cause if some activists were arrested and this was reported in the popular media. More innovative policing of protest and demonstrations, has, in fact, involved the negotiated arrest of protesters with leaders of protesting organisations. These 'staged' arrests (rather than mass arrests) have proven very successful as they reduce conflict between police and protest organisers and they provide a

177

mechanism for bringing public attention to the cause at hand. Members of the public are usually sympathetic towards protestors whose freedoms have been curtailed when their actions are peaceful.

While the selective arrest tactic is definitely preferable to a mass arrest approach, this tactic could also lead to an escalation of conflict between police and protesters. The protesters have declared that they do not want to cause any damage. They might therefore expect the police to employ tactics that are more distant and non-invasive. Such an approach would mean that protestors would be aware that the police are present, but in the background, facilitating public protest while at the same time ensuring that they are able to intervene if protest becomes damaging to persons or property or if public disorder breaks out. A line of police trained in public order policing would then need to be available and ready to disperse and arrest, if necessary. They would be placed some distance from the planned protest to avoid unnecessary antagonism between the police and the protesters. Direct police intervention here would be a last resort, rather than a first response.

Given that the leaders of the environmental groupings refuse to negotiate, it will not be possible for the police to prearrange a staged arrest. However, the ACC could arrange for plain clothes police officers to become part of the protest and to use their 'insider' position to inform leaders of this possible strategy at the point at which the protest takes place. Should this tactic be used, it is likely to be a very delicate arrangement. Protesters might 'out' the police, and this has the potential of antagonising the multinational companies who will feel that the police have 'sided' with the protestors. Moreover, if protest leaders do not have tight control over those engaged in the demonstration, conflict could erupt between the police and those protesters who might feel that the police are undermining their right to demonstrate and speak freely. While the police may be under pressure from government and from industry to disperse protesters as early in the event as possible, ACC Andrewski should bear in mind that once the police engage in mass dispersal tactics (often using force), disorderly behaviour is likely to result. This was evidenced in the case of the World Trade Organization protests in Seattle where protesters began to break windows and throw objects at the police only when police used force to disperse en masse (Postman and Carter, 1999).

ACC Andrewski will be acutely aware that he has a responsibility to protect the bystanders and onlookers at any protest event activities that may emerge. As far as possible, he should make use of tactics that least impact (physically and emotionally) on non-participants and bystanders. It is for this reason that it would be unwise for the police to make use of tear gas since tear gas is fairly indiscriminate in its reach and its use can lead to a fair amount of panic from those who have not been exposed to tear gas previously, or are unaware of its impact.

If tactics such as a planned and negotiated arrest are not feasible, other forms of intervention might be required if a protest action is embarked upon which brings condemnation from government, the private sector, or the public. The possibility of this occurring is strong given how emotive this situation is. It would therefore seem wise for the ACC to deploy his officers around the outermost perimeter of the buildings which are to be 'hijacked', but to do this in a way that is distant and non-interventionist. A small but robust team of police, such as an intervention or special task unit, needs to be available as 'invisible' back-up/reinforcement. This highly skilled police group should have the capacity, skills, and equipment to be able to move swiftly onto the scene and arrest those who are involved in harmful activities. They should also be able to quickly apply less-than-lethal force to deflect those protesters who are engaged in damaging or harmful activities.

The larger contingent of police officers deployed at the scene should then be instructed to be present and visible at a fair distance from the building that is likely to be invaded. They should then be able to form a perimeter around the site at short notice if required. They should have excellent cordoning skills. Given that the protesters are unlikely to be armed, the officers should be equipped with shields for protection against objects that might be thrown at them, and with water cannon to facilitate dispersal if this is required. The police should be instructed to avoid the use of any weapons or equipment that could lead to injury, but they must have adequate equipment (such as shields and helmets) to protect themselves against any form of attack from onlookers and from protesters.

These 'reinforcement' officers' should not be highly visible unless acts of disorder, public or property harm, occur. It has been shown time and again that the very presence of police with heavy body armour, riot helmets, and visible weapons may in itself be a symbol of antagonism and appear antithetical to claims to democratic policing methods and outcomes (Jefferson, 1990). Protesters viewing heavily armed police may respond more aggressively than might have been the case with a less threatening police presence (Gillham and Marx, 2000). If the police do engage in 'rough tactics', news of this is likely to spread quickly leading to an increased sense of solidarity among protesters, as well as solidarity between protesters and onlookers/bystanders. Having said this, environmental activists might even resort to what Button et al (2002) refer to as 'ecotage'. This includes, according to Button et al (2002), sabotage of equipment, vehicles and publicity materials, and even the intimidation of (senior) police officers. Should this occur, reinforcement officers should be prepared to cordon off areas that could be identified as targets either through the use of fences or through forming a police line separating protesters from crowd members. Shield cordons are another tactic that should be considered to facilitate moving a crowd backwards. This would mean that reinforcement officers must be equipped with long shields that can be locked together. Shield cordons are a useful means for allowing police officers to dart into a crowd in order to arrest 'provocateurs' and then bring them back behind the line.

Engaging the Media

The anticipated event is likely to attract a fair amount of attention from the media since nuclear energy and service delivery are very sensitive issues, both for the general public and for government. Holloway (1998) has made the point that MEAs tend to exploit the press as much as possible as a way of achieving their objectives. The press is important to MEAs since they document the debates surrounding environmental issues, as well as the standpoints of environmental activists. The media also publicise campaigns and events organised by environmental groupings, and the interventions of the government in regard to protests and demonstrations. MEAs use the press to garner public support which will put pressure on government and the private sector to facilitate a public inquiry into proposed developments or plans that are viewed as environmentally damaging (Lamb, 1996). The ACC needs to bear in mind that in most environmental campaigns the activists are joined by a diverse range of other groups and individuals. Middle-aged, middle-class men and women, and prominent conservatives often protest alongside radical activists (Button et al, 2002: 27). This means that police planning must be proactive and must account for possible antagonism by varied population groupings should the police act aggressively or give law and order primacy over the right to freedom of expression and association.

Given the fact that the MEAs make very effective use of the popular media, as well as the reality that the policing of such events is at any rate of public and political interest, it is critical that a well-informed police communications officer be in constant contact with the media, informing them about the issues at hand, the conflicting standpoints of the various stakeholders, and the plans that the police have to deal with protest action. Having one or more outstanding police press liaison persons cannot be overstated. Police who have been involved in policing such sensitive events in the past have pursued a range of strategies to maintain ground with the media.

The police could consider exploiting the public media to communicate directly with the protesters and to ensure that everyone is aware of what the police are prepared to offer and what tactics they are likely to employ in particular circumstances. This would provide the police with a means of openly communicating their operational planning, but would also serve to restrict the leadership of the MEAs through making them aware of the likely consequences of violent and disorderly protest and inflammatory public statements.

ACC Andrewski might also be well advised to engage a private public relations specialist 'to help them get their message over and counter the protesters' "spin"' (Button et al, 2002: 30). The police (or their 'sub-contractors') dealing with the press (and other stakeholder groupings) should be as candid as possible about their plans, and should as far as possible keep to their word about what their strategic interventions are likely to be given situations that may emerge. Gillham and Marx have demonstrated in their work on the complexity and the irony of policing and protesting that a 'lack of candor by authorities, along with the protesters' belief that police [do not] keep their word, [contributes] to the view that police [are] hardly neutral protectors of the public' (2000: 228).

As far as possible, the police should not be seen as having a natural affinity with government, although this is extremely difficult for police commanders to achieve (Della Porta and Retier, 1998). This is important also because of the background information Andrewski has about the increasing difficulties of maintaining the reactor's safety. If something happens the police don't want to be seen as siding with 'the enemy'. The police commander, and his officers, should communicate to the broad public a dedication to facilitating peaceful protest as well as a commitment to protect the government's ability to provide energy to the public in the most efficient, cost effective, and sustainable manner possible. The communications officer would need to be properly briefed about the debates around the use of nuclear energy and the standpoints of the various stakeholders, ie government, the private sector, and environmental groupings. If action is to be taken against the protesters, this should be explained in terms of public safety, and not in terms of the 'wrongfulness' of the stance of the environmental activists. Ultimately, what should be clearly communicated is that the police are there to protect all parties and installations and to promote peaceful demonstration.

Multi-agency Approaches to the Policing of Environmental Protests

Protests such as the one identified in this scenario impact on a range of stakeholders and are likely to involve security interventions and intelligence gathering from a plurality of actors. It is now fairly widely accepted, even amongst police officers themselves, that most forms of policing require inter-agency partnerships (Davies and Thomas, 2003). This reality is greatly enforced when, as is the case in this scenario, the public police are faced with policing in private spaces. In these private spaces, for example big companies, private security industries will be involved in securing property, life, and information (Button et al, 2002). Bryant (1996) has documented the great quantity of resources that companies expend in 'securing' against environmental activists. They have made use of private security companies to instal security fencing and access control systems. Many companies have also introduced private security guards who are involved in intelligence gathering about protests and demonstrations, and who also 'police' company private property.

It could even be argued that the police, while overseeing the planned events from a distance, take a backseat in the policing of this situation, allowing the private security operatives, already mobilised, to do the 'dirty work' of policing in this complex and emotive situation. It is our view that such an approach would not be advisable. The public police are far more likely to be sensitive to public concerns and interests which the protests tackle. Private security operatives, while sometimes better at preventative strategies than the public police, tend to address narrow interests (those of their clients), and their organisational culture is often punitive and reactive (see Singh and Kempa, 2007). The presence and strategic involvement of the public police is therefore required not simply to demonstrate a concern with broad public safety, but also to ensure that a more rights-based approach to policing is adhered to.

There is no guarantee that the private police, left alone, will make use of reasonable force either in preventing the protest or in ejecting demonstrators. Given the narrow interests of the private security industry, as well as their potential for responding unsympathetically to the MEAs, ACC Andrewski must be cautious in not aligning himself too closely with the plans and 'thinking' of the company's security personnel. But the fact that a security nexus does exist means that thought must be given as to how best to mobilise existing resources, skills, and capacities in maintaining public order, ensuring the safety of all persons and property, and in facilitating peaceful protest. Given this, the public police would be best advised to work collaboratively with private security operatives, but also to seek out other potential policing collaborators. In this vein, ACC Andrewski would be wise to encourage the protesters to identify their own marshals (or monitors) to assist with the peaceful flow of the event. This is one of the best strategies that can be employed to control protesters who are likely to engage in violent and disruptive actions, which fall outside of the state commitment to organisers to non-violent action (Gillham and Marx, 2000). These marshals may have been identified by environmental protest leaders prior to the demonstration. If this is not the case, the police should make every effort to encourage the mobilisation of marshals once the event has already commenced. If the police are able to secure such non-police marshals and monitors, demonstrators will develop a web of 'insider' accountability, and will not feel that their actions are determined and controlled by the police.

The policing of environmental public order events is an excellent example of where policing is heading. Policing in the 21st century is likely to be nodal, or plural, requiring the police to rethink their identity, core mandate, and mechanisms for governing security (Shearing and Marks, 2011). A diverse range of policing agencies will have to be involved in the policing of events such as the one under discussion. These agencies will not only be involved in regular or traditional patrol, order maintenance, and dispersal operations, but also in intelligence gathering and in dealing with the media. The police and local authorities as public agencies are going to have to find ways of coordinating the activities of these multiple actors to attain policing outcomes that are rights-respecting, dynamic, and ethical (Button et al, 2002).

In public order situations such as the one under discussion, much as in other 'tricky' policing circumstances, what is now required, as Shearing and Marks put it, is

> ...police officers who are able to join up with other groupings to diagnose social problems and to mobilise all existing capacities, skills and resources in resolving these problems. We require a public police who are willing to think strategically about when they are required to intervene using their specialised skills, knowledge and resources. And the police need to be able to negotiate their roles with other network actors. (2007: 217)

In so doing, the nightmare of police being everywhere all of the time, trying to think of every possible strategic solution to a problem, can be prevented. As a range of actors from all sectors come together, dynamic solutions can be found and responsibilities can be shared. Public order events, like those organised by MEAs, require innovation, knowledge sharing, and an ethical framework that can be referred to in de-escalating conflict and disorder. ACC Andrewski would do well to consider coordinating a network made up of the following actors: the public police, private security personnel, marshals from the environmental social movements, representatives from the MEAs (who may or may not refer to themselves as leaders). Representatives from government, the companies who have an investment stake in nuclear sites, and members of the press should also be called in to find creative solutions in balancing protest and order in the situation under review. Other actors may also be brought into the network when required. These include health and safety officers, building inspectors, and road traffic managers.

Having all of these actors on board will produce outcomes that are not necessarily determined by a narrow police mentality, or by the demands of one group that has power and capital. It is important to remember that forms of capital that dominate will change. While it might seem that political and social capital are the determinants of policing strategies, the cultural capital that MEAs might garner could shift power dynamics dramatically, requiring fundamentally different ways of building police legitimacy and effecting outcomes that result from negotiated management strategies. Without doubt, these types of arrangements are difficult to coordinate. Approaches and strategies will differ, and getting a centralised coordination of intelligence (even just between the various policing agencies) is extremely difficult to achieve. However, the time when the police thought they monopolised policing will not return, and the quicker the public police acknowledge this, the better.

As Button et al rightly argue, 'the policing of environmental protests has provided new challenges to policing organizations and also provides a valuable insight into the changing nature of policing' (2002: 31). None of this is to say that the police give up on their core functions or allow their symbolic authority to be diminished. They remain, for now, central actors in the policing of all major public order situations or situations that could result in significant social conflict (Thacher, 2009).

Conclusion

There are no straightforward answers to how a police commander such as ACC Andrewski should approach this anticipated protest event. But the recommendations we make include operational independence on the part of the ACC, the mobilisation of multiple policing agencies in the policing of (environmental) protest events, the strategic use of arrests, and absolute caution in the use of force. Policing of such events has to be intelligence-led and dynamic. The ACC needs to determine appropriate intervention mechanisms based on police intelligence, strategic planning, public police mandates, and the constant requirement to balance order and civic liberty. While the ACC should not be beholden to 'political masters', he will have little choice, as a public police officer in a command position, but to be sensitive to the needs of government. Nevertheless, it is crucial that police and government officials become aware that a new mentality of environmental protection should replace dominant existing mentalities that focus on cost-effectiveness, new public management, and dominant social ordering. MEAs have played an important role in shifting consciousness of state and non-state actors, but their causes will be best achieved if they maintain a commitment to peaceful protest and to negotiated management of demonstrations.

What we are proposing here is that a hard and fast law enforcement approach not be used in dealing with this situation. Preventing any form of protest or engaging in mass arrests will have many negative consequences. It will exacerbate tensions between the various stakeholder groupings and could even transform peaceful protest to violent protest. A strong law enforcement approach is also likely to evoke increased sympathy from the public for the protesters and this is likely to have significant political costs. The environmental groupings may feel that they are forced to operate in increasingly 'underground' ways to avoid the scrutiny of the police and to be able to outwit the police. This is not a situation that police, government, or private industry can afford.

References

Bryant, B, *Twyford Down-Roads, Campaigning and Environmental Law* (London: Chapman and Hall, 1996).

Button, M, John, T, and Brearley, N, 'New challenges in public order policing: The professionalization of environment protest and the emergence of the militant environmental activist' (2002) 30 *International Journal of the Sociology of Law* 17–32.

Davies, A and Thomas, R, 'Talking cop: Discourses of change and policing identities' (2003) 81(4) *Public Administration* 681–99.

Della Porta, D and Reiter, H, *Policing Protest: The Control of Mass Demonstrations in Western Democracies* (Minneapolis: University of Minnesota Press, 1998).

Gillham, P and Marx, G, 'Complexity and irony in policing and protesting: The World Trade Organization in Seattle' (2000) 27(2) *Social Justice* 212–36.

Holloway, J, 'Undercurrent affairs: Radical environmentalism and alternative news' (1998) 30 *Environment and Planning* 1197–217.

Jefferson, T, *The Case Against Paramilitary Policing* (Milton Keynes: Open University Press, 1990).

Lamb, R, *Promising the Earth* (London: Routledge, 1996).

Lee, MF, 'Violence and the environment: The case of Earth First!' (1995) 7 *Terrorism and Political Violence* 109–27.

Shearing, C and Marks, M, 'Being a new police in the liquid 21st century' (2011) 5(3) *Policing* 210–18.

Sheptycki, J, 'Policing political protest when politics go global: Comparing public order policing in Canada and Bolivia' (2005) 15(3) *Policing and Society* 327–52.

Singh, A and Kempa, M, 'Reflections on the study of private policing cultures: Early leads and key themes', in M O'Neill, M Marks, and A Singh (eds), *Police Occupational Culture: New Debates and Directions* (London: Elsevier, 2007).

Thacher, D, 'Community policing and accountability', in P Grabosky (ed), *Community Policing and Peacekeeping* (Boca Raton, FL: CRC Press, 2009), pp 57–70.

Waddington, PAJ, 'Coercion and accommodation: Policing public order after the Public Order Act' (1994) 45(3) *British Journal of Sociology* 367–85.

Waddington, PAJ, 'Policing public order and political contention', in T Newburn (ed), *Handbook of Policing* (Cullompton: Willan, 2003).

Addressing the Scenario
Public Order Command: Dilemmas of Police Practice

Michael Messinger

Background

Clearly the issue of nuclear power, its generation, the storage of the waste products, government policy to provide sufficient power supplies in the immediate future, give rise to some profoundly significant issues of public policy. The decision by government, in this scenario, to sanction the building of private nuclear power stations has clearly provoked strong feelings and opposition in a wide group of environmentalists and other similarly minded organisations and individuals. It also seems that there will be a significant number of groupings with both legitimate and illegitimate points of view and a wide variety of both genuine and perceived vested interests, all of whom will wish to oppose the proposed building of a nuclear power plant by the particular company depicted here.

The role of the police in situations such as those described and implied by this scenario is to enforce the law (including laws on human rights and civil liberties), facilitate peaceful protest, and also ensure that the normal life of any potentially affected communities, including businesses, can continue with a minimum of disruption. The detail of government initiatives, commercial imperatives, corporate reputations, and protester preferences and tactics are all informative and must be considered when developing both a strategic response and also in informing the choice of tactical options. However, the primary considerations must be that any policing response or intervention must be lawful, proportionate, reasonable, and achievable. It should also be remembered that policing with discretion in a liberal democracy is a significant privilege and must not be compromised or abused.

When considering the proper policing response to any given set of circumstances an obvious choice is that the police could 'do nothing' and allow the protest to take place, only responding if and when alleged breaches of the law have been committed. Clearly this would be unacceptable on several levels. It would be an abdication of the primary policing role of prevention of crime and protection of both people and property. It would also be unprofessional and would attract very justifiable criticism from the news media and others in public life, if not formal censure from politicians (for example, through select committees of either House of Parliament, the judiciary, either sitting in court or chairing a public inquiry).

Is Nuclear Power a Special Case?

Nuclear power stations by their very nature are secure and protected places, with a significant range of legislative obligations placed on them because they form part of the critical national infrastructure, which makes protest action much more than a 'private' quarrel. By failing to police any protest at such a high profile and publicly perceived 'high risk' location—both in terms of its power source and its importance to the life of the nation—police would be seen to have abdicated their primary responsibility for preventative policing and would be rightly challenged and heavily criticised. This would potentially have an adverse effect on police/public relationships both locally and nationally and would be unacceptable and professionally negligent.

This situation puts the police between the proverbial 'rock and a hard place'. On the one hand, if this was any other commercial undertaking, it could be regarded as a dispute akin to that of a strike. If the protesters were successful then it might jeopardise the profitability of the business, which might be forced to cease trading. That is a legitimate interest that would need to be balanced against the human rights of protesters to express peacefully their opposition to the nature of the business being conducted. Of course, if they acted or threatened to act violently against people and property, then the protest would no longer be 'peaceful' and those involved would be liable to arrest and prosecution. However, the purely commercial costs of the protest would be borne by the company, as they are involved in a boycott by retailers or customers. If potential clients are dissuaded from doing business with the company because of the protests of activists, then that is simply a cost of doing business. There may be civil remedies to which the company has recourse and these may involve the police as it does when bailiffs eject protesters from private land. This point is crucial: in English law trespass is normally a civil tort, not a criminal offence. However, English law was extended by legislation in 1994 that created a criminal offence of 'aggravated trespass', which aims to outlaw trespass accompanied by the obstruction or disruption of a lawful activity, and/or the intimidation of those engaged in such activities.

Let us imagine for the moment that Jason Andrewski was dealing not with a nuclear power plant, but with a cosmetic firm, the development of whose products involved animal experimentation to which protesters took strong objection and planned to trespass on the premises, but to inflict no damage. In these circumstances, even if people who worked in the cosmetics firm felt intimidated by the presence of chanting, placard waving protesters, this would not necessarily occasion police intervention. The protest is unlawful, but it is also peaceful. As Her Majesty's Chief Inspector of Constabulary, Sir Denis O'Connor, reminded the police (2009a, 2009b), they not only are duty bound to abstain from preventing peaceful protest, they are duty bound positively to *facilitate* the protest. The cosmetic company may employ security staff who would be entitled under civil law to eject the protesters, but the police would not likely be involved in that ejection themselves.

What is the difference between a cosmetic firm and a nuclear power plant? In a commercial context there is little to choose between them: if the cosmetic firm's products are not on the shelves, consumers will be denied the opportunity to use these products to beautify themselves. Hence, the company will lose sales and income, and might go out of business as a result. This could be seriously damaging to those previously employed in the firm, its investors, and suppliers. It could prove serious for a local economy where the firm was a major employer. Yet, none of this makes the protest action anything other than 'peaceful' and hence the Article 10 and 11 rights of the protesters would prevail. If the power generators cannot sell their electricity to customers, the same will befall them.

However, there is a distinct difference between the cosmetic firm and the nuclear power plant because the latter is a vital component of the 'critical national infrastructure'. Until the 1980s electricity generation was the task of a nationalised industry. This was because electricity generation was regarded as a 'strategic industry' upon which rested the entire economy. Hence, ensuring sufficient electricity to turn the wheels of industry was not regarded as something that should be left to market forces. When (in the 1970s and 1980s) coalminers sought to exert industrial pressure through strike action and picketed power stations and other plants that were essential to electricity generation, they came into direct and forceful confrontation with the police. The duty of the police in these circumstances was not to be neutral arbiters of competing human rights, but defenders of the state's strategic interests. That said, there was still an expectation that all police activity would and must be undertaken within the law that pertained at the time. One must always remember that the police themselves are always accountable to the Law and given their specialist role the level of expectation can and will be higher. Since the 1980s, electricity generation has been privatised. It is now entirely equivalent to cosmetics production, except that unlike cosmetics the entire economy still rests on electric generation—it remains critical national infrastructure. Yet, companies engaged in electricity generation remain free to act in their own commercial interest. Hence, a company is not compelled to generate electricity if it is unprofitable to do so. So, in this case the company is entitled to conclude that the disruption to its activities is sufficiently damaging that it will no longer invest in building and operating plants in Britain. However, this might prove calamitous for the economy as a whole. Even the threat of disinvestment could have a 'domino effect' on the investment plans of other manufacturers who might at least stall their investment plans until it became clear what the future of electricity generation was. There is a wider possible impact of successful protest leading to the disinvestment of a major international company, and that is upon market confidence. This was glimpsed when animal rights activists targeted Huntingdon Life Sciences (HLS)—a commercial company that conducts animal experiments. So successful was the campaign that the company's share price virtually collapsed and the company moved its head office overseas, out of reach of campaigners. So seriously did the government regard this that they pressed the police to take effective action against the campaigners for serious criminal offences, leading to the prosecution of many activists. One concern of government was that if HLS collapsed or relocated abroad, it would send a damaging signal to the markets and to potential investors in other high technology companies.

Moreover, any civil nuclear power plant is guarded not only by private security personnel, but by its own police force—the Civil Nuclear Constabulary (CNC)—that possess full constabulary powers not only within the plant, but also within a five-mile radius of it. They are also routinely armed. On the other hand, the Civil Nuclear Police Authority, which exercises public oversight of the CNC is also a 'public authority' and hence bound by the ECHR, as much as any other police force.

This tangled private–public arrangement, with its complex set of obligations, interests, legal powers, and constraints, which both compete with, and supplement, each other comprise the 'rock and a hard place' between which are sandwiched ACC Andrewski and officers under his command. 'The rock' is that the electricity generating company is a commercial business like any other, whilst the 'hard place' is that it is far from equivalent to any other, because the interests of the whole nation rest upon it. If the protesters succeed, then lights may dim and eventually be extinguished throughout Britain. This, therefore, must be considered when calculating the proportionality of the police response.

Given this unenviable situation in which ACC Andrewski finds himself, it is vital that as many of these third party interests are incorporated into the policing operation, so that officers know what they are doing, why they are doing it, and how they are expected to achieve their collective goals. A partnership strategy is needed to bring as many disparate groups together as possible and a clear public and press relations strategy is formulated.

Policing Options

The policing challenge is clear in that there will always be an imperative to base any policing response on the best possible information and ensure that it is as appropriate and proportionate as is possible. The views of the many and varied groupings that make up the constituent parts of any protest (in favour of and against the aims of the protest, vested interests, communities, innocent passers-by, statutory agencies, governments, police staff and their families to name but a few) have to be taken into consideration and weighed in terms of relevance, importance, and urgency. It also has to be expected that there will be significant 'advice' available to those in decision-making positions to adopt one or other positions. These sources of 'advice' may well come from affected business inter-ests, politicians, community groups, and activists themselves. All deserve to be carefully listened to and considered when making strategic decisions. However, police commanders must also remember that they not only have to deal with the current issues but will have to police the communities and those within it after the matter is resolved—one way or another. If 'mutual aid' is required from other police force areas, then it is essential that they too fully understand that this will only constitute an episode in the life of the community, however long it might last.

Given that police are aware of the real likelihood of protest then a proportionate policing response is both necessary and appropriate. The fact that the protesters have refused to comply with the notification requirements of the Public Order Act or enter into any communication, still less negotiation with police, does mean that any protest march would be prima facie potentially unlawful. However, a static assembly—for instance, outside the main gate—would not necessarily be unlawful, but anyone engaged in it would not be covered by the immunities offered to a 'picket' that is 'in furtherance of a trade dispute'. Hence, the company would be free to seek redress under the civil law and, if successful, that might extend to an injunction the breach of which would constitute a contempt of court. The fluid structure of the protest group would make it difficult for the com-pany to proceed against them collectively or each one individually. Also, because it is not a picket 'in furtherance of a trade dispute', the protesters would be con-strained by all the provisions of the Public Order Act 1986, which would enable a senior officer present at the scene to impose restrictions reasonably intended to prevent 'serious public disorder, serious damage to property or serious disruption to the life of the community'. Equally, if there are reasonable grounds to believe that the purpose of those organising the protest 'is the intimidation of others with a view to compelling them not to do an act they have a right to do, or to do an act they have a right not to do' (s 14[1]) then police can impose restrictions. However, all this is subject to the overriding consideration that '*peaceful* protest' is protected by the European Convention on Human Rights (Articles 10 and 11).

ACC Andrewski can expect to come under considerable pressure from power-ful vested interests to suppress any protest. Strict enforcement of the law is rarely an attractive or realistic option from several very practical points of view. It would be hugely demanding in terms of police resources. It would involve the police in taking action that was very likely to be resisted, which would be potentially counter-productive as it would leave a policing challenge that became both more diffuse and potentially more committed, focused, and disruptive. It would also be questionable as to whether a professional policing response could be maintained if the protest were to continue in an overtly adversarial manner over an extended period of time. A further consideration would be the possibility of reputational risk to the police image and an associated loss of trust from the local communities in particular and the wider public in general.

A further option could be for the police to employ a very open approach to the potential protesters through the use of and engagement with various media channels raising the real policing concerns and their desire to seek the cooperation of and discussion with protest groups to organise, plan, and facilitate a lawful protest. This might then encourage the less militant groupings to come forward and discuss issues with the police. It would also put the issues relating to protest at this plant into the public domain in a very potent and open fashion and could well allow the police position to be clearly communicated and offer opportunities for open discussion and debate prior to any protest taking place. If this was to work well then it could be beneficial both in policing terms but also in energising debate and getting all areas of opinion surfaced. However, it would also have the potential to increase the size, shape, and nature of any protest thereby exacerbating the potential policing challenges. It would also allow for the less militant and potentially passive protest groups and their issues to be 'highjacked' and the positive intentions could become subverted. On the other hand, neither the government nor commercial interests might welcome a public debate that highlighted the issues arising from the privatisation of critical national infrastructure. They might prefer that the issues be couched in terms of policing and public disorder.

On balance some form of public appeal may be helpful but it would have to be a part of a wider strategic approach that would be capable of dealing with a wide range of possible outcomes. Whereas, for the police, the advantage of a public appeal to negotiate would place the policing operation within its wider context and highlight some of the issues involved and the likely challenges that will be faced by the affected communities. However, whilst having some potentially very positive aspects, most notably highlighting any failure of protesters to engage in negotiations that would leave the police little option but to impose restrictions, it is finely balanced by the prospect that it might exacerbate tensions without developing any meaningful negotiating platform.

An additional strand would be to continue to build a comprehensive intelligence picture of the possible size and shape of any protest and then to facilitate its policing, whilst at the same time continuing to attempt to establish a dialogue with the protesters to enable meaningful and mutually beneficial negotiations.

Clearly there would also need to be conversations with the management of the power station to establish their needs, priorities, and responsibilities as well as discussions with other groupings that would have a legitimate interest or concern over the possibility of protest and the likely effects that would flow from it. Gathering as much information and intelligence as possible will allow more informed decisions to be taken.

Finding the Balance

On balance the preferred option would be to facilitate the protest and then police it accordingly. It would allow for a planned and properly resourced policing response to be built. It would also ensure that the correct policing resources could be brought together to facilitate the protest whilst also enforcing the law. By facilitating the protest it would allow for a more realistic appreciation of the challenges to be faced and the ability to continue to attempt to develop dialogue and establish lines of communication with all parties. Thus it would provide a more realistic possibility that the proper demands and limitations to be met by protesters could be communicated in a realistic and auditable manner. This therefore indicates that some form of policing response that is properly planned and resourced is necessary.

This approach, which should be based on known facts, information, and intelligence, does mean that there will be a policing response in place as and when any protest takes place. It does have the benefit of helping to reassure communities that are likely to be affected. It also allows the police to undertake their duty of enforcing the law, protecting individuals, and preventing disorder. It also goes a significant way to allowing for the proper oversight and facilitation of lawful protest whilst providing a response to unlawful activity. That said, it will place a significant demand on policing resources that would otherwise be providing more general routine policing elsewhere and will place additional burdens on budgets, staff, and limited resources. Nevertheless, part of the policing function is to be able and prepared to respond to incidents in a proportionate and appropriate manner irrespective of the notice given.

The lack of meaningful negotiations with protest groups will mean that any strategic and tactical planning will be potentially excessively heavy in terms of both human and specialist support resources. This is an unavoidable consequence of having to prepare a policing plan on the basis of incomplete and imprecise information. It is a case of preparing to deal with the unknown whilst hoping that the reality is significantly less challenging and demanding. This can, of course, be mitigated by planning on the basis of what is definitely known or considered possible based on information, intelligence, and past experiences elsewhere. However, there will always be a need to resource an imprecise 'what if' factor in the short to medium term until more certainty—and precise information—becomes available.

A major challenge that will have to be faced is that the exact nature of the protest is not known. Guerrilla tactics by protesters are always difficult to counter and are hugely demanding on both personnel and other resources. Part of any plan to police protest must involve a clear and agreed understanding of what areas will and will not be dealt with by police and what the management and staff of the power station will be responsible for providing. Security at such sites needs to meet certain standards and it would be reasonable for that to be enhanced to a degree by the company in light of the available information. However, it would be both unwise and unreasonable to expect or allow the site management to go any further than their own legislative requirements or agreed operating procedures. On the other hand, it will be hugely beneficial if a professional working relationship can be continued between the management of both the plant and the policing response. It is very helpful if police properly understand and appreciate the key performance challenges that the management and staff of the plant face and that there is a clear and shared understanding of their contingency arrangement and safety critical vulnerable areas. This will allow the policing response and approach to be geared to facilitate lawful protest whilst at the same time minimising both risk and inappropriate disruption to a legitimate business activity.

Minimising Negative Policing and Maximising Favourable Consequences

It is vitally important that any police response deals with what are strictly policing issues and does not enter into a debate about the pros and cons of the issues that are about the focus of the protest. The police role is to enforce the law when necessary and to facilitate peaceful protest. Clearly individual officers will have private views on the issues of the nuclear power. However, that must not be allowed to colour or affect their professional policing response. That needs to be made clear at the outset and must be reiterated as and when necessary.

Understanding the protest

However, as part of the strategic planning process it would be both proper and advisable if all the major issues that have led to the potential for protest are considered, investigated, and discussed at a strategic level.

Clearly having a full grasp of the circumstances and outcomes of similar protests is vitally important information that will aid the planning process. It would also be very beneficial to understand and have a comprehensive grasp of the primary drivers that have led to governmental decisions that have caused the possible conflict and the attitude that is current as to the potential for protest. Outcomes of previous discussions concerning the key areas of nuclear power, nuclear waste disposal/storage, the processes of letting contracts to foreign companies, and the real situation as to the relationship between statutory organisations and commercial companies in terms of appetite for protest and possible disruption to build programmes and the like and the likelihood of that being relevant to the current circumstances would be both useful and very helpful to informing the decision-making processes being taken by police at both a strategic and tactical level.

Similarly, police would be wise to continue to use all opportunities to make contact with, and start a debate with, possible protest groups. They would be wise to make clear that peaceful protest would be facilitated but unlawful or violent behaviour would not be accepted. It may well be that public meetings with local communities may provide an opportunity to air the general policing approach, whilst not going into significant detail as to police planning but providing general reassurance and thereby getting the message across more indirectly. Continued efforts to start a relationship with protesters must be both necessary and advantageous.

The police would wish to maintain a neutral stance on all of these issues. However, the more detail and contextual information that can be obtained the better informed will be the eventual policing strategy.

The failure of protesters to discuss their wishes and intentions is clearly both disappointing and unhelpful. However, attempts to strike up discussions must continue whilst planning and tactical options will have to be developed on the basis of known information and past experiences and outcomes of similar protests and activities by known participants.

Other interested parties

There needs to be a continuing discussion with the power station management, at varying levels, to ensure that there is a clear and shared understanding of what is proposed and in place and what is and what is not acceptable. Clearly there should be a policy of 'no secrets' as far as is possible whilst also maintaining a professional relationship and a proper 'distance' between the commercial imperatives of the company and the need to deliver power and continue with re-development and a policing operation that is intended to facilitate lawful protest and deal with unlawful behaviour.

Another constituency is the local communities who will possibly suffer some significant disruption to their quality of life due to the presence of protesters in what they perceive to be 'their area'. Many local residents may also be workers at the plant and would therefore be unhappy that their livelihood was being challenged by what they might consider an ill-informed and disruptive group of protesters.

Similarly, it would be very important to have the benefit of a comprehensive community impact assessment that is updated on a regular basis. Clearly communities have a legitimate interest in issues that are likely to affect their areas and so it is proper that they are part of the debate and their views are understood and catered for as far as is possible.

Similarly, contact needs to be made with affected local authorities at an early stage to ensure that they are aware of the potential for protest and also that their contingency plans, as they relate to a disruption of, or catastrophic failure of, the power station are checked and are fit for purpose and capable of implementation should it be necessary. This may seem to be a somewhat 'heavy handed' or alarmist approach given that the only known information is that the more militant protesters intend to stage a very elaborate publicity stunt. However, given the reaction and outcomes that flowed from a similar event in the USA it would be wise to ensure that the means to minimise panic and cope with unforeseen consequences of such activity are available and appropriate.

There is also a need to have as much definitive information as possible regarding the various statutory agencies' attitude to the emerging information concerning the current operating company and the revelations made public by investigative journalists. Whilst this is clearly going to be information that would need to be obtained on a 'need to know basis' it would be proper to seek it as it goes to the very heart of considerations about strategic options and tactical responses.

Given the potential nature of the protest and the issues that have been brought to light it is clear that any protest and its policing will be of some considerable interest to the media. It is therefore important that a media strategy is developed as a matter of urgency. It is also important that it is re-visited on a regular basis as more information becomes available to ensure that it is still fit for purpose. It would also be wise to consider inviting the media to briefings to explain the police approach and their desire to facilitate peaceful and lawful protest. It would also be wise to ascertain what, if any, press briefing the company is intending to undertake and also establish their appetite to engage with the media and on what grounds. Clearly, the more consistency in any media briefings the better whilst always accepting that differing organisations may have different priorities that they would wish to emphasise.

Given the importance of the power station to the national infrastructure it is to be expected that government departments will be interested in the issues that have led to the potential for protest and also in the proposed policing response should a protest materialise. This is both proper and necessary and an early decision will need to be taken as to the methods by which information is shared between police and the various government departments. Clearly, this needs to be an effective process and thus it should be discussed, agreed, and operated from an early point so that all agencies are properly informed and updated. Consistency of briefing and consistency of message are important here to ensure that accurate and relevant information is shared as and when necessary.

Human rights

Similarly proper consideration needs to be given to the suggestion that Articles 10 and 11 of the European Convention on Human Rights (enacted into UK law

195

by the Human Rights Act 1998 safeguarding freedom of association and expression) could well nullify any criminal action against protesters if they were to infiltrate the power station to stage their publicity stunt.

Clearly the Human Rights Act needs to be considered when any policing operation is being planned. Both of the Articles quoted have an impact on the possibilities for policing the protest and this must be accepted. However, both Articles need to be considered in the wider context of the balance between individual (or group) rights and those of the wider public interest. Clearly any definitive decision as to whether an individual's rights have been infringed will be a matter for the courts, should it go that far. However, in the case of the circumstances that relate to this particular case it is likely that the wider public interest in terms of electricity consumers being able to receive a secure power supply and thus conduct their normal daily activities in a reasonable and acceptable manner would take precedence over the right to protest. Similarly, the right to stage the publicity stunt to draw attention to a particular cause may be outweighed by the community's right to lead a settled and undisturbed life that is not significantly disrupted by a possibly well intentioned—but in reality disproportionate—response to a prank or elaborate publicity stunt. Clearly the relationship and relevance of the rights and their limitations set out by the Human Rights Act are very real and present issues and legal advice as to the relative weightings and relationships with other legislation would be very valuable prior to finalising a strategic approach.

By its very nature the policing of public order events will involve the need to balance priorities, make value judgements on the veracity, or otherwise, of information and intelligence, and plan to deliver an appropriate and proportionate policing response.

The challenges faced by strategic commanders in such cases are self-evident. The available policing resources are finite and need to be used to the very best effect to support and police communities. Thus any interference with that primary role, for whatever reason, must be both justified and be the absolute minimum commensurate with need.

The fact that the scenario involved in this case study involves a very high profile and emotive issue merely adds to the challenges faced by the police. Such issues provoke significantly strong feelings in a very wide range of groups and individuals. Others are more concerned that the underlying governmental decisions are wrong or ill considered and thus wish to highlight that debate. Yet others see this as an opportunity to promote some other totally unrelated issue or set of beliefs safe in the knowledge that they are unlikely to be easily identified as they will be shielded by the large grouping of less assertive activists.

Against this set of issues are the priorities of the generating company who are a commercial organisation and accountable to their customers, their shareholders, and the other statutory bodies. Their concerns will be to continue to do business without the possible disruption caused by a protest of imprecise proportions. No doubt there will be other business driven pressures that they would not wish to be made public or to be highlighted in any reporting of the potential protest.

Media interest

Balancing and assessing the relative importance of all of these issues and the proper concerns of other vested interests—local authorities, governments, multinational business interests, the media (to name but a few)—will always be a challenge. However, the police service does have a very positive record of success in balancing and evaluating the challenges they are quite properly required to face and in delivering an appropriate response.

They are also very well aware that their decisions will be closely questioned and that their strategic and tactical decisions will be open to proper questioning and inspection both in fast and slower time. This is the challenge faced by police commanders and is one that they accept without question. The need to uphold the law is paramount and must continue to be so. However, this must also be done in a proportionate manner and all the related priorities and opinions given the proper consideration. This is the basis on which policing by consent and with discretion is based and it is also why it should be treated with the proper seriousness and professional application.

A very real option would be to publicise the fact that similar protests in other parts of the world have used the stunt of faking a nuclear accident by covering vital buildings with a very realistic cover that simulates a crack or other damage. If this were to be undertaken and publicised widely it would go a long way to ensuring that there was no public panic. It would also take a great deal of the potential 'sting' out of the entire protest. However, before this was done there would need to be very careful investigation as to where the information had come from, whether publicity would put anyone at real risk of injury—or worse—and whether there were any other competing priorities that would make such a course either unwise or impossible. This will need to involve significant negotiations with other statutory agencies, the power generation industry, and the government. However, at the end of all this the decision will rest fairly and squarely on the shoulders of the strategic police commander who must weigh all the issues and ensure that any decision made is proportionate, justifiable, and lawful. ACC Andrewski will also need to consider whether any short-term benefit would outweigh the very likely deterioration in relationships with protest groups and put at risk any other ongoing policing activities. This is a heavy responsibility but one that can be achieved and one that he must be ready to be held accountable for making. Hence careful consideration, record keeping, and analysis are vitally important. He should also remember that what may seem to be a very effective short-term 'win' may well be a causal factor in the 'loss' of longer term desired outcomes. That does not mean it should not be done but it does mean that it requires very careful consideration of all the options and possible consequences. It should also be recognised that whilst it may 'draw the sting' of the protest it could equally increase its ferocity and determination and worsen the possible outcome.

Priorities

All protest will involve competing priorities and there will be a very wide spectrum of views across the entirety of the debate on the issues involved. The police role is to enforce the law in a proportionate and lawful fashion whilst also accepting and taking into account legitimate issues that impact upon it. Mr Andrewski has got a big job on his hands and there is a great deal to be considered in reaching a solution that will achieve the strategic policing objectives whilst acknowledging and minimising other concerns. Let's consider for instance a scenario in which a Head of State makes a state visit to a country where their policies at home and abroad are not 'universally popular' with a significant section of the host country's population. Clearly the host government would be only too well aware of the negative feelings but considered that the potential benefits to be gained from the visit outweighed any possible negative reactions. The policing role is going to involve ensuring that the public part of the visit is achieved with due ceremony and dignity whilst at the same time facilitating any peaceful protest. Rather like the scenario discussed, there are some very real competing priorities that are not easily balanced. There is no realistic chance of stopping the state visit and no one—particularly government and the media—would countenance anything that may seem to be 'heavy handed' policing of peaceful protest in a liberal democracy. The answer in this case would be to 'flex' both the visit and the protest opportunities to ensure that the security and dignity of the Head of State were maintained whilst also facilitating real and meaningful peaceful protest. The watchword would be to hope for the best whilst planning for the worst and work very hard to make as much of your own luck as possible. It would be a high risk strategy and could go badly wrong. If that were the case then acceptance of reality and a new career choice might be a real and likely option!

Ultimately, Mr Andrewski can only make the very best informed decisions as to the overall strategy based on the facts and intelligence he has at his disposal. He will also have to take into account the restrictions and opportunities offered by relevant legislation in force at the time and the resources that he will have available to deliver the operational consequences of the strategy. He can possibly influence some of the major 'points of conflict' and could draw the sting from some of the publicity stunts. However, all actions will have consequences and they must be carefully considered too. He and his strategy (together with its operational delivery) will be judged with the wisdom of hindsight by government, industry, the media, and communities. He must do all that is legally possible to get the best overall outcome whilst also supporting his staff and maintaining the good name of his police service and its ability to deliver proportionate policing in a free society. I know that is 'eminently doable' and I wish Mr Andrewski a significant amount of good luck.

References

Her Majesty's Chief Inspector of Constabulary, 'Adapting to Protest. 1' (London: Her Majesty's Inspectorate of Constabulary, 2009a).
Her Majesty's Chief Inspector of Constabulary, 'Adapting to Protest. 2' (London: Her Majesty's Inspectorate of Constabulary, 2009b).

21

Editor's Commentary

PAJ Waddington

Dealing with people en masse is fundamentally a task for the police. Indeed the bloody suppression, in 1819, of an outdoor meeting called by a radical orator to demand universal male suffrage (which became notorious as 'Peterloo') was a prominent influence encouraging the formation of a lightly armed police in London in 1829. However, it is rarely a task that receives the attention that it deserves. Almost universally policing is popularly equated with crime-fighting and one danger that arises from this equation is the tendency to fit all gatherings into the crime category. Terms like 'rent-a-mob' are popularly employed to suggest that those who gather, especially if the gathering is accompanied by violence, are merely 'riff-raff'. This is seriously misleading and many generations of police officers have been misled. First, gatherings of people occur for a wide variety of reasons, from the most innocent and indeed virtuous to the most dangerous. Hundreds of thousands of people attend royal ceremonies in Britain and they gather to commemorate the deaths of the famous and the fallen, without the slightest hint of wrongdoing of any kind. At the other extreme, deadly ethnic riots (Horowitz, 2001) have claimed the lives of thousands, as witnessed, for example, in the Rwanda genocide in 1994 and the bloodletting that followed the assassination of Mrs Gandhi, the Prime Minister of India, ten years earlier.

Secondly, gatherings are only rarely violent or disorderly. We notice those that are, steadfastly ignoring how commonly people simply gather informally and organise themselves so as to accomplish some task, from watching a spectacle, such as a firework display, to rescuing those afflicted by some tragedy (McPhail, 1991). This is also true of that category of gatherings that unfairly, perhaps, is often associated with violence—political demonstrations and assemblies, most of which are entirely peaceful (Waddington, 2003). Even those gatherings that do turn violent tend only to become violent in brief episodes; most of the time people wander about waiting for something to happen. Thirdly, there is a considerable difference in the composition of gatherings as compared to the characteristics of those engaged in criminal activity. Criminals very disproportionately comprise those with little of what sociologists call 'social capital' and 'cultural capital'—that is, they tend to be isolated and they tend also to lack education and intellectual acumen. Even participants in the kind of rioting and looting that was briefly seen on the streets of some large English cities in the summer of 2011 tend to depart from this characterisation of criminals. People with criminal convictions are not more prominent in episodes of violent disorder than they are amongst the general population (Kerner, 1968; Field and Southgate, 1982). Protesters, including those who are most militant, tend to be distinctively well-connected and they tend to be better educated than those who participate in crime. This is no accident: most spontaneous gatherings are organised through networks of acquaintances and assembling a protest requires a modicum of organisation. So, police officers should beware of the 'myth of the madding crowd' (McPhail, 1991).

This is not to say that protesters are any less challenging than 'common criminals'. On the contrary, they are likely to prove far more difficult to police, for they are likely to know their rights and be eager to educate police officers in the limits of their powers. Amongst their number there are likely to be professional people and most protest groups enlist the services of sympathetic lawyers ready to attend a protest. Equally, they may pose a much greater threat than a burglar or robber is ever likely to do. If the militants amongst those gathered to oppose the construction of a replacement nuclear power plant succeed, then it could gravely hobble economic prosperity for the foreseeable future. If they were to be successful in creating the impression that a massive crack has appeared in the wall of the containment building, then the panic that predictably might ensue could place thousands of people in jeopardy. People who feel passionately about an issue may accept that extreme measures are justified to achieve their goals. Compromise is something that they might see as betrayal. In their own eyes they are not acting out of self-interest, but seeking the good—even the salvation—of society and humanity as a whole. Terrorism—especially if it enjoys any success—is almost invariably the most violent extreme of social movements. The 1970s terrorists of the Red Army Faction (aka Baader-Meinhof group) or the Brigate-Rosse (or Red Brigades) were motivated by radical Marxist ideology; the IRA and ETA were the terrorist expression of radical nationalism; al-Qaida and its affiliates are similarly violent manifestations of the much wider movement of radical political Islamism. Terrorists who are unconnected to such movements are vulnerable and tend quickly to be killed or captured. These wider communities, of which militants tend to form relatively tiny hard cores, sustain the militants, by offering practical support, sympathy and understanding, as well as doubting the militants' detractors. Support for social movements can be likened to a nest of concentric circles in which the innermost circles are the most militant and outermost circle tends to be moderate and difficult to mobilise into action. It follows that those occupying the most peripheral circles are also the most numerous. If those occupying the outermost circles can be detached from the innermost circles, this amounts to the significant erosion of support.

In both the contributions contained in this section, contributors emphasise the need for police to *negotiate* with the protesters. The aim of negotiation is to persuade the persuadable outer rim that they can and should make their case verbally, rather than take militant action. If successful this places militants in a difficult situation, because either they abstain from taking possibly extreme measures for fear of alienating their soft support, or they remain committed to their militancy and isolate themselves. As with any negotiation, this involves meeting, preferably face-to-face, with opponents and persuading them to adopt a course of action that they would not otherwise choose. I witnessed many such negotiations when observing the London Metropolitan Police's public order officers dealing with a diverse array of major gatherings in central London during the early 1990s (Waddington, 1994). I described how officers exploited strengths, such as 'the home ground advantage' in which prospective protesters were welcomed, treated as guests, offered help and assistance with the organisation of their protest, gently steered away from doing anything that would threaten not only violence, but also any unavoidable disruption to the life of the capital city. These officers were remarkably successful at doing so, but they were utterly unaware of their skills and abilities, and expressed surprise when they read what I had written. This is the problem with 'negotiation'—it is a craft! It must be performed in order to be perfected. The context is everything: there is no recipe that works for every situation. On one occasion that I witnessed, a group of militant anarchists planned to march through the heart of government in Westminster, which caused much concern to the police. This threat led the police to mount a major operation to defend locations such as Downing Street and the Palace of Westminster. A few days prior to the demonstration, the officer in overall command invited the anarchist leaders to meet him. He deliberately wore his full uniform, including his cap. He was a strikingly tall man and he strode confidently into the conference room where the anarchists were assembled. Walking the length of the room, his face burst into a broad smile and he stretched out his hand in welcome. Somewhat bewildered by this display, the anarchists rose from their seats, grasped the outstretched hand in sequence and mumbled some acknowledgement of his greeting. The officer then removed his hat and sat down next to the anarchists. He lent forward and said in barely audible but earnest tones that the anarchists must be assured that the Met Police would protect their right to protest as vigorously as they would protect anyone else. Then he was gone! It was a studied performance and had the desired effect: a somewhat stunned anarchist leadership acceded to the police proposals and the protest march was held without incident. The senior officer confided in me that he would not dream of repeating such a performance with what he considered 'ordinary decent protesters' like trade unions, or the Campaign for Nuclear Disarmament.

This places the contributors to this volume in some difficulty in describing how ACC Andrewski should conduct the negotiations. In this respect it is like other aspects of policing (see particularly Part Four in this volume), just as it applies to any other vocation that relies on craft skills: medical doctors need to hear the sounds of bodies through their stethoscopes in order to be able to discriminate a sign of pathology from the gurgling and gushing of a living human being. Many professions rely upon such *practices* and the police should not only recognise their own practice, but seek to teach it through practical instruction, mentoring, and guidance.

What the contributors are more able to identify are the traps that need to be avoided, obstacles that need to be surmounted, and options that need to be excluded. Marks and Tait, writing from a South African perspective in which the police are more accustomed to using significant amounts of coercive force, are eager to exclude the use of the most forceful options, such as water cannon. Messinger, writing from a background of public order policing in Britain, hardly mentions using force at all. This tells us something: what is acceptable in any society is relative to its culture, history, and politics. The use of coercive technologies does not simply rely upon a rational appraisal of what works. Neither can the same technologies be used against all protesters, for some protesters attract more sympathy than others. For instance, police can afford to be much more heavy-handed in controlling soccer supporters or proponents of racist and right-wing causes, than they can with those who support more endearing causes. What exactly is 'endearing' also cannot easily be stipulated. Police commanders need to be aware of the 'public mood', which can be quite volatile. In the summer of 2011, armed police in London shot and killed a man in controversial circumstances. A couple of days later, the man's family led a small demonstration to the local police station to protest about the killing. There was some confusion on the part of the police about how they should handle this sensitive issue, which left the family feeling ignored. Younger, perhaps more aggressive, members of the protest began using social media to summon acquaintances to join the protest and to voice their anger with greater stridency. Eventually, police vehicles were attacked and then a bus was set alight and shop windows were smashed. To many viewing these scenes live on their televisions, this seemed to be an understandable, albeit unwelcome, expression of rage. However, in the days that followed, the public mood changed, as roaming gangs of youths invaded shopping areas far from the location of the shooting, and began looting them for desirable commodities. A furniture store was gutted by flames started by arsonists. Photographs in the news media showed people leaping from first floor windows to escape the conflagration. Public sympathy for the family of the dead man and concern about the manner of his death remained, but were eclipsed by outrage at what was seen as an orgy of acquisitive crime disconnected from the shooting. 'Riots'—like other gatherings—are not singular occurrences and part of their management lies in understanding the fluctuating mood that shifts the boundaries of what is publicly acceptable.

A central dilemma—recognised by all our contributors—is the use of covert intelligence. On the one hand, the more information the police have regarding the intentions and capacities of the protesters, the more precisely can they modulate their response. However, this must be balanced against the risk that any intrusion will be discovered and regarded as an unwarranted curtailment of privacy. In 2009 militant environmentalist protesters planned to occupy and close down a conventional coal-fired power station in the Midlands of England. They were arrested; those who pleaded guilty were dealt with in 2010, and the remainder were due to stand trial in 2011. Then it was disclosed that a Metropolitan Police Officer, Mark Kennedy, had infiltrated the group in 2003 and was maintaining surveillance of them during the planned occupation of the power station. The trial collapsed amid accusations that the officer had become an agent provocateur. It also came to light that during his infiltration of the group, the officer (who was married) had formed at least two sexual relationships with female activists. By the time of the trial, the officer had resigned from the police and was now expressing remorse for his betrayal of the group. There was the usual flurry of media speculation and revelation, and the Surveillance Commissioner published an inquiry (Rose, 2011). It was a damaging episode for the police that highlights the dangers of covert surveillance. First, environmentalism is a cause that enjoys a generally favourable public image. The prospect that environmentalists could cause damage or pose a risk to innocent people is not one that is often entertained. Hence, any covert surveillance would need to surmount a very high threshold to be justified. Secondly, environmentalism is an articulate social movement that draws upon science for its rationale. Any covert surveillance officer would need to become familiar with the web of self-justification that is woven around environmentalism: climate change, habitat destruction, the threat of 'resource wars', and so forth. The danger is that this web can ensnare the conscience of officers and lead them into sympathising with the cause. Daily close contact with other activists in a climate of secrecy and threat forges close personal relationships—a 'band of brothers' as well as 'sisters' and 'lovers'. Finally, surveillance can only be effective at very close range (see discussion of the terrorism dilemma in this volume, Part Five), which requires treading the perilous path between legitimate surveillance and becoming an agent provocateur.

Messinger points out that much information can be acquired from 'open source' materials. Campaigners need to broadcast their message. Al-Qaida may be secretive about its operations, but on 3 November 2001 Osama bin Laden broadcast a proclamation announcing what he regarded as a holy war that specifically identified the Australian intervention (on behalf of the United Nations) in East Timor as an affront to Islam justifying jihad. Eleven months later Australian tourists were slaughtered in the Bali bombings. Secret intelligence services devote significant resources to reading newspapers and listening to broadcasts in those parts of the world that are of interest. Police need to learn that 'intelligence' is not only gained from surveillance and infiltration, but from *understanding* one's opponent. Treating radicals as little more than criminals does not advance understanding, but undermines it.

Since the police in this scenario believe they know what the intentions of the militants are—to unfurl a banner that depicts a crack in the wall of the containment building—they must now decide what to do with that information. They could keep it to themselves and make contingency plans to frustrate the accomplishment of the plan. Alternatively, they could decide to inform protesters that they are aware of the plan and negotiate a purely symbolic act of allowing it to be unfurled in the full glare of media publicity, but with assurances to everyone that this was not a real threat. This would achieve the demonstrative purpose of the moderate protesters in compliance with Articles 10 and 11 of the European Convention, whilst avoiding any disruption to the functioning of the plant. This disclosure would, of course, warn the militants that their plans had been discovered and they might then respond by taking an alternative course of equally militant action. They may even have one prepared—a 'plan B'. Equally, the police commander cannot be sure that the intelligence is accurate: it could be false information deliberately leaked to the police to mislead them. A means of addressing this uncertainty might be to develop a contingency plan that if militants seek to scale the containment building and unfurl the banner, this will not be prevented, but preparations would be made to counter any fears that the crack was real. As part of that contingency plan, measures would need to be taken to prevent any further incursion or attempt to disrupt the functioning of the plant.

Military planning commonly employs what are known as 'red teams', whose task it is to plan and respond as one would to an enemy. Police involved in public order are not engaged in 'battle' with an 'enemy'—far from it, protesters should be recognised as engaged in a political virtue, that is participation in the political process (Waddington, 1995). However, police and protesters tend to seek incompatible goals and police commanders should seriously consider tasking a few of their most able officers to form a 'red team', to forecast how protesters might respond to police actions. This should rest upon an understanding of how protesters perceive the situation: *their* goals, *their* perceptions, and *their* priorities.

Police have other resources—as all contributors recognise: partnerships. What is also apparent, especially from Messinger's contribution, is that this too needs to be carefully managed. The interests of the power generating company and the police may overlap considerably, yet may not align completely. This too is part of the intelligence function, for who can be relied upon for what is of vital interest to the police. Public order commanders, in situations as fraught as those contrived in this scenario, would be wise to form a dedicated cell acquiring, assessing, and integrating information about the intentions and capabilities of partners. Of critical interest here will be the CNC and private security, because depending on their reliability the commander will need to determine where to 'dig' the proverbial 'ditch to die in' (Waddington, 1994). It would be attractive to have such a final line of defence as far inside the plant as possible, so that there can be no question about the intentions of the militants.

Finally, all contributors regard the use of force as the least favoured option, and rightly so. Police officers often over-estimate the deterrent effect of force, believing that putting crowds to flight by baton and mounted charges, and use of munitions like CS smoke will be something that protesters seek to avoid. On the contrary, provoking the police into the use of force is a sure and certain recipe for capturing headlines and allows protesters the opportunities to complain to the news media, politicians, and the courts about police brutality and denial of human rights. One reason (I believe) why protesters hate the tactic popularly known as 'kettling', is that so little force is used. If protesters seek to break out of the containment, then it is they who must initiate the violence, whilst the police officers act defensively. This may not entirely deny them access to the 'moral high ground', but it does make occupation of it much less secure.

References

Field, S and Southgate, P, *Public Disorder: A Review of Research and a Study in One Inner City Area* (London: HMSO, 1982).

Horowitz, DL, *The Deadly Ethnic Riot* (Berkeley: University of California Press, 2001).

Kerner, O, *The Report of the National Advisory Commission on Civil Disorders* (Washington, DC: US Government Printing Office, 1968).

McPhail, C, *The Myth of the Madding Crowd* (Hawthorne, New York: Aldine de Gruyter, 1991).

Rose, RHSC, 'Ratcliffe-on-Soar Power Station Protest: Inquiry into Disclosure' (London: Office of the Surveillance Commissioner, 2011).

Waddington, PAJ, *Liberty and Order: Policing Public Order in a Capital City* (London: UCL Press, 1994).

Waddington, PAJ, 'Public Order Policing: Citizenship and moral ambiguity', in F Leishman, B Loveday, and SP Savage (eds), *Core Issues in Policing* (London: Longman, 1995), pp 114–30.

Waddington, PAJ, 'Policing public order and political contention', in T Newburn (ed), *Handbook of Policing* (Collumpton: Willan, 2003), pp 394–421.

Index